by **Peter S. Prescott**

A WORLD OF OUR OWN:
Notes on Life and Learning
in a Boys' Preparatory School

SOUNDINGS:
Encounters with
Contemporary Books

A DARKENING GREEN:
Notes from the Silent Generation

THE CHILD SAVERS:
Juvenile Justice Observed

The Child Savers

PETER S. PRESCOTT

The Child Savers

Juvenile Justice Observed

Alfred A. Knopf New York 1981

THIS IS A BORZOI BOOK
PUBLISHED BY ALFRED A. KNOPF, INC.

Library of Congress Cataloging in Publication Data
Prescott, Peter S. (date)
The child savers, juvenile justice observed.
1. Juvenile justice, Administration of—
New York (N.Y.) 2. Child welfare—New York (N.Y.)
I. Title.
HV9106.N6P73 1981   364.3'6'09747   80-2705
ISBN 0-394-50235-3 AACR2

Grateful acknowledgment is made to Random House Inc. for
permission to reprint three lines from "In Time of War" by
W. H. Auden, from *W. H. Auden: Collected Poems;* copyright
1945 by W. H. Auden.

Manufactured in the United States of America

for Antonia,
who early knew
what justice is

Contents

Introduction
3

I A Case of Murder 2 12

II The Coming of Family Court 47

III The Black Hole of the Bronx 76

IV Natural Families 114

V The Friends of Robert Levy 144

VI Caring, Kind Environments 177

VII The Key to the Quality of Life 218

The Child Savers

Introduction

At the time I decided I wanted to write a book about juvenile justice I knew no more about it than do most people who watch television news, or read the papers:

BOY, 15, ELECTROCUTES
WIDOW, 80, IN BATHTUB

and

JUDGE FREES
KILLER KID
———
Mayor Angry

Like everyone else, I had heard that the problem was getting worse and that nothing effective was being done about it, probably for the same reason that nothing effective seemed to be done about what our society considers more important problems: inflation, energy, various Islamic eccentrics. As a nation we have, understandably, a limited collective attention span, and some problems are not going to hold our interest for longer than it takes to get from one TV commercial to the next.

I came upon this subject in a backwards sort of way. My first book had been a study of an exclusive boys' preparatory school, an examination of the ways in which students and the adults who taught them fended for themselves in a time of crisis against a benevolent, super-annuated autocracy. Having dealt with one end of our country's social and economic spectrum, and after writing two more books, I thought I might take a look at another institution that had been established for the alleged benefit of young people in our society. This book I would make something of a mirror image of the first. I would deal with children at the other end of the spectrum: the outcasts, the inarticulate, the violent.

Moreover, I had two reasons for wanting to write about the law. The first was practical: courtroom trials are essentially dramatic to read about. A trial is an arena of combat for civilized people, and the law is perhaps the least of the factors that will decide the victor. The second was more temperamental: like most people who have read Kafka, or worried about Vietnam and Watergate, I worry about what is done to people by their governors in the name of the law, in the name of their own good. I wanted particularly to write about some aspect of the condition of human rights in our society today. It seemed to me that if, as I suspect, these rights are not a stable commodity, children (who are often held by our society to be marginal citizens) might have the most difficulty maintaining theirs. Perhaps the best place to watch these rights deteriorating would be a courtroom from which both press and public are excluded.

Finally, I wanted to write a book about how things happen. About the conflict between idealism and apathy, between noble plans and insufficient resources. About the way things get done, or more often don't get done. Our juvenile justice system did not instantly present itself to me, but by the time it did I was ready to see that I had been looking for it all along. Within its intense and narrow focus, the juvenile court offers not only examples of process and deterioration of rights, of idealism and apathy. In addition, the dramas that are played out there every day expose the most violent and most delicate ruptures of family life. The grief, the frustration and the frenzy that develop each day within the court cause most of those who work there, from the judges to the stenographers, to erect (sometimes with self-critical irony) elaborate defenses.

Many books and articles had been written about the history and theory of juvenile justice, but none had been attempted from the inside of the machine, as it were, or at least as close to the inside as a reporter can get. Reporters, like lawyers, shy away from juvenile courts for at least three reasons. The first is apathy. The public, as I have said, can't find time to think coherently about the problem. Sweep these kids off the street, is the common man's prescription: out of sight and the need for thought, preferably to some secure detention for life or until they become sober citizens. As for lawyers, most of them scorn the juvenile court; in the profession's opinion it is not a forum for real law (and certainly not for real fees). The second reason for this general avoidance is the court's complexity. I didn't know when I began work on this book that I would have to learn (and try to explain to my readers) a kind of law so different from ordinary trial law that many attorneys who appear before the court are embarrassed by their ignorance and prove incapable of effectively representing their clients. The third reason is that the juvenile court is reluctant to be examined. Early in 1975, when I started my investigations, the Family Courts in New York State were off limits to the press; they still are today, though a journalist may gain temporary admittance if he can obtain permission from the judge presiding over the case he hopes to observe. The argument given for such secrecy is that children have a right to make mistakes and are entitled to protection from publicity that may damage them in years to come. Beyond this, one comes inescapably to another conclusion: what happens in these courts is often not fit to be seen. By barring the press—or by letting it in for only a day or two, not long enough for it to sort out what is going on—the courts stave off a public cry for reform.

My own request to observe New York City's Family Court for an entire year was rejected by the court's administrative judge. I renewed my application and, as reporters will, enlisted the aid of parties influential in the court. Delicate negotiations proceeded for some fifteen months. The judge hedged and stalled; I audited classes in juvenile law by night at New York University. The judge had, of course, more pressing problems than mine, and there was always the chance that if he exercised a kind of pocket veto I would get tired and go write about dog fights instead. After twelve months, the judge relented, but no sooner had I presented myself in the Brook-

7

lyn Family Court than I was removed under guard to the Court
Clerk's Office, where I was left to cool my heels, wondering whether
I was under arrest or free to beat a retreat to the nearest subway.
No explanation was forthcoming—though I was at last told that the
judge had changed his mind and needed time to reflect—and the
court clerk saw no need for me to tie up one of his many telephones.

Had I known then how the Family Court works, I would have
taken my experience as an encouraging sign—as indeed it was, for
with no more than three months' further delay I was in the court for
good. The judge, incredibly, issued me an undated pass, which I used
for not one but two years.

Once in, I had no difficulty determining what kind of book I wanted
to write. I had never intended to write a study of the causes of juvenile
crime, or of how the poor live today, or *what we must do*. Many
reporters—particularly the blacks among them, and those with a
facility in Spanish—are better qualified than I to write such books.
And, of course, many such books have been written. What I had just
then the exclusive franchise to do was to write about the process of
justice as it is applied (or misapplied) to children. I was, for instance,
less interested in why young Zachary was gang-raped his first night
out in the shelter home than in why, when his case came to court, it
seemed difficult to prove. Why Angel ran his knife through an older
man's heart concerned me less than the extraordinary maneuvers his
lawyer undertook to get him back on the street, and what his lawyer
thought about what he was doing.

Nor did I intend to offer wide-ranging programs for "solutions"
to infinitely complex problems that are probably really as intractable
as they seem. Reporters are not social engineers, though some have
seemed to think they are; the business of the journalist is to point
out the situations that exist. By his emphasis he can imply what he
thinks of them. Clearly, the system can be improved by liberal lashings of decency and efficiency, of responsibility and long-range planning. Beyond that, it would be presumptuous for me to offer lec-
tures.

Above all, I decided that, confronted with such a broad and complex subject as juvenile justice, I would be making a serious mistake

if I reduced it to a touristy sort of book—a broad, superficial, touch-all-bases general survey of the state of the problem across this wide nation of ours. There is, I suppose, a use for the kind of book that reports the opinion of a judge in Muncie and of a newspaper editor in Tulsa, and the interesting experiment that may or may not succeed in Seattle, but that kind of book has never appealed to me. I have always felt that a reporter can range further by working concentratedly from a narrow base. By hanging doggedly about a single court for weeks and even months on end, I worked to gain the acceptance, then the trust, and finally the alarming confidences of everyone who works or appears there: judges, lawyers, even the court clerks, stenographers, probation officers and guards. So much time in court is spent doing nothing at all—the proceedings are always being interrupted, often for no discernible reason—that I could chat also with policemen, witnesses, social workers and psychologists, as well as with petitioners, respondents and their relatives.

Granted the need for a narrow focus, there was never any doubt in my mind that my focus had to be on New York City. The juvenile court was invented in Illinois and the most important case in juvenile justice originated in Arizona—my book could easily expand to accommodate such history—but New York is the unavoidable place for such a study. The city's age and size infuse its problems with an intensity and a despair with which younger cities, west of the Hudson, do not have to cope. A significant part of the juvenile justice dilemma in New York results from the political clout that its indolent agencies have acquired since they were founded as church-based institutions a century or more ago. But if most things are worse in New York, some are also, in some remarkable ways, better. For the fact is that our nation's laws involving the rights of juveniles and procedures in juvenile courts originated here. When, in 1967, the U.S. Supreme Court awarded to children most of the protections of due process already enjoyed by adults, it followed a model that New York State had five years previously enacted by statute. Few people understand that it took a small revolution in our social and legal philosophy before children were allowed *any* legal protections when confronted by a court that could send them to jail for years. Fewer still are aware that the immense labor which brought about that revolution resulted

from one man's determination. That man serves as a central character
in this book.

I am also writing here about wasted lives, destroyed lives and an
institution set up by society to ease grief and pain but which inadvertently—helplessly, knowingly—increases the anguish. Many people
who know a little about New York's Family Court think that it should
be done away with, replaced with something harsher. Others, who
know a little more, think that it should be done away with because
it is not effective, because it is not performing the task it was assigned
to do for troubled children.

Curiously, most people who have anything to do with Family Court
express ambivalent feelings about its goals and purposes: dismissive
feelings from the gut, more decent feelings from the heart and head.
People intimately involved with the court and its works can, within
the course of a few minutes, reveal both their contempt for the people
in general who appear before it and their concern for *individuals* who
are clearly victims in need of help. As a commuter to the courts, I
found the same ambivalence at work in me: no matter how often I
encountered these children at close range, the further I withdrew
toward my exurban home, the more abstract, the more severe, my
thoughts about what should be done with them became.

Because these contradictory emotions afflict everyone involved in
the courts—and are usually not perceived by them to be a contradic-
tion—it is perhaps not curious that everyone in the court—judges,
prosecuting and defending lawyers, social workers—feels that he and
his colleagues are the good guys in the daily dramas that unfold.
Everyone in Family Court is aware that the court exists for the "best
interests" of the child; therefore, since *he* is working in behalf of the
child, his opponents have to be the bad guys. Right? Yet the thought
that perhaps he isn't the good guy after all torments most of those
who, after the erosion of years of service, retain any sensitivity in this
court. The dilemma goes with the franchise.

In this book, I have tried to reveal, rather than explain, such
conflicts. Too much else needed explaining. The first chapter, for
instance, puts forward a great deal of law and procedure peculiar to

juvenile justice: the basics of what the reader will need to know. To make it less formidable, I have arranged it around a case of homicide. As will become clear in the final chapter, this particular case, if tried today, would be tried differently, under different regulations. I observed these courts over a number of years, and as I watched, a harried legislature kept changing the rules of the game. But the important point is not whether the prosecutor belongs to Corporation Counsel's staff, or to the district attorney's—or even, really, whether the case is tried in Criminal Court or in Family Court. Details change, but the essential dilemmas do not.

In between these two chapters I have placed five more. One has to do with the history of juvenile justice from its origins in England's chancery courts to the present day in America. Another attempts to show just how badly the system can work, in this case through a portrait of the old Bronx Family Court in its pustulant extremity, a year before it was closed down. This is followed by a chapter devoted to the most poignant of juvenile cases—cases of child abuse and neglect. In another chapter, I track a single law guardian—that is to say, a lawyer whose job it is to represent indigent children—through a variety of cases. Still another chapter is devoted to the exquisitely brutal treatment afforded children in institutions outside of the court —institutions which, I need hardly say, were created to treat and care for these same children.

I must make two final points. The first is that this book is unbalanced in the attention it gives to violent crimes. There *are* children from whom society must be protected as soon as possible. I have come into contact with a number of them—large, muscular individuals, but children, nonetheless—who have killed and maimed, raped and sodomized, without considering their actions at all. There can be little doubt that they will do the same again. The press makes much of them, and so do judges and lawyers, who concentrate most particularly upon them, making what happens in such cases eminently reportable. What the press doesn't tell us, however, is how few of these sensational cases there really are, what a small percentage they represent among the hundreds of thousands of children who run afoul of

the law. If the violent children were the only ones we had to think
about, our task would be easy. It is the presence of the other children
—disturbed children, children whose parents can't or won't take care
of them—that tests our social conscience. The press rarely speaks of
them, and they have no way to speak to us. But they are there, and
they are in terrible trouble, and even if we don't want to think about
them, even if we find it convenient to lump them together with criminal children, their presence poses a mute question: What kind of
society do we think we are?

My other point: Except where the name of a child appears in the
public record of a court other than New York City's Family Court,
the names of all children in this book have been changed. So, too,
have the names of their relatives and witnesses involved in the proceedings, the names of three or four other adults, and the digits in the
only docket number to which I refer.

I have been engaged intermittently with this book for nearly six years
and in that time have been helped in a variety of ways by more people
than I can possibly acknowledge. My principal debt is to the Legal
Aid Society of New York City, which assigned its overworked attorneys to instruct me in the labyrinth of juvenile law. Other Legal Aid
lawyers suffered my presence and my endless questions; others still
volunteered to coach me in the practical aspects of courtroom tactics.
All this they did in a disinterested way: no one at Legal Aid ever
suggested what I should think of what I saw; no one ever asked to see
what I was writing. I must stress that this book has not been approved
by the Legal Aid Society; such errors as it may contain are mine alone.
I am particularly indebted to Harold H. Healy, Jr., past chairman of
Legal Aid's board of trustees; to Robert B. McKay, past president of
the society; and to Archibald R. Murray, Legal Aid's executive director and attorney-in-chief. The depth and range of help provided me
by Charles Schinitsky, attorney-in-charge of the society's Juvenile
Rights Division, will be apparent throughout these pages.

I can thank by name only a few of the several score attorneys, not
only from Legal Aid but from New York City's Corporation Counsel
and other agencies, who unprotestingly allowed me to impose upon

their time and patience: Robert M. Levy, Thomas V. Curtis, Susan Larabee, Judith Levy Sheindlin, Carol Sherman, Wendy Lauring, Michael J. Dale, Michael Gale, Edward M. Kaufmann, Larry Schwartzstein, William Logan, Thomas Esposito and Judge Mara T. Thorpe. I am grateful also to Fern Schair, executive director of the Fund for Modern Courts; Merril Sobie; the late Arthur B. Tourtellot; Eleanor Lake; Orville Prescott; Shirley Katzander; Alexis Gelber; Martin Guggenheim; Susan B. Lindenauer; Lawrence Lader; Maurice Nixon; Charles Elliott; and Miriam Kerster, director of Legal Aid's Juvenile Services Unit. I am indebted to my wife, Anne Lake Prescott, for years of encouragement and sacrifices to make time for me to work, and to uncounted judges, social workers, court clerks, Probation officers, court reporters and uniformed court officers who helped me understand the daily dramas in which they are involved.

Without a generous grant from the John Simon Guggenheim Memorial Foundation, research for this book could not have been completed. Had not *Newsweek*'s editors allowed me two periods of time away from the magazine, it could not have been written.

I

A Case of Murder 2

Children are really loved here, even by the police:
They speak of years before the big were lonely,
And will be lost.

W. H. Auden, *In Time of War,* XXV

There came a time (as lawyers say) when it appeared that everyone in the Family Court building in New York County except Tom Curtis knew that one of Curtis's clients had been picked up the night before on a charge of Murder 2. The news, like so much garbage hurled into a stagnant pond, rose quickly from the fifth floor to the ninth. Corporation Counsel leaked it to the court officers in Intake A, where, amid much shaking of heads, the law guardians picked it up. On this morning, June 30, 1977, Thomas V. Curtis, a young attorney employed by the Juvenile Rights Division of the Legal Aid Society, is occupied with a child abuse case in Part II, and therefore virtually inaccessible; the courthouse consensus is that when he emerges he will not be greatly elated by this turn of events. The putative murderer, a fifteen-year-old boy named Angel Sanchez, is "known to the court." Translated from the jargon, this means that Angel, at the time he allegedly committed his murder, was on parole, awaiting trials for three other crimes of violence. Not a few in the court wonder why the little bastard has been let loose so many times to do his thing again, but their wonderment is strictly pro forma: this kind of nonsense happens all the time, and besides, Curtis is a good lawyer who does well the job he has been told to do, and he takes justifiable pride in his ability to return his clients to the streets. Nevertheless, Angel's is an unusual case. Contrary to popular belief, the school of juvenile delinquency does not offer murder as part of its curriculum. Almost invariably, the children who kill people have never been in trouble with the law.

At 10:15 this Thursday morning, Detective Richard J. Joyce of Manhattan Homicide Zone One is interviewed by Charles Emma, an attorney employed by the Corporation Counsel of the City of New York, in room 5B4 of the Family Court. The tone and substance of this interview might suggest to an ignorant observer that its purpose is to prepare an indictment that will lead to the arraignment, trial, conviction and sentencing of a teenage murderer. Not so. Were Angel Sanchez a year older—were he sixteen instead of fifteen—Detective Joyce's interview would be taking place a few hundred yards away in Manhattan's Criminal Court at 100 Centre Street, where adult offenders are indicted by assistant district attorneys. But because Angel is a juvenile, he is, according to the law, incapable of committing a crime. He will be charged instead, in the document that Charles Emma is drafting in pencil, with "an act which, if done by an adult, would constitute the crime of MURDER 2nd as defined by 125.25 of the Penal Law, a Designated Felony Act, pursuant to section 712 of the Family Court Act." Consequently, there will be for Angel no indictment, no arraignment, no trial, no verdict, and if, after all these events that do not happen, he is found to have killed a man, there will be no sentence and no prison. In their place, Angel faces a petition which will be supported by Corporation Counsel first at a brief Intake hearing before a judge, and then at a longer fact-finding hearing before another judge in this civil court which is admonished to think first of the welfare of the child who stands before it. Should a finding be made against the respondent (never a defendant) at the conclusion of this hearing, there will eventually be a dispositional hearing before the same judge, at which time Angel may be locked away for years by a maneuver known as a placement with a training school. Some there are in Family Court who have no use at all for this pollution of the language of the law.

Emma's interview with Joyce is encouraging. There seems no doubt that the kid did it, and that the case can be proved in court. Joyce has with him the arrest report, prepared at 1:00 that morning in the 7th Precinct. In the large block reserved for "details," the booking supervisor, with a fine disregard of the euphemistic language of juvenile law, has typed: "Deft did stab one Jose Rodriguez thereby causing his death." In handwriting he has added: "Mother Juanita ntfd." Other information, entered in the appropriate blocks, reveals that the location of the "occurrence" was a park at Norfolk and Houston streets on Manhattan's Lower East Side, that the complainant's name is "People," that the arrested party was neither fingerprinted nor photographed—the law then forbade such records in the case of a juvenile —and that he had no funds in his possession. His race is "H" (though many Hispanics might object to being considered a race apart, the classification has less to do with genetic science than administrative ease), his weight is 105 pounds, and his height is 4 feet 9 inches.

"Angel," says Detective Joyce, "has a complex about his height." He also has scars on his face, the result of a fire.

Joyce gives to Emma a Police Department complaint report, filed by Police Officer George Allen of the 7th Precinct. According to this report, on June 29 Officer Allen "at approx. 2205 hours responded to a 10-85 at Bellevue Hospital where the undersigned was informed of a felonious assault. At 2315 hours complainant"—the complainant at this point was not "People" but José Rodriguez—"was pronounced DOA by Dr. Godfrey of Bellevue Hospital."

"Could it have been an accident?" Emma asks.

"The knife was thrust four inches into his heart," Joyce replies. The assumption is that no one can accidentally propel his heart four inches deep onto someone else's knife. Still, it seems that Rodriguez, twenty-four years old at the time of his demise, was a junkie.

"Was it self-defense?" Emma asks.

"I may have said to Angel that it looks like self-defense," Joyce says. This is, for Emma, a matter of concern. He hopes Tom Curtis will not hear of it. "Tom Curtis," Emma says, "is a damn good lawyer," and a damn good lawyer is likely to challenge the admissibility of the written confession that Joyce obtained from Angel at 2:00 A.M. that morning.

Eight days will pass before Curtis sees a copy of Angel's confession.

After Joyce had read the boy the so-called Miranda warning of his rights, and another policeman had translated the warning into Spanish for his mother, Angel took two pieces of paper and wrote:

"This junkie was walking in the park at Norfolk St. between Houston and Stanton. She droped her purse and I pick did up. And the knife felt out. I pick up the knife and Jose who was staning next to me said don't steal from the lady. I said Jose I don't steal from nobody. I'am not like you stealing from all my friends. He said shut the fuck up. How are you talking like there. Jose went to hit me the pocketbook. I pick up the knife opened and I poinied it at him. He swung the pocket book again. Has he swung his body came right into the knife. I saw blood coming from his chess I was worried about him but people in the block will not let go. Somebody told my mother that I was in troublen. She came running and got me. I'am came back to the block. And my mother saw *Det.* Joyce and told me to give myself up. I told *Det.* Joyce what happened.

"I'am making this statement of my own free will. I was advised of my right and my mother was present."

What with the paperwork and the interviewing of witnesses, this case has kept Joyce up all night. A pleasant-looking middle-aged man with a florid face, silver hair and a brogue from County Cork, he is Central Casting's idea of a senior Irish cop; his placid demeanor suggests enormous competence. He has been on the force for twenty-four years and, since he became a detective, he has handled eighty homicides, many of them committed by adolescents, though Angel is only the second juvenile he has had to book for murder. He is proud of his office, Manhattan Homicide Zone One, which covers six precincts, including Chinatown, deals with 130 homicides a year, and has received a citation for solving cases. Nowadays, Joyce spends half of his duty time each year in courtrooms, and he is aware that this diversion of his energies has impaired his ability to solve homicides: "I would have to say that my special skills have become courtroom skills." His familiarity with criminal courts has made him contemptuous of district attorneys who, he suggests, manage to combine laziness with overwork and who will allow two killers immunity if they will testify against a third, "when all three of them should fry." The criminal courts, he insists, and the Family Court for good measure, should be "wiped out and reorganized from scratch. Pretty soon, the way we're going, there'll be a murderer in every family."

Angel, for instance, though he rather likes Angel. "He's a gentleman. I wouldn't want to punish him. I'd like to see him get into an institution, get treatment. But I'd keep him there three years." In fact, Joyce would not mind being the judge in this case: "What this kid needs is a father. A big brother."

By 11:15 Emma has finished the draft of the petition. Bearing the docket number D-2414/77, which means that it purports to be the 2,414th delinquency petition to be filed in New York County Family Court so far this year, it charges that Angel "did with intent to cause the death of one JOSE RODRIGUEZ, did cause the death of such person by stabbing him with a knife, and such death was caused under circumstances evincing depraved indifference to human life, in that he recklessly engaged in conduct which created a grave risk of death to said person." Emma takes it to a typist, who will stamp on the finished document "Designated Felony Act Petition," which means that this is a particularly serious case and must be treated in a special manner conceived by the New York State legislature only last year in response to what the legislators take to be a cry from the voters that somebody must do something about all this juvenile crime. Emma thinks that with luck the petition will reach Intake A by the 1:00 lunch break.

In Intake A, on the fifth floor, Judge Philip W. Thurston presides. A seemingly amiable man in his sixties, he has a toothy grin which he flashes at the unfortunates assembled before him—whether in human commiseration or in reflex defense against the serial horrors that command his daily attention, no man can say. It is Thurston's job, this month, in this Part, to give brief audiences to all parties who have a claim on the court's time, excepting cases involving child abuse, which because of their special urgency are rushed to a Part reserved for them alone. Thurston has numerous options available to him for each case that is called before him, but his principal responsibilities are three: he must assign counsel to the participants in each case; with the help of his clerk, he must schedule these cases for hearings according to the time that is available on the calendars of each of the Parts in the court; and in matters involving children accused of offenses, he must determine, with the help of a Probation officer, whether they are to be paroled to their homes while awaiting a hearing, or remanded either to the Juvenile Center in the Bronx, a place of secure detention, or to one of the city's agencies or shelter care homes.

Because there are a great many cases pressing against the double doors leading into Intake A, and because few final decisions are made here, matters tend to move quickly. Many who appear before this Part have no idea that it represents only the beginning of things, do not understand what is happening, or why they cannot expatiate upon their grievances at length. Thurston, for instance, has no intention of listening to the man now before him, who wants to explain something. "I'm sorry, mister!" Thurston seizes the next file as a court officer hustles the man, who looks like Marlon Brando gone even further to seed, toward the door. *"Outside!"* the court officer says, and Thurston flashes his teeth: "He wanted to tell us the story of his last seven years. I can see why that grandmother didn't want him to see his children. He's something of a character."

In rapid order, Thurston refuses to set bail for a Chinese child escaped from Chicago, and dismisses a lawyer's argument that a mother's petition against her unruly daughter is improper. The Chinese boy never had a chance: "The law," Thurston says, "is clear: no bail, and besides, this is a Designated Felony petition." He's right: children do not have the right to post bail; indeed, were they to obtain the right, the issue in most cases would be moot, since few children who appear before this court could raise the money. The boy is accused of conspiracy to commit murder. According to court rumor, the Ghost Shadows, a juvenile gang in Chinatown, imports hit men —actually Chinese hit boys—from around the country to settle its disputes with rival gangs. The would-be assassin had been flown in from Chicago, and because of the approaching holiday weekend he must be remanded until July 5, which, his lawyer correctly observes, is more than the seventy-two hours allowed by statute. Thurston is unconcerned with such niceties.

As for the ungovernable daughter, she is a surly black girl who turns around in her chair to face the back wall. Thurston insists she face the court. The girl's mother, however, can't face the court either;

she is so fat she must sit sideways to the judge, because her chair is bolted to the floor before an immovable table. "The daughter thinks this is all a big joke," Thurston says. She lives with her father, but it is the estranged mother who has complained of her orneriness. While mother confers with Corporation Counsel for two minutes—all the time for preparation that her lawyer has—the girl's lawyer argues that the father, who hasn't bothered to appear in court, hasn't complained, so the mother is out of order, not being in residence, not really knowing what she's talking about. Thurston lets the petition stand, and the child will have a hearing later to see whether she must be removed from her father's home. "It seems," says Thurston, "that neither parent is doing much to help this child."

With so much justice accomplished, the Sanchez case is called. Angel's mother enters, chewing her fingernails, followed by an interpreter and by Tom Curtis, who, like all Legal Aid lawyers, carries a sheaf of files and a fat yellow-covered book on family law. Angel is brought in from a detention room, in handcuffs; one of the court officers takes a position behind him. Angel is a dark-skinned, compactly built boy, but he *is* astonishingly short. Disconcerting as the scars on his face are, he has limpid brown eyes and an alert demeanor, and might be taken, by an unwary observer, for a cute little nine- or ten-year-old. When it becomes clear that the handcuffs are to stay on, Curtis objects—uselessly, because the Administrative Judge has ruled that violent children are to be so restrained.

Curtis informs the court that Angel's father is flying up from Puerto Rico tonight to hire a private lawyer, which means that the case must be adjourned until the next day. Privately, Curtis is somewhat miffed; although he doesn't really need a complicated murder trial added to his case load, he has had a lot of experience with Angel and understands the boy's problems. Besides, as everyone in Family Court knows, private lawyers do not fare well in this court. Most private lawyers strenuously resist appearing here, where they feel they are treated badly and due process seldom applies. It is true, they *are* treated badly, even rudely on occasion, by judges and court officers, but it is also true that most of them are unfamiliar with the peculiar vagaries of family law (hearsay testimony, for instance, is permitted in child abuse cases, much to the detriment of the parents whom the

private lawyers defend), and many seem unfamiliar with a basic premise of trial practice, which is that the business of a defense lawyer is
to defend his client vigorously, and not condescend to him or, having
predetermined his guilt, conspire with judge and prosecutor to arrive
at a semblance of equity. Curtis correctly assumes that by virtue of
his experience with this kind of law and with this particular court, he
can defend Angel more effectively than a private lawyer can, but he
doesn't want to be put in a position where Angel's mother wants him
and the father wants someone else.

Today, however, there is nothing to be done. Still in handcuffs,
Angel kisses his mother and is remanded to Juvenile Center. Such
displays of familial affection are rare in Family Court.

Toward evening, in his office on the ninth floor, Curtis broods about
Angel's situation. Curtis is in his early thirties; a thin, intense man
who wears gold-rimmed aviator glasses, a trim mustache and bushy
blond hair, he strides quickly through the corridors, his features knit
in a frown of concentration. In court, he grimaces and shakes his head
at questionable rulings. "He involves himself in every case up to
here," says an opposing lawyer, holding his hand above his head.
"He'll be a candidate for King's County"—a mental hospital—"soon
himself." Once an exasperated opponent said, "Stop trying to save the
whole world, Tom!"—which only irritated Tom. Saving the whole
world is not the point; saving a few of the world's casualties is. Curtis
does not care for the assumption that Legal Aid lawyers are necessarily bleeding hearts; as a token of his own conservatism, he serves part
of each year as a captain in the National Guard.

Curtis wonders whether Angel's seemingly uncontrollable violence
results from a prescribed drug, methyltestosterone, he has been taking. Two years ago, Angel and some other kids attempted to light a
fire for an indoor barbecue by throwing gasoline on the briquets; the
gasoline fumes collected in the room and finally exploded, leaving
Angel badly scarred. To enable his hair to grow, and to enable him
to mature sexually—for Angel's principal problem is his stunted
growth—he has been taking large doses of male hormones, which may
have a side effect of making him violent. Curtis thinks, too, that brain

damage may be a possibility: "So many of our clients were born to mothers who have no idea at all of prenatal care. The mothers are fourteen years old, have lived for years on a diet of Pepsi and Cheez Doodles, and as soon as possible they feed their infants Pepsi and Cheez Doodles, too—when they remember to feed them at all. Some of these mothers were junkies when they were pregnant. We get psychiatric reports on these kids, their average IQ is maybe 65 to 75, just barely the minimum to function, and the psychiatric reports say 'minimal brain damage.' It's the usual diagnosis, nobody knows what it means, maybe we're all 'minimally brain damaged' to some extent. The only doctor these kids have is the Emergency Room at Bellevue, when they get a leg cut off. Often the first doctor they see is the doctor at Juvenile Center, when they get arrested."

If any of these factors apply, Curtis thinks that Angel must be considered one of the victims of his acts, a boy who deserves treatment rather than punishment. If he can get the court to agree, then it is legally the court's responsibility to see that Angel is properly treated, but in this area, as in so many others, the court is inefficient and has few resources to draw upon, so if Angel is to get what he needs, it will be up to Curtis and the Legal Aid social workers to arrange it. This extralegal function, which occupies much of the Legal Aid attorneys' time, was anticipated by the framers of the Family Court Act, which defines the defenders of juveniles as "law guardians."

First, however, Curtis will have to persuade a judge that Angel is not in fact a hardened criminal. Considering Angel's present legal position, this will be difficult:

• Angel faces trial on a charge of assault with a knife. Like many street kids, he carries an illegal weapon called a "double-oh-seven," a folding knife that opens with a flick of the wrist. Corporation Counsel has talked about "attempted murder," about Angel's cutting the throat of another boy, when, says Curtis, he only scratched the boy's shoulder in a fight over a girl. Such scrapes between acquaintances are so common in New York City that they rarely draw an arrest; Curtis thinks that if Angel had been an adult, there never would have been a case.

• Angel is scheduled to stand trial for intimidation with a sawed-off rifle. He and a friend had been in a hardware store. The proprietor, says Curtis, "thought they were stealing stuff and beat the shit out of the other kid. Angel returned the next day with the rifle and threatened the man's life." In a pre-trial hearing, Curtis managed to suppress the rifle—meaning it could not later be used in evidence—because the police had not taken Angel to the station, as they are required to do, and had not read him his Miranda rights. "The police are anxious to suppress reality out there," Curtis says.

• Angel is faced with another charge of attempted murder. A group of kids tried to kill another in the lobby of a movie theater. Seemingly the most serious of Angel's prior dilemmas, Curtis believes it the least worrisome. Angel is innocent of this one, he says: "We know who did it." After the assault, Angel calmly went back into the theater to see the rest of the movie—it was about the life of George Jackson—which, says Curtis, he would have been unlikely to do had he been guilty.

As each of these cases works its tortuous way through the court, Angel, thanks to Curtis's skill, has remained free on parole. Curtis sighs: with this fourth charge confronting him, Angel is unlikely to be paroled again.

On a wall in Curtis's office hangs a large reproduction of a painting, Hudson River School, which shows a white-clad figure standing in the stern of a bark emerging from some kind of Freudian tunnel. A beacon gleams from this figure's forehead. The painting is called "Childhood," one of four from Thomas Cole's "The Voyage of Life," a series which, for its insipidity, was widely reproduced a century ago. "It's not the experience of my kids," says Curtis, who at this time has no kids but his clients.

At 5:00 the courthouse empties. Nearly everyone in the large waiting room outside Intake A has gone home, their cases put off until another day, yet just now a woman starts to shriek. A court officer looks nervously about—this kind of behavior, particularly at the end of a long, hot, frustrating day, can become contagious—then tries to calm the woman down. Nothing doing: hysteria has set in, and within a few minutes it is clear the woman could not stop screaming if she wanted to.

"It's an act," says a Probation officer as he gathers his files. "We just remanded her son for the umpteenth time. He's in here once a week."

"Give her an Oscar and she'll go home," says another.

"We don't give Oscars here. Only remands."

The woman is alone and the court is not equipped to handle such a situation, so after twenty minutes no one even bothers to watch her as she howls to herself, crouched against a wall.

The new Manhattan Family Court building, which was opened in 1976, is an eleven-story, black-granite affair, the very image of what can be accomplished in the Bureaucratic Modern style for $28 million. Its reflecting façade suggests to observers that they mind their own business; its parking lot, which wants $1 an hour in quarters, three hours maximum, suggests that no one will be detained here long, certainly no one poor, though no one has ever been known to come out of its revolving doors in three hours, let alone one. According to courthouse legend, a woman once left her children alone in the court while she went to feed quarters to the parking meter; when she returned, the children were gone, vanished, not to return for a week. This courthouse stands at 60 Lafayette Street, on the corner of Leonard Street, a few blocks from City Hall. The U.S. Customs Court is nearby, and (in the language of Family Court) "across the street" is the Criminal Court, where adult criminals engage in plea bargaining. The phrase implies a handy proximity: once the kids, at age sixteen, are rotated out of the Family Court's revolving doors, they will be welcomed to their new home "across the street." Between Lafayette and Centre streets there is a pleasant little park with lots of trees and benches not yet broken; on a summer afternoon the latter are studded with sleeping bums. Here and there one can see still a number of forlorn turn-of-the-century buildings with elaborate crumbling cornices that stand in human contrast to the judicial architecture that occupies so much of the area, and to the neighborhood's most striking edifice, the New York Telephone Building, now in the process of completion. Looming above these narrow streets, this awesome structure with its weird Martian vents—very large, and placed very high

—bespeaks an inhuman authority; it demands, in fact, to be seen from a distance, but there is no distance.

On July 1, as on every working day, all those with business before the court are ordered to attend by 9:30 in the morning. Mothers, occasional fathers, private lawyers, social workers, relevant relatives, witnesses, policemen, complaining parties, the children who are the subjects of these proceedings (except those detained at Juvenile Center; they will be delivered by bus an hour later) and their siblings too young to be left at home alone are expected to present themselves to the court officers who stand with clipboards in the lofty waiting rooms outside the various Parts. Some of these people will indeed arrive on time, but only rarely does everyone involved in the same case arrive on time, and so everyone will wait. Quite likely they will wait into the afternoon, being told nothing, until at the day's end they are told to come back tomorrow, or on August 13. Each Part has its calendar, which suggests an order in which the cases will be called, but the order is entirely fanciful: a case cannot progress if the respondent's mother is home sick, or a policeman doesn't show, or the law guardian is trying another case, or the judge is juggling his calendar according to some priority known only to him. Many people wonder why, since delay is inevitable, the court insists on calling all its business for the day together at the beginning of the day—why not tell some people to come in the afternoon? Judges have been known to postpone cases for which all parties, six or eight of them, are ready, because these judges want to see which cases are *not* ready, and therefore can be adjourned; by the time these unready cases are put off, it is often too late to hear the case that was set to proceed.

And so, in these light and airy waiting rooms, the assembled citizens may pass the day sitting on bright blue and orange contoured plastic chairs that have been fastened in rows set at angles to each other (arranged this way, no doubt, so that antagonists need not glare directly at each other), but they may not smoke, or drink coffee, or eat anything at all. A few literate veterans of the waiting rooms may be seen reading paperbound copies of *Shogun* and *The Rise and Fall of the Third Reich,* books of an appropriate length for their owners' ordeals. Others peer at the Part calendars set beneath glass in large and ugly stone sculptures that have dangerously sharp corners and are said to have cost $18,000 apiece. This morning, outside Intake A, where Angel Sanchez must appear again, some jester exercising his freedom of symbolic speech has inserted next to the calendars a nearly exhausted roll of toilet paper. Nearby, a very small mother addresses her very large son: "I'm gonna beat the shit outta you. You think I can't? You think 'cause you're in a court I won't beat the shit outta you?" In another row of chairs, a Chinese gentleman explains to his daughter, in French, that she must tell the judge the truth.

The buzz among courthouse personnel this morning concerns a boy who escaped last night from one of the secure detention rooms, room 5J5, in the labyrinthine corridors behind the public areas of the court. The boy had been left locked in the room, awaiting his appearance in Part I, in a case that was never called. From the evidence of the damaged room, it appears that the boy pulled two tiles loose from the ceiling to make a very small hole (but then the boy was very small) in a corner that could not be seen from the glass partition in the door. The boy climbed into the hole and waited there amid the air-conditioning ducts until everyone had gone home. He was apparently forgotten; anyone looking into the room through the reinforced glass would have seen only an empty room. At some time after five, the boy jumped down, carrying a metal strut he had pried loose from the works above. With this he broke off the door handle, but the door remained locked. Using the handle, the boy banged about the walls —the circular indentations are plainly visible—until he found a soft spot in the exterior wall. He then kicked a large hole in the wall, took the elevator down to the lobby and strolled away. A Probation officer observes that every air-conditioning machine installed in obscure corridors where the children never go is covered with expensive, gleaming stainless steel, but the walls of the detention rooms are made of particle board, junk so weak that an undersized kid can stick his foot through it. "Typical," he says. "Typical of the kind of thinking you find everywhere in this court."

Though Tom Curtis, that morning, has reason to think he will not act as Angel's lawyer in the Rodriguez case, he has already been to the scene of the crime. "On the scene you can intuit a lot," he says, "and what you get by intuition is often more important than the hard evidence." Curtis is nevertheless extremely careful about going into his clients' neighborhoods alone. Once he drove his car up to 144th Street on Eighth Avenue to look at a scene a boy had described. Some kind of war for control of the drug trade had been going on, and in the previous few months twenty-five people had been shot in the vicinity. "I didn't get out of the car," Curtis says, "but I did open my briefcase in the car, and instantly two cops appeared and looked inside. They thought I was delivering dope." Sometimes Curtis takes Charles Gilly with him—Gilly, a former policeman, is an investigator for the Legal Aid Society and licensed to carry a gun—but yesterday evening he went alone. He took off his lawyer clothes, put on a T-shirt and his oldest jeans, and walked about the Lower East Side. Once this was a notable Jewish neighborhood—Orchard Street and Rivington Street are not far from where Rodriguez was killed—but now it is mainly Puerto Rican, though many of the stores still have Hebrew signs in their windows. Across Norfolk Street there is a six-story tenement building, badly deteriorating, where Angel lives; Mrs. Sanchez was sitting on a chair on the pavement outside the building's door, chatting with her friends. Curtis nodded to her, but did not stop to speak; he was concerned that the dead man's friends, who were surely on the street as well, would regard Angel's Anglo lawyer with hostility. Across the block lives another of Curtis's clients, also once charged with murder: this neighborhood, though not so bad as some in the Bronx, or even in Brooklyn, is about as tough as Manhattan affords.

The park where José Rodriguez had been killed the night before is a small one at the corner of Houston and Norfolk streets. A chain fence surrounds it, but the gates are missing. There is an ugly brick gazebo in the middle, with reeking toilets on either side; in the shade and stench of urine that this structure offers, winos sleep on benches. Angel had mentioned some possible witnesses to the killing—two girls he doesn't know, who were sitting on a metal stump, and a man he does, who was shooting a basketball at a rim without a net—and Curtis hoped, since the other side will try to find these people, that he could prove the killing took place around a corner of the gazebo, out of their sight. But he found a red stain on the asphalt, which might be blood, and the stain is, unfortunately, in plain view of both the stump and the basketball rim.

On the morning of July 1, Tom Curtis has little time to think about Angel's case. He is tied up in Part III with a disposition and a fact-finding hearing, neither of which goes well for him. In the disposition, a lawyer from the Bureau of Child Welfare recommends the return of three children who were taken from their mother by reason of her insanity. Mother seems better now, but she may relapse—no one can really tell. A BCW case worker who, like most of his colleagues, is barely articulate, offers the usual evidence about a tidy house, clean clothes, enough furniture, the children looking forward to visits from their mother, but he strenuously resists allowing his immense and disorderly file to be introduced as evidence. BCW case workers are held in even more contempt than BCW lawyers by virtually everyone in the court; not only can they never find what they want in their files, they find it difficult to remember that their role is to be skeptical of parents who have neglected their children. Curtis forces this case worker to admit that he has in his file material that would suggest the children should *not* be returned to the mother, which is why he is understandably reluctant to turn his file over to the court. The mother's lawyer argues that if Judge Joseph A. Esquirol, Jr., rules against the mother, so must he rule in all cases where the mother seems to have recovered. Esquirol does not appear to disagree. He returns the children, subject to guarantees that a Puerto Rican group, the New York Foundling Hospital and the BCW will observe them closely. Curtis has little confidence in this decision.

In the fact-finding hearing, Curtis makes a motion for suppression of identification—and loses. Two black boys—one thirteen, the other seventeen—"acted in concert" to knock over an eighty-four-year-old woman and steal her purse. The woman testifies that she was punched in the head and pushed to the ground, and though she doesn't know by which boy, she saw Brian Washington, the thirteen-year-old, running away. A policeman some distance away saw the boys counting money; when he rushed them, they gave it to him. The policeman then found a purse containing food stamps and a Macy's charge plate, which led him to the victim. He drove the boys in a patrol car to the old woman's home and showed them to her. Are these the boys? Yes, indeed. This is what Curtis objects to: it is called a "show-up," and has been ruled by the Supreme Court to be not a fair identification. Boys handcuffed in a police car are too easily assumed guilty; a proper identification should be made from a lineup at the station. The older brother, who is retarded, has already been sentenced to five years' parole in Criminal Court; here he testifies that only he was involved, that he had told Brian to beat it, that Brian had not hit the woman. Brian, looking cute, tells the same story. No one testifies that Brian hit the woman or took the purse, but Esquirol finds against him anyway. Little law has come to bear here, and Curtis is disgusted, but he is confident that since this is Brian's first offense, the case will be thrown out at disposition.

That afternoon, when Angel's case is recalled in Intake A, Curtis learns that the father, who lives with a woman in Brooklyn ("We're just good friends, your honor"), has no money for a private lawyer. He learns, too, from Angel that when Detective Joyce asked if he wanted to make an oral confession, Angel refused; Joyce then said, "Well, why don't you write it, then?" Curtis tells Judge Thurston that he will ask for a probable cause hearing to suppress this confession and asks for this hearing to be held before some other judge than Joseph A. Doran, who now presides in Part IV, the Designated Felony Part, and who will conduct the fact-finding hearing. Curtis knows Doran, a judge who normally sits in the Bronx, only by reputation— he is supposed to be bright, but also the most prosecution-minded of the judges—and dreads having to try Angel's case before him. He has another worry, as well:

Curtis: "I would object to it being put down for a probable cause in that Part of the court. I would point out to the Court that the standard of evidence that is set out by Section 739b of the Family Court Act and by reference by the Criminal Procedures Law are such that very often materials which would not be admitted in a full fact-finding or preliminary hearing are admitted at a probable cause hearing. I would therefore think that my client's rights would be prejudiced if the judge sitting in the Designated Felony Part, who in all likelihood will be the trial judge, were to hear the probable cause hearing also."

Thurston: "Motion is denied, counsel."

Inwardly, Curtis seethes. The judge hears all this inadmissible evidence. How is he to put it out of his mind during the trial? It's got to influence him. Aloud, he says: "Would the Court expound upon the reasons for denying my motion?"

Thurston: "As I understand the statute here, once the parties are here and everything is ready, the case then goes to the Designated Felony Part, period."

Curtis: "I think the aspects of the judge there—"

Thurston: "I think a lot of things should be changed, but I am not the legislature, counsel."

Curtis: "This is not the beginning of a trial. This is in fact a separate hearing. I would note my objection."

Thurston: "Certainly." He offers him a date in Part IV: July 7 or 8.

Curtis: "I would note that a delay of that nature is clearly outside of the three-day limit set by 739b of the Family Court Act."

Thurston: "I don't think that section or three days applies to homicide cases, counsel."

Curtis: "Your honor, I have my calendar in front of me. I have ten cases on the 8th, including a number of delinquencies with hearings in Part III. I would ask for the 5th or the 6th."

Thurston: "Counsel, it's either the 7th or the 8th."

Curtis: "Can the Court explain why I can't have the hearing within the three days required by the statute?"

Thurston: "I don't think it applies to homicides, in my estimation."

Curtis: "My client has been incarcerated now through the Court since yesterday."

Thurston: "Well, you know his history very well, counsel."

Having lost that one, Curtis tries another: "I understand that my client made a written statement to the Police Department."

Thurston: "This case is adjourned to July 7, 1977, Part IV, Designated Felony Part, for a probable cause hearing. Remand of respondent is continued."

Curtis: "I understand that my client has made a written statement which I gather is in the custody of the Police Department, your honor."

Thurston: "If so, you are entitled to it. Do you know anything about it?" Thurston is speaking now to Larry Schwartzstein, who is the head of Corporation Counsel in the Manhattan court. Schwartzstein will prosecute this case. Most law guardians have little regard for him; they believe he is ambitious to be a judge, which is why he usurps the important cases—because if you want to be a judge, it looks good to have won important cases. Schwartzstein, however, is no fool, and brushes Curtis's ploy aside.

Schwartzstein: "I am in the process of investigating it. Between now and over the weekend I will attempt to obtain not only the statement but also some medical documents and turn them over to Mr. Curtis." It is a generous-sounding statement, but it means only that Curtis will have to sweat awhile before he sees the confession and the autopsy, without which he cannot prepare his defense.

Thurston: "I'm sure you will. All right."

So matters rest. This sparring for legal advantage has been not so much translated as it has been summarized and interpreted for Mrs. Sanchez, who understands little except that her son's trial has been again postponed.

In its regular session of 1976, the New York State legislature, responding to voters who demanded that the courts get tough with violent kids, enacted the Juvenile Justice Reform Act to create a category of offenses called Designated Felonies. The result was that beginning in February 1977, children of fourteen or fifteen years of age who were, like Angel, charged with serious offenses—first- and second-degree murder, first-degree kidnapping, arson, manslaughter, assault, rape, sodomy, robbery and a few other specially qualified antisocial acts— would be tried in a special Part (with a locked door) which was enjoined to keep the need for the protection of the community in mind, as well as the needs and best interests of the respondent. If one of these older children was found to have committed such an act, he could be incarcerated for a period extending to five years, instead of the previous three, and the judge would have the power to extend this period, a year at a time, until the youth reached the age of twenty-one. Release from such confinement, or the transfer of the child to a lesser degree of confinement, would be made much more difficult; indeed, under the old statute, children convicted of delinquent acts rarely were locked up for longer than seven or eight months. Moreover, procedures during the various hearings were to be tightened, to make sure that these Designated Felony cases moved right along and were not so often adjourned that they simply crumbled away. The increased severity seems to have accomplished what its framers and their constituents intended. In July 1978, the director of the state Division for Youth, which takes charge of these serious offenders after the court has ruled on them, reported that the Designated Felony Parts had achieved an 85 percent rate of conviction—a higher rate than can be obtained in the adult courts.

One reason for this success may be that judges assigned to these special Parts tend to be tougher and more experienced than their colleagues. Such a man is Joseph Doran. At sixty-nine, Doran is one year from compulsory retirement. Irving Cohen, formerly head of Probation in the Bronx, knows his record and thinks him one of the good judges: "He's foreboding," Cohen says. "He knows the law. He takes no shit. He acts as a judge should act. He's not charming." In fact, Doran, who began as an Appellate lawyer, was a law professor for twenty-two years. Now, at the end of his career, he is alarmed at the changes overtaking the city. "We're not miracle workers," he says, "and yet people expect miracles from this court. That's why we have such a bad reputation. I'm deeply disturbed by the number of people who use this court to settle family problems. We can't do much. I had a mother in here recently who complained that her fifteen-year-old son assaults her. The boy hasn't lived at home since he was thirteen. He has a five-month-old baby and lives by stealing. He burned a house down on commission so the owner could collect insurance. He told his mother he'd do it, and he did. I got him in here on a warrant—I don't issue summonses to kids, they won't obey them—but there's nothing I or the court can do to help this kid. He'll be picked up on some felony soon and do some time.

"Some blame it on the abolition of the hairbrush, or the razing of the woodshed. Time was, a father would beat his kid and the kid would learn something. But if the father beats his kid today, you know what they call it? Child abuse. I'm aware there *are* cases of child abuse, when a baby is hurled against a wall, but if a child has a bruise on his behind—why, the BCW workers call that neglect, at least. And then they think they have the right to take the kid away from his family and put him with another—while *they* decide the case—all this at great expense to the public."

By the end of the day, Doran is tired—"physically tired, as I would be in Criminal Court, but emotionally tired, too. These people come in, are emotionally upset, and some of it wears off on you. We don't have criminal trials here, where the lawyers do most of the work, draw out the facts for a jury to evaluate. We have no juries here. *I* have to draw out the facts and evaluate them. It's tiring." The lawyers are tiresome, too. "The law guardians and Corporation counsels are so young they enjoy the futile scrapping. They think they're still back in moot court." Once Doran summoned opposing counsel to a conference at the bench. "I've learned something in Manhattan County," the judge from the Bronx told them. "I've learned that lawyers from both sides try to paint me into a corner. I've leaned over backward to accommodate both of you and I always end up in the corner." Doran paused, arched his gray eyebrows and smiled: "But you can't win against the guy up here," he told the lawyers, "because *I* hold all the trumps. You can't win. Now you've got to start all over. If you like to work, go ahead. I just sit back like the Cheshire Cat and grin. I know how to avoid the end runs."

"You have to be an amateur psychiatrist to be a judge in this court," Doran says. Unlike most of his colleagues, he doesn't mind the shortages of staff and time, and as for money: "We'll never get any more money into these courts. I get through my cases, but you don't see me rushing." Sometimes, when the pace is slow, Doran takes a catnap between cases, right there at the bench. "That's not uncommon," says Janet Fink, a law guardian. "You have to be careful not to be talking, or not to let your witness talk, while the judge is sleeping, or signing papers, or chatting with a visitor."

.   .   .

Angel Sanchez's probable cause hearing convenes a little after 11 A.M.
on July 7 in Part IV, the only courtroom that operates on the sixth
floor of the building. Like the other courtrooms, it is small, even
intimate; only a few chairs line its octagonal walls, because neither the
public nor the press is allowed access to any of the Family Court's
proceedings. The furniture inside the room is also arranged octagon-
ally: from Judge Doran's perspective, the court clerk sits to his right;
the witness stand is to his left; across the room, the law guardian, the
respondent and his mother sit at a table on Doran's right; Corporation
Counsel has a table to his left. Inside this octagonal arrangement of
bench and tables, there is a well, a kind of sacred space that serves
to distance the antagonists from the majesty of the court. Officials
assigned to this Part feel at home within this space: the court reporter
sits there with his stenographic machine, halfway between judge and
witness; the court liaison officer, who represents Probation in these
proceedings, has a file-covered desk inside this area; and the uniformed court officers—the house policemen—stride back and forth
across it, carrying documents from counsel to the clerk or to the
judge. All parties to the case, however, are hustled around the outside
perimeter of the tables, and even the lawyers seem to hesitate before
entering this interdicted ground.

Irritated as he is by so much of what happens in Manhattan, Judge
Doran cares neither for the new Family Court building—"an archi-
tect's dream"—or his courtroom. The colors of the furniture—bright
orange and blue—are too jarring for people who are already of unstable temperament. Also, the octagonal arrangements: "It's unsettling,
too many corners, each wall seems to have its own door, and who
knows what's going to come out from those doors?" Nor does he
believe probable cause hearings have any purpose in this court. In
Criminal Court, such hearings are used to determine whether the
defendant should be held in jail in anticipation of further actions by
a grand jury, but since there are no grand juries in Family Court, why
bother? There are, nevertheless, two legitimate functions for probable
cause hearings in this court: Corporation Counsel is obliged to prove
(in Angel's case) that death was by other than natural causes, and that
there is evidence that ties the killing to Angel. Larry Schwartzstein
should have no difficulty here, so from Doran's point of view, the
hearing is useful only to determine whether Angel should be paroled

before his trial. Doran does not know Angel's history—the law says he must not be informed of it—but he does know that Judge Thurston has kept Angel on remand in Juvenile Center, so he is not likely to entertain seriously any motion from Tom Curtis that Angel be freed. Nevertheless, both Schwartzstein and Curtis want to have a probable cause hearing: for Schwartzstein it means that he will have fourteen days, not three, to round up witnesses and prepare his case; for Curtis, the hearing can, if he is skillful enough, be used for "discovery"—to find out what Schwartzstein knows, what strategies and witnesses he plans to use.

Curtis, this morning, is dressed in his most conservative style: white shirt, dark tie, blue pinstripe suit, his hair slicked back forcibly against his head. "It's not an afro today," Schwartzstein observes. "He looks like a prosecutor now. Kinky hair is for law guardians." Immediately the hearing begins, Curtis moves for a conference at the bench—much of what happens in Family Court happens off the record—and Doran invites counsel to his chambers. There Curtis explains to the judge what his motions are going to be and the order in which he will present them. "I have a tendency to talk very fast," Curtis observes later, "but I don't want to antagonize the judge. What good would *that* do? I get more of my clients out on the street than those who irritate judges do. So I was trying to keep the atmosphere very courtly. The scene in court had to be orderly. After all, it's what's on the record that counts, and the stenographers have trouble when three people talk all at once. Sometimes the record is a mess. I want to be sure this one is clear."

Forty-five minutes later, the hearing resumes. As the courtroom settles down, Detective Joyce, who is unruffled by Curtis's intention to suppress his confession ("I've got the murder weapon. I've got three witnesses. It won't matter if they throw the confession out"), sticks a needle into Tom: "Ah, you're the enemy."

This is not to Curtis's taste. "I'm *not* the enemy. I'm a good guy."

"Aren't you the law guardian?"

"Yes."

"The enemy."

Annoyed, Curtis shakes his head. "I've just spent two weeks in the National Guard protecting you."

"I've been doing that all my life."

Curtis is interested. "Where?"

"The police."

On the record, two minutes later, Curtis asks Judge Doran for a suppression hearing on what he calls Angel's "statement to the police." He argues that the suppression hearing—in legal terms, a voir dire, or a Huntley hearing—be heard *before* the probable cause hearing. Curtis hopes to prove either that Angel's confession was given involuntarily, or that it was extracted from him in flagrant violation of his rights. If he can bring this off, and if the confession is found inadmissible, he hopes to persuade Doran to disqualify himself from any further hearings on the grounds that he has been exposed to the illegal evidence.

It is arguments like this that prompt many people who should know better to complain that the Legal Aid lawyers get their clients off on "technicalities"—and, of course, since Angel was arrested no one has argued the facts of the alleged crime, but only matters of law. When the law guardians hear the "technicalities" complaint, they shrug resignedly. "The *technicalities,*" they patiently point out, "are the Fourth, Fifth and Sixth Amendments to the Constitution of the United States." The real problem here is not one of technicalities, but simply whether children who are faced with proceedings that may lead to their removal from their homes, and perhaps to incarceration, are endowed with the same rights that any literate adult knows have been his since this country began; the law says they have these rights, or very nearly all of them, but there's no question that many people would prefer the courts to act as if they hadn't.

Larry Schwartzstein, no stranger to technicalities himself, opposes Curtis's motion: "It has been my understanding that in Family Court when we are dealing with a Court absent a jury that all matters are before the same tryer of fact. As a matter of fact, the Court of Appeals in the matter of *People* v. *Brown* cited at 24 New York 2d 168 299 New York Supp. 2d 199 concluded as follows: 'Since a jury trial is not constitutionally required referring to Family Court proceedings, respondent's claim to the right of a separate hearing is without merit absent a jury trial. All questions of fact, including those dealing with the voluntariness of any statement, are determinable by the same judge who presides at the trial.' " Schwartzstein goes on to argue that the validity of Angel's statement is not a question to be determined before the fact-finding stage of the proceedings, that the existence of a statement, whether admissible or not, is sufficient to establish probable cause.

Judge Doran agrees: there will be no separate hearing for suppression. Curtis immediately asks that the case be sent back to Intake A "so the probable cause hearing could be heard by another judge." He reminds Doran that because inadmissible evidence may be heard in the probable cause hearing, it is essential that the judge who will preside over the fact-finding hearing—in this case, Doran—remain uncontaminated by it.

Schwartzstein opposes this motion as well. Judge Thurston, in Intake A, has already denied this motion. "I don't think that once we have a ruling by an Intake judge that we have to send it back to another Intake judge for another ruling." In fact, with the elapse of time, another judge now presides in Intake A.

Doran agrees again. The rotation of judges among the Parts is a matter so arbitrary that it alarms most people who have anything to do with Family Court, so Doran may well not, after all the delays, hear the fact-finding part of this case himself. "But apart from that," he says, "since the motion is that I refer this matter back to Intake A, I am not disposed to do that. I question my authority to do it. I may add I don't see any substantial merit that would require the Court to take such action." The only merit, from Curtis's point of view, is not one of law, but of defense strategy: the new Intake judge might well rule differently from Thurston. "Accordingly, Mr. Curtis, the motion to refer back to Intake A is denied."

Curtis: "Note my objection."

Doran: "Certainly. Are there any further applications at this time?"

Curtis has one. He wants to change the phrase in the petition that reads "and such death was caused" to read "and/or such death was caused." The emendation makes some legal sense.

Doran: "So this will be an and/or pleading?"

Curtis: "Yes."

Doran: "Grammatical purists would be horrified by that pleading. I don't want to take any responsibility for whatever legal complications may arise from grammatical improprieties." But he allows it. "Are we ready to proceed, gentlemen?"

They are. Schwartzstein introduces a certificate of death, an identification of the body by the police and another by a relative of the deceased. Curtis continues to object: "I would note that I think no proper foundation for their admission has been laid. . . . I would submit that further perusal of Section 190.30 of the Criminal Proce-dures Law makes me object to the submission of the third document," and so on.

Schwartzstein: "I will take it back. I merely offered it. It is my position and my position always has been to give the Legal Aid Society as much information as I have." The very image of the prose-cutor anxious to cooperate with the defense: this is Schwartzstein's style, and Curtis shrugs; he knows what will be withheld.

Curtis: "I withdraw my objection."

Doran: "I would think you would."

Detective Joyce is then sworn in. He testifies that he "responded to Bellevue about 11:15 P.M. June 29th at the emergency ward. One male identified as José Rodriguez was being operated on, emergency opera-tion. He expired a couple of minutes later." Ten minutes later, he took five men, friends of the deceased, to his office in the 13th Precinct. At 12:30 A.M. he went to the park where Rodriguez was stabbed. "A group of Spanish people flagged me down. Amongst them was Angel Sanchez and his mother." He identifies Angel and Mrs. Sanchez as being present in court. "Angel spoke to me and said, 'I stabbed José.' I took Angel into custody. A second police car had turned the corner and I borrowed handcuffs from one of the officers." Joyce drove Angel and his mother to the 13th Precinct. While in the car, Angel told Joyce that he was fifteen, which alerted Joyce to the special problems he faced in dealing with a juvenile. At the precinct, he took Angel to the "designated area for juveniles"—a room that must be of a certain size, on the ground floor, with a window. He offered Angel and Mrs. Sanchez coffee and sodas, which were declined, and then, because Mrs. Sanchez speaks little English, he had to cast about for an inter-preter, finally coming up with a bilingual policeman at 2:00 A.M. "I proceeded to advise Angel and his mother in English of their rights under the Miranda warnings. As I did that, Officer Alicea did it in Spanish." He then gave Angel pencil and paper. The confession was written and signed, then read aloud twice, once in English and again in Spanish.

Schwartzstein: "Did the respondent indicate any participation in a crime?"

Curtis: "Objection. It is not established my client's rights were afforded him. I would note at this time my request for a voir dire on the admissibility of the statement at the probable cause hearing."

Doran: "It hasn't been offered yet."

Curtis: "He's been asked if my client indicated his involvement in a crime. I would submit the answer would be the fruits of inquiry which has not been established."

Schwartzstein protests: "I am attempting to give the Legal Aid Society as much of an outline as they can have so they can prepare for trial." He is, he says, only "indicating" that a statement exists, its admissibility to be determined later.

Doran: "Objection overruled, Mr. Curtis."

Curtis: "Note my exception."

Doran: "Surely."

Further questions from Schwartzstein elicit the information that Angel stabbed José Rodriguez once with his knife, that Joyce informed Angel that Rodriguez had died and that Joyce had interviewed three witnesses to the killing, who referred to Angel as "Shorty."

Schwartzstein: "Did they indicate that they observed what transpired that evening in the park?"

Curtis: "I'm going to object to this line of inquiry on the grounds that it is hearsay. Hearsay is excludable under the rules of evidence set forth in Section 193."

Schwartzstein: "If we were on trial, there is no question that the information which is being elicited from the detective would be hearsay. It being probable cause, I'm trying to gain for Legal Aid as much information as I can," and so on. Curtis's objection is again overruled, and Schwartzstein introduces the confession in evidence. Curtis objects again and is again overruled.

On cross-examination, Curtis runs over Joyce's testimony again until Schwartzstein objects: "The information being elicited at this time is not material for a probable cause hearing."

Doran: "Objection sustained. Exception noted." He seems faintly amused. Throughout all of this, Doran, who appears hard of hearing, has screwed up his face and cupped his hand behind his ear. Seeing this, Curtis raises his voice, but then allows it to fade away again. "All judges here," Curtis says later, "see themselves as part of the law enforcement process—and that's not so. All judges pay too much attention to what the police say—as if that were fact. It isn't, necessarily." Now, Curtis protests that "180.60 of the Criminal Procedures Law says I have a right to cross-examine this witness."

Schwartzstein: "I would take exception to the comment that Mr. Curtis has made. I think Mr. Curtis is being given the opportunity to cross-examine this witness."

Curtis loses again. Doran says, "I have already made a ruling." In a probable cause hearing, as opposed to a fact-finding hearing, the judge has the discretion of limiting cross-examination. He must allow some, but he will never allow as much as the law guardian, who is trying to discover as much as he can of the prosecution's case, would like. "They play games," Doran says, "but I can play games, too."

Curtis makes a final stab: "Officer, you said you interviewed three individuals. Who were those three individuals?"

He doesn't have a chance. Schwartzstein is on his feet. "I would at this point object to the identity of these three individuals for the following reasons: one, for their own protection, and two, because I want to be sure they will come forth at the date of the trial without being harassed or being bothered by investigators or anyone of the Legal Aid Society."

Doran: "Well, counselor, probable cause hearing is not a substitute for discovery. Objection sustained."

Curtis: "I would submit that we have a right to interview those witnesses if they wish to be interviewed. We can't force anybody to be interviewed if they don't wish to be." Doran is impervious to such pleas. "I would note my strong objection," Curtis says. He believes he has a right to know who the opposition's witnesses are. "With research," he says later, "you can often prove that they couldn't have seen what they'll swear they saw." But if after talking to them, Curtis sees his case is weak, he may persuade Angel to plead to Murder 3, manslaughter, and get him sent away for a year and a half instead of five. On this matter, Curtis is mistaken: unlike federal law, New York State law does not require the disclosure of witnesses.

Having lost these skirmishes, Curtis declines to call his own witnesses. He tells the court that probable cause has not been proved at this hearing because the disputable confession "indicates that my client *accidentally* caused the death of this individual." Schwartzstein replies that it is for the fact-finding hearing to determine whether death was "accidental." Doran agrees, finds probable cause has been established and sets a trial date for July 22. Firing his last bullet, Curtis asks Doran to disqualify himself from hearing the trial on the grounds that he has heard evidence that might be suppressed later on. Doran brushes the idea aside.

Without protest from Curtis, Angel is remanded to Juvenile Center until his fact-finding hearing. Had Curtis moved for his client's parole, Seymour Gottfried, the court liaison officer, who represents the interests of the Probation Department in the courtroom, would have opposed it. The law says specifically that a juvenile may *not* be held in detention unless there is a substantial probability that he will not appear in court on his return date, or if there is a serious risk that he may, while on parole, commit another crime. "I argue from the evidence," Gottfried says, "the evidence in that file." He points to the hefty file that Probation has assembled on Angel. "That kid will kill somebody else as soon as he has a chance. Often, though, the law guardians will try to negate my evidence. I've been severely put to the test. Even on dangerous assaults, the use of knives and weapons, I've been put to the test." Gottfried has been doing this kind of work for twenty years. "I was in this court before the law guardians got into it. And believe me, the rights of the kids were often ignored. The judge would act as executioner. Nowadays the cops constantly screw up their cases and these law guardians, they're sharp, they get the kids off free, the judge has to throw the case out." But Gottfried was confident from the start that Curtis wouldn't ask for parole this time. "That Sanchez kid, he'd as soon stab you as look at you. He's really mean. That's what Tom doesn't want me to say to the judge."

Indeed, Curtis doesn't. Since Doran will preside at the trial, he doesn't want him to hear a thing about Angel's past. He tells Angel he won't argue for parole. "I don't want the judge to hear your record." Angel nods. The prospect of a couple of weeks' imprisonment, so terrifying the day before, has suddenly become less so: Angel has heard from his mother that if he is released he may be killed by Rodriguez's friends.

The days just preceding Angel's trial leave Tom Curtis tense with frustration. Although he has offered the court reporter three times the going rate, he has not yet received the transcript of the probable cause hearing. He has not received the autopsy on José Rodriguez, nor the toxicologist's report, which would indicate whether the deceased had been high on drugs at the time of his death. Rodriguez, Curtis has learned, was probably a drug dealer, but because he showed kids like Angel the tricks of breaking and entering, he was popular in the neighborhood. Curtis suspects that Rodriguez was a violent man, and if he can develop that theory he may be able to support Angel's claim that Rodriguez had attacked him with the junkie's purse. Did Rodriguez swing the bag at Angel and fall on the knife? "Maybe," Curtis says. Then he pauses. "Not likely." Besides, he has heard a rumor that the autopsy will show not one knife wound, but four. "That destroys my case. He kept jumping on the knife? Not likely."

Curtis also suspects that the three "witnesses" the prosecution intends to produce are friends of the victim who will happily perjure themselves. One of them, it turns out, is a client of one of Curtis's colleagues in Legal Aid, which poses an insuperable ethical problem: Curtis does not act for himself in a trial, but for the firm; he cannot, having access to his colleague's files, fairly attempt to discredit one of his firm's clients. For a few days, Curtis thought he would have to drop the case—Angel would get a private lawyer after all—but then Larry Schwartzstein announced that he was so confident of victory that he didn't intend to use the tainted witness. This strikes Curtis as odd, because he has learned that this boy, and several others, forcibly walked the profusely bleeding Rodriguez to a clinic six long blocks from the scene of the stabbing. "*They* killed him, really," Curtis says.

On July 22, the confusion in Part IV is worse than ever. Tom Curtis received the autopsy report and the transcript of the probable cause hearing only the night before, and the toxicological report—a test for

the presence of alcohol and drugs in the deceased's blood and kidneys
—only minutes before the court convened. "The autopsy," Curtis
says, "always has an effect on judges that is detrimental to my clients.
The description of the wounds, the fractures, the contusions, the
defensive wounds on the victim's hands—that has a strong effect." In
Judge Doran's chambers, Curtis says that he must ask for an adjournment of the trial. The autopsy shows that José Rodriguez was killed
by a single blow, which may help Angel's claim that the death was
"accidental." The toxicology report shows the presence of morphine
and quinine, a compound used to cut morphine in the manufacture
of heroin. "I need time to consider this."

"It takes twenty seconds to read," Larry Schwartzstein says in an
aside. "We should proceed. This shows the stupidity of this Part.
Nothing's going to be done. Why shouldn't it be tried? I brought in
six people. This is the day it's *supposed* to be tried!"

But Curtis cannot be rushed. What was the effect of the morphine?
he wonders. What did it make him do? "My kid is confronted in a
park by a drug abuser who's been to prison. It may be self-defense."
Curtis wants the "yellow sheet"—the Police Department's arrest record—on Rodriguez; this can be subpoenaed, but it will take time to
get.

Time is the problem: Detective Joyce is about to start his vacation;
when he returns, Schwartzstein begins his. The scheduling mess is
impossible. "Let's do it the easy way," Schwartzstein says to Curtis.
"Take a plea." He offers Curtis Manslaughter I, which will result in
a five-year term: one year in restricted placement, two years in a less
restricted facility, two more years elsewhere. Self-defense, however, is
Manslaughter 2, worth only a year and a half.

Back in the courtroom, Curtis requests his adjournment.

Doran: "I grant your application. This is a serious matter." Curtis
suspects that Doran, who will return to the Bronx in ten days, would
just as soon not get tangled in a case that might bring him back to
Manhattan, or be reversed on appeal.

Doran calendars the case for September 6 and continues Angel's
remand. Curtis objects. Doran gives him a wintry smile.

. . .

Afterward, Curtis is very upset. In a corridor behind the courtroom, he paces nervously back and forth, his hands clasped tightly behind him. "I'm feeling very defensive about this," he says. In fact, he knows he has not prepared his record well for a writ of habeas corpus that he wants to file in the state Supreme Court to have Angel tried as soon as medical records can be obtained. For an hour in the judge's chambers they argued the question of adjournment. Curtis had wanted the trial to proceed the following week and had said so, but there was no court reporter present and his arguments were consequently all off the record. He should immediately have made the same argument on the record when they went back into the courtroom, but he forgot. He could, too, have asked the judge to substitute Angel's pressing case for another on his calendar that involved a boy at home on parole, but he did not. If all this were not damaging enough, Curtis is in the awkward position of reversing himself: during the probable cause hearing, he had argued that Doran should *not* hear the trial, and now he wants to file a writ arguing that Doran *must* hear the trial. These omissions and contradictions may very well sink his writ, because the Supreme Court justice who hears it will be guided by what the record shows. Allowances will not be made for Curtis's legal lapses. "I've made a bad record," he says.

In the courtroom, just before leaving, Curtis turned to Janet Fink, a law guardian who had stopped by to watch the aborted proceedings.

"It *was* a bad record, wasn't it?" he asked her.

"No," said Fink, exhibiting at the same time her customary unflappable demeanor and the extraordinary team spirit that prompts the law guardians to be supportive of each other. And then, because professional candor is important too, she adds: "I've seen better."

Curtis broods. Perhaps he has been thinking too hard about getting Angel back to the streets, where he may be murdered; too much about the trial and not enough about the disposition. "Maybe a year in a state hospital would be better for him." He denies that he is concerned with that bugaboo, "the best interests of the child." "I don't know what that means. I'm talking about an easier sentence." It seems that Angel was supposed to be taking half of a five-milligram pill of methyltestosterone each day, letting it melt under his tongue, but instead he was swallowing the whole pill: a double dose. Might *that* have precipitated the killing?

"This is an unusual case," he says. "I've had homicides before, but I can't get a hook on this one. Every time I try to get something on it, the lead melts away. Here's an example. Last summer I had a client, fifteen, who was arrested for murder. He and a buddy were approached by a junkie who accused them of throwing beer bottles at him. These two kids attacked him. My client hit him with a stick about the head while the other stabbed him in the chest and stomach seventeen times. Previously, a woman had tried to hold them apart. She was a Corporation Counsel witness. My kid had no record and didn't actually kill the man—the blows would not have killed him—so we got the sentence reduced to Manslaughter 2. Which meant a year in a secure facility, and he hasn't caused trouble since. That was the hook, you see: he didn't have a record. He didn't deliver the fatal wounds.

"Here's another case. Four kids chase three guys from Ecuador through Harlem. One guy breaks away. My kid follows him. While he's chasing him, one of my kid's buddies kills one of the other Ecuador guys. All four kids were arrested for murder, but the hook was that mine was a ways off, pursuing another man. He got off.

"But what's the hook on this one?"

Curtis sits on his briefcase and begins writing notes for his writ. He is tempted to move for a jury trial. Never mind that the U.S. Supreme Court has ruled that juveniles are not entitled to jury trials. Never mind that the Family Court has no facilities for a jury trial. "That's not my problem," Curtis snaps. There's a statute which says that any person who may be incarcerated for a year or more is entitled to a jury trial, and under this new Designated Felony Act such incarceration is what Angel faces.

"I'm losing sleep over this," Curtis says.

The writ fails, or, more accurately, is made moot. In the interim, Angel has been convicted in one of his other cases, the knifing case, and he has been remanded for a statutory twenty days pending his other trials. Curtis had applied in his writ either for a speedy trial in the matter of Angel's alleged homicide, or parole until the September 6 date. He thought he might be ordered to go to trial the next day, unprepared, but instead the Supreme Court justice ruled that since

Angel was legally remanded until the middle of August, the writ would be adjourned. Curtis had not expected that. By mid-August, Angel has been found guilty again: in the rifle case, the charge of menacing is dropped because Angel cooperated in returning the rifle, but he is found guilty of petty larceny, for taking a packet of plaster from the store.

A few weeks later, Angel is tried for the attempted murder in the movie theater. The trial takes two days. The victim is present. He hasn't seen Angel since the incident, but very coolly he points his finger at him and says, "He stabbed me."

Curtis is surprised. He still thought Angel innocent of this one. "I don't like being surprised in the courtroom," Curtis says; he doesn't approve of a complainant's coming into court, looking over at the defendant's chair and saying: "You." He thinks the complainant was lying; he thinks there should have been a proper lineup, but with Angel's runty figure, what good can a lineup do? "It would have been a futile gesture. But then, that's what the law's about: futile gestures."

This case is heard before Judge Stanley Gartenstein, who presides in Part IV in September. On September 6, a few days later, Curtis makes pro forma gestures to persuade Gartenstein to disqualify himself from hearing the Rodriguez case. Gartenstein declines. What's the use? Curtis asks. He's heard the other case, he knows Angel's record. Curtis confers with Schwartzstein and accepts a plea: Manslaughter 2 in the Rodriguez case, combined with an Assault 1 finding in the movie theater case. The two admissions together should result in no more than a three-year sentence: a year "inside," Curtis estimates, followed by two years in a residential facility. No question, of course, of consecutive sentences being imposed. "He who commits more crimes gets punished less," Larry Schwartzstein observes.

So now, after all of Curtis's legal maneuverings, there will be no trial in the Rodriguez killing, but only a formality to be observed. Curtis rises to address Judge Gartenstein, motioning for Angel to rise with him. Law guardians have a standard spiel for the record to run through when making an admission; the exact words vary from lawyer to lawyer, but not much. Curtis tells Gartenstein that he has advised Angel of his rights, explained what those rights mean and what is likely to happen to him if he pleads guilty in court. He says that Angel knowingly and voluntarily wishes to admit to a charge of Manslaughter in the second degree.

The judge, for the record, must then go over all this territory again.

Gartenstein: "Angel, do you know who Mr. Curtis is?" A mumbled assent. "Did he advise you of your right to remain silent?" Another mumble. "What does that mean to you?"

Angel: "I've kind of forgot. I'm nervous."

Gartenstein: "Just relax. We don't bite. Do you know what 'remain silent' means?"

Angel: "I don't have to speak without a lawyer."

Gartenstein: "Mr. Curtis, coach your client. I want no ambiguities on the record."

Curtis and Angel confer in whispers. Angel then tells the judge what happened in the park: Rodriguez swung the purse at him, and Angel stabbed him in the chest.

Gartenstein: "Have any threats been made to you, any promises made to you, to get you to say these things?"

The question, necessary for the record, is nearly meaningless. Promises have not been made, for the attorneys cannot know what a judge will do, and Gartenstein is a tough judge who, at Angel's disposition two weeks hence, will insist that the two sentences must run consecutively, much to Curtis's horror. Curtis: "The legislature *never* intended that!" Gartenstein: "Show me where they didn't." Nevertheless, today an understanding seems to have been reached: you make life easier for us and we will make yours considerably easier for you. But because no one mentions this arrangement openly in court, Angel mutters his obligatory no.

It is all over now, except for the really hard work. Curtis, without much help from Probation, must work to get Angel remanded to the Bronx State Hospital, which is set up to deal with violent kids, and not to Goshen, a prison upstate which is the only other maximum security facility mandated for children convicted of Designated Felonies. Goshen confines the worst kids in the state—most of them look like adults—and there the undersized Angel would be further victimized, sodomized, perhaps even killed.

Angel is led away, and Curtis picks up his files. Whether Angel's ordeal will extend for a further three years, or six years, he will remain

Curtis's client; Curtis will be involved in whatever problems he encounters in the course of his confinement. Curtis shudders. The day has not gone as well as it might have, and he has a fever, has been ill for several days. As he leaves the courtroom, he is told that another client of his has just been brought in on a homicide charge.

"It's very unusual for a lawyer to have two homicides," Curtis says. For a moment he hopes that this boy won't want him to represent him. Then he shoves the thought aside.

II

The Coming
of Family Court

For it is most certain, that our Law hath a very
great and tender consideration for Persons naturally
disabled, and especially for *Minors.* The Law
protects their Persons, preserves their Rights and
Estates, excuseth their Laches, and assists them in
their Pleadings. . . . *The Judges are their
Counsellors, the Jury are their Servants . . . and the
Law is their Guardian.*

Anon.: *Infant's Lawyer* (London, 1697)

On June 16—two weeks to the day before Angel Sanchez was brought
in on his charge of Murder 2—Judge Margaret Taylor, presiding in
Part II of Manhattan's Family Court, picked up the papers before her
and threw them over her shoulder. "I give up!" she yelled. "I don't
know why I took this job. Don't talk to me!"

It is 4:10 in the afternoon, and court is in session. Judge Taylor, on
loan from the Civil Court to which she was elected, has been trying
a particularly brutal case of child abuse. She is a trim, attractive
woman of perhaps fifty, her hair just beginning to turn gray. Her
manner is brisk, she speaks very fast, yet she manages to muster a
warm smile for the unfortunates who respond to her morning calendar call. The law guardians love her. "She really believes in due
process," says one. "When the prosecution collapses, she throws the

case out of court. She doesn't try to build it up again. Every other judge does." In fact, Taylor overrules herself. She admits to ignorance of the law. She will say "Shut up" to the lawyers, then agree to listen, then let them do what they want.

Counsel: "Can I have a little more time on that, your honor?"

Taylor: "No. How much time do you want? All right."

"Everybody hates her," says Marvin Epstein, a lawyer for the Bureau of Child Welfare. "When I'm trying a case before her, I'm fighting two lawyers. She's counsel for the defense." Robert Olzman, the court reporter in Part II today, agrees. As his hands play over his stenographic machine, he rolls his eyes to the ceiling whenever Judge Taylor makes a ruling. "No one else wants to work in this Part," he told the judge this morning. Taylor nodded. "Perhaps they're trying to tell me something." She meant to make a joke, but Olzman nodded vigorously: Yes, ma'am, you bet they are.

And so it has been all day. Judges in Family Court must hear cases involving adults as well as children, and Taylor's morning began with a support case: a woman is demanding $384.60 a week from her estranged husband. Taylor can hardly believe that she must hear such a plea. "I ask myself, why am I *listening* to this? These people with all their advantages could settle this. I have all *those* people out there" —she gestures to the waiting room crowded with children and their parents—"who have *real* problems. What we need in this court is an R&R Part. Rest and Recreation. After nine months in a tough Part, one month in R&R with these long, boring support cases. If I tried this case, it would take three days." To the husband and wife before her, however, she says only that under Section 1049 of the Family Court Act she is required to give preference to cases involving neglect, abuse and children in remand. "I must say it will be hard for you to get a hearing in this court." Why don't they try the matrimonial division of the Supreme Court instead? "We are five judges short, which shows what the public thinks of the Family Court. I have cases involving children who have been remanded for over a year."

In fact, she has thirty-two cases on her calendar today. Few will be heard in their entirety, some not at all. Each case she does hear proceeds to a certain point and then is adjourned for one reason or another. In one case this morning, involving the permanent removal of a neglected child, the mother doesn't show. That would seem to be evidence enough of the mother's indifference, but Taylor balks. She will not order the child's removal from her mother's home without talking to the mother. "To explain what it means, that she'll never see her child again." She turns to the mother's lawyer.

Taylor: "Do you know where your client is?"

Lawyer: "No, your honor."

Taylor: "Why didn't you bring her here with you?"

Lawyer: "I just got this slip. It says only to be here today."

Taylor: "You didn't try to get in touch with the mother?"

Lawyer: "If I'd been told to find the mother, I would have tried."

Taylor sighs. "There is no way this court helps anyone without stigmatizing them: the mentally ill, the juvenile delinquent, the PINS. It goes on their records for the rest of their lives. I think this is an outrage that we have to do this. Therefore, I do everything I can to avoid a finding. That's the shocking, terrible thing that we do in this court: if they agree to neglect or mental illness, they are found *guilty.* I'm not going to fool around with euphemisms. That's why I want to arrange a *voluntary* surrender of this child."

The mother's lawyer, turning aside, says, "Jesus Christ." This lawyer is all for giving the kid up for adoption; he knows his client, the mother, is no good, and the kid's "best interest" is what matters. He tries to explain this elementary idea to Judge Taylor, who immediately declares a mistrial.

Taylor: "You must represent the mother, *just* the mother. You must not take the position of the Court."

Lawyer: "You're talking a blue streak. No one else can say anything."

Taylor: "It's the obligation of a lawyer to represent his client."

Lawyer: "The record is clear. What's the use of that?"

Lawyers, Taylor believes, never represent the mother. "It's shocking. I have to do it myself." To this lawyer, she says: "I can't even believe we're having this conversation. You're a lawyer. It's not my job to represent your client. I will not permit due process to be violated in this court."

Lawyer: "When your honor is out of breath, I'll try to say something."

Half an hour later, confronted with another support case, Judge Taylor turns to one of the lawyers and asks, "What would *you* do?"

Lawyer: "With all due respect, your honor, this is the kind of attitude that makes this court a laughing matter. Why don't we throw up our hands and walk out, your honor? You and I could do it right now."

And so, with this kind of thing going on all day, Judge Taylor ends the afternoon by throwing her papers all over the floor. She turns to a court officer and says: "Go outside and adjourn every case until September. Everybody's remanded till September. All their motions are denied. All the other judges do it this way, why shouldn't I? Maybe the other judges are right: don't give a shit. The lawyers shout at me. What am I going to do? I give up. I don't know what to do. I really don't know how to handle the Family Court calendar."

All of this is off the record, because the stenographer has gone to the toilet. For the past few hours, lawyers in the cases that Judge Taylor has been trying to balance have been arguing about their vacation schedules; no one agrees just how much time he has spent waiting for his case to be heard.

Lawyer: "Counsel says he's been here for four days. I've only been here for two days."

Taylor: "Oh, that's very significant. Let's talk about that for a while."

Now Taylor says, "I want a long argument, no short arguments. This is the way Family Court works, right? We normally adjourn cases for two months. This is the way things are normally done." A lawyer tries to get some of what Judge Taylor has just said on the record, but she denies his motion. "I'm tired. It's the end of the day. Everyone wants to make a statement. I ask, why? Is it possible that anyone has a perspective on this case? Lawyers argue; I really don't understand it. It's wasting people's time. Everyone corrects everyone else. Lawyers' statements do not ring bells with me."

From the waiting room outside, lawyers, hearing that their cases have been remanded to September, try to enter Judge Taylor's courtroom to protest. She refuses them: "I don't want to talk to lawyers." A motion is made to transfer the case at hand to the state Supreme Court, but Taylor brushes it aside. "It doesn't solve this problem. Family Court does try, does care."

When all but two lawyers have left the court, Taylor again admits defeat. "I've just given up. I think you should do just two cases a day and adjourn everything else. Let the cases take two years. If you don't let a lawyer talk for six hours, they complain."

One of the lawyers says, "This kid, in this case, has been traumatized."

Taylor: "Every child in this court is traumatized by everything. The only conclusion I can come to in Family Court is that parents are destructive of their children. They do terrible things to them. They say terrible things. Neither parent should have the child most of the time. I know this case could have been finished in half the time, but *how?* Everything takes so much time. In Supreme Court, you know, seven to ten Parts are not working *every day* because they have nothing to do."

One of the lawyers mentions one of the more colorful Family Court judges. "Why don't you do what she does? Pay no attention to the rules of evidence. Cut off testimony. Act on common sense."

"But," says Taylor, "she was reversed all the time. Her cases kept coming back. That doesn't save time. Energy. My spirit."

"It's the system," a lawyer says.

"The system stinks," says the other.

"It's Charley Schinitsky's fault," says the first. "I say to him, '*You* started all this. *You're* responsible.' "

Many people—the cynics and some time-serving civil servants in the Family Court—would like to blame Charles Schinitsky for the mess the court is in today. Schinitsky is attorney-in-charge of the Juvenile Rights Division of New York City's Legal Aid Society. Twenty years ago, virtually singlehandedly, he wrought a revolution in the juvenile court system of New York State, a revolution that spread rapidly to other states and became mandated by the federal courts as well. What Schinitsky did, in essence, was to bring lawyers into the court to represent the children. One might think that a courtroom was a congenial habitat for lawyers, but until recently they were not wanted in the juvenile courts; the consensus of the preceding sixty years had been that lawyers would make a mess of the kindly ministrations these courts were established to provide. And so, depending on how you

define "mess," they have: no one is as obstreperous or as profligate
of precious court time as a lawyer concerned with due process, rigorous cross-examination of witnesses, the presentation of evidence and
testimony favorable to his client, and the insistence that troubled
children receive the services to which, by law, they are entitled.

Nevertheless, the mess that is Family Court cannot be laid at
Charles Schinitsky's door. That this court *is* a mess is the result of
numerous confusions and incompetencies, many of impressive historical venerability. From its inception in medieval English chancery
courts, juvenile law has been of all legal disciplines (possibly excepting
law relating to mental health) the least firmly grounded in the assumptions and traditions of "due process." From its inception, juvenile law
has been carefully isolated from the rigors and precedents of common
law; in fact, its philosophical underpinnings derive not from law
but from humanitarian concerns and from prevailing fashions in
sociology.*

The earliest expression of such concern, deriving from the time of
the chancery courts, may be found in the doctrine of *parens patriae,*
which is a legal provision allowing the state to assume, in the event
of presumed parental default, responsibility for the custody and protection of children within its jurisdiction—and of their property interests as well. Impressive as the Latin phrase may sound, the doctrine
has no basis in common law. In common law, children under seven
were considered incapable of criminal intent; children over seven were
treated as adults. Legal historians today tend to view *parens patriae*
with irony or contempt, as a kind of quasi-legal camouflage that can
be used to cover a multitude of legal sins. Speaking for the United
States Supreme Court in *In Re Gault,* the most important case involving juvenile rights, Justice Abe Fortas said: "The Latin phrase proved

---

*The best description—albeit of a textbookish sort--of the history and philosophy of
juvenile law is to be found in Frederic L. Faust and Paul J. Brantingham's *Juvenile
Justice Philosophy: Readings, Cases, Comments* (St. Paul, 1974). More general, but also
useful, is Ellen Ryerson's *The Best-laid Plans: America's Juvenile Court Experiment*
(New York, 1978). To these, and to a seminar taught in 1976 at New York University
Law School by Martin Guggenheim and Alan Sussman, I am indebted for much of
what I say here, from the role of the chancery courts to the invention of juvenile court
in Illinois in 1899.

to be a great help to those who sought to rationalize the exclusion of juveniles from the constitutional scheme; but its meaning is murky and its historical credentials are of dubious relevance."

Thus it can fairly be said that the confusion surrounding a child's position at law dates from the earliest time that he was thought to have a special, or privileged, position at all. Chancery courts, whose jurisdiction lay in equity rather than in common law, were held in suspicion by American revolutionaries determined to reject the prerogatives of monarchy, of which *parens patriae* was one. Nevertheless, Americans, like their English forebears, have never had to look far for reasons to intervene in the privacy of family life. In our colonial days, we were quick to adapt the English Poor Law of 1601, which allowed for the involuntary removal of children from parents thought to be undeserving; such children were apprenticed to more proper families without litigation and without their natural parents being informed of their whereabouts. The legal question of whether a child has a right to be raised by his parents (and this question's more subtle permutations—is it the right of the child? of the parents? or of both?) was not, until this century, much bruited about in the land.

The first center for the forcible detention of wayward children was established in this country in 1824. The motivating idea behind the New York House of Refuge, a humanitarian idea based on the best social theory of its time, was that troubled children should be removed from the fate that awaited them in adult prisons. Only one type of serious offender—the kind of child we would today call a juvenile delinquent—was ever confined there. The rest were those who could never have reasonably been sent to jail: children who were neglected or disobedient. Conditions at the House of Refuge were harsh. The day began with two hours of classes preceding breakfast, followed by eight hours of labor (piecework, for the most part, contracted for from local industries), then two more hours of schooling. The children were locked in their rooms at night and ordered to observe strict silence. Nathaniel Hart, the superintendent of the House of Refuge, remarked, "We will be fathers to them if they obey the rules." From these rules and this regimen it was assumed the children would learn the values of thrift, honesty and individual responsibility.

These expectations failed. Undeterred by what the law might do to them, juvenile gangs flourished in the city, causing one reformer to warn against the day when "the outcast, vicious, reckless multitude of New York boys, swarming now in every foul alley and low street, [will] come to know their power and *use* it." Nor could the House of Refuge and similar reform schools modeled on it achieve their stated purpose: the few children who were so confined were not reformed.

As if to compound the confusion of dubious law and more dubious social theory, the phrase *parens patriae* resurfaced for the first time in America in 1839, when a mother in Pennsylvania brought her daughter, Mary Ann Crouse, to court on a complaint that she was unmanageable. The court agreed and dispatched the girl to a reform school. Mary Ann's father objected, claiming that his daughter's confinement without trial by jury was unconstitutional. Pennsylvania's Supreme Court dismissed his claim in a one-page opinion, maintaining that the purpose of Mary Ann's and other children's confinement was improvement, reformation, wholesome restraint, and protection from depraved parents or environment. Therefore, no jury trial was necessary. "The infant," the court declared, "has been snatched from a course which must have ended in confirmed depravity; and not only is the restraint of her person lawful, but it would be an act of extreme cruelty to release her from it." Citing *parens patriae,* the court continued: "It is to be remembered that the public has a paramount interest in the virtue and knowledge of its members, and that of strict right, the business of education belongs to it. That parents are ordinarily intrusted with it is because it can seldom be put into better hands; but where they are incompetent or corrupt, what is there to prevent the public from withdrawing their faculties, held, as they obviously are, at its sufferance? The right of parental control is a natural, but not an inalienable one." In this portentous decision the murky Latin phrase from chancery court was used to justify not only the removal of children from their parents, but the right of the state to do so by extralegal means.

Fundamental to the attitudes of those who, in the nineteenth century, were concerned about children in trouble with the law was a departure from the classical theory of criminology as it was developed in the eighteenth century by the Englishman Jeremy Bentham and the Italian Cesare Beccaria. Bentham and Beccaria, appalled by the cruel and often arbitrary punishments meted out to the criminals of their day, suggested that the law should devise penalties only severe enough to achieve security and order; anything more was tyranny. Believing that the offender operated from his own free will, and anxious to limit the powers of the state, they advocated a laissez-faire approach to crime: punish the criminal only after the crime has been committed, and make the punishment specific; thus would future criminals be deterred from committing offenses. Beccaria maintained that rewarding virtue would deter the unvirtuous from their schemes. Bentham, believing that men sought pleasure and avoided pain, argued that men would avoid the pain that the punishment of criminal acts would entail. Laudable, however, as their attempts to rationalize the treatment of criminals may have been, their assumptions about human nature were, to say the least, inadequate. One wonders what either Bentham or Beccaria would have made of a man who, devotedly served by his wife, methodically tortures her son by a prior marriage because he himself had been tortured by his father.

It is safe to assume that these reformers never encountered such a man—but then neither did the reformers of the nineteenth century who jettisoned the classical theories. These were middle-class, well-intentioned people, concerned with preserving the status quo, anxious about the threat posed to the traditional rural quality of American life by the growth of urban slums and the uncontrollable behavior of those who bred there. These reformers, more interested in the criminal than in the crime, adopted the spirit of the engineer rather than that of the detached observer. Unlike Bentham and Beccaria, they discounted the role of free will in criminal behavior, which was, according to the new philosophy, determined by forces outside the criminal's control. Unlike the classical theorists, who advocated deterring men from crime, the positivists (as these new theorists came to be known) emphasized treatment and rehabilitation of the criminal. Deriving their scientific determinism from the ideas of Darwin, Marx, Freud and an Italian criminologist, Cesare Lombroso (whose theories they understood only in part), they argued that punishment was obsolete and the criminal sick, that crime was the result of environmental pressures and the disintegration of family control. In their scientific way, they discarded not only the classical model of an impartial and impersonal justice, but notions of moral culpability and responsibility as well; in the vacuum thus created they collected data about criminals and built composite portraits of criminal types. Sin, they suggested, must be understood to mean misfortune, and the offender's moral defects were to be treated as one would the bad nutrition or defective eyesight that were the probable cause of the offender's antisocial behavior.

When put into practice, these ideas of European origin proved entirely suited to the American temper—its can-do optimism, its hustling determination to do good, to do the impossible, to straighten out intractable problems with liberal lashings of generosity and technology. If human beings can be changed by changing their environments, then by George we'll change those environments, never mind that the premise is unsubstantiated and may be entirely misconceived. And if rehabilitation is the aim of what we now call our correctional approach to criminology, then what better arena is there to test its validity than that of juvenile justice? If, as these nineteenth-century reformers believed, children are essentially innocent—that is to say, without responsibility for their antisocial behavior and possessed of a basic inner purity—then they cannot be perceived as hardened criminals. And surely those who are not yet enslaved by vice are most susceptible to rehabilitation. Sentimental the theory may have been, and fundamentally unsound, but there was a nobility to it as well, and, as so often happens with unsound philosophies, it resulted in sound and necessary reforms. Upon this theory, developed a century ago, the juvenile courts were founded, and upon it such faith as yet remains that these courts may do some good is sustained.

Once it had been decided that children were not to be treated as criminals, it became imperative to remove them from corrupt environments where they would learn antisocial behavior. Throughout the last century, wayward children were mixed with adults in detention cells, courtrooms and penal institutions. The reformers now demanded that children be segregated from adult offenders. In Massachusetts, between 1870 and 1877, measures were taken to create separate Parts in which juvenile cases might be heard, separate detention cells and rehabilitation centers, separate dockets and records systems. These, however, were only partial steps. Not until 1899, with the establishment of the country's first juvenile court in Cook County,

Illinois, did the reformers achieve their goal of having cases involving children dealt with by civil, not criminal, proceedings. And with the invention of the juvenile court came—as a kind of by-product—the invention of a new status of person in America: the juvenile delinquent.

The enacting legislation was deliberately broad and vague. Although the juvenile court was to be a civil court, endowed with all the far-reaching and coercive powers of the state, it was also to be something of a friend to the child: the state as the wise adult sitting in for the child's defaulting parents. If justice in this court was to be "personalized" and "socialized," then constitutional restraints and due process were out of order, and so was the idea of equality under the law. This was not, as everyone kept emphasizing, a *criminal* court. Whatever the court did with a child—and once the child was under the court's jurisdiction it could do pretty much what it wanted with him—it would not leave him stigmatized with a criminal record. The idea was to treat the child fairly, to understand his problem and his needs and to arrange for those needs to be met. Since the child was not perceived as a criminal, he had no need of constitutional guarantees when appearing before this court. The court, in fact, went so far as to hope that it might intervene in the life of this child *before,* not after, he committed an antisocial act.

Because prevention and rehabilitation were the court's primary concerns, rules of evidence were discarded lest they inhibit the court's attempts to gain a whole picture of the miscreant's circumstances. To this end, hearsay evidence—inadmissible in criminal proceedings—would be allowed. The court's decision would not be made on a determination that the child had "beyond a reasonable doubt" done something specific, but upon "the preponderance of the evidence" relating to the child's overall pattern of behavior. That the court might more efficiently determine what to do with this child, the proceedings would be kept informal. For its further ease, and to protect the child's privacy and future reputation, the court would also be closed to all who might raise troubling questions: lawyers, for instance, were clearly not needed, nor was the press, nor was the public.

The result was that no one knew what was going on in these courts.

Because lawyers were not permitted to make appeals, the appellate courts didn't know what was going on. Because the definition of delinquency was so vague, young people were being adjudged delinquents pretty much according to whether their behavior differed markedly from the judge's experience of what a child's orderly demeanor should be. Because the court's mandate was to assume jurisdiction over any child who needed help, any child who was picked up off the street could be charged with something in court. But then, the court was the child's *friend.* It acted in his "best interests." Could anyone disapprove of that?

The invention of the juvenile court in 1899, with its conception of justice hitherto unknown to any jurist in history, was a revolution indeed.

Three-quarters of a century later, in his fifth-floor office at 189 Montague Street in Brooklyn, the author of the second revolution in juvenile justice reflected on the juvenile courts as they spread from Cook County across the country. In this winter of 1976, Charles Schinitsky is sixty. A quiet, robust-looking man with a full and pleasant face, his gray hair is cut close about his scalp, his gray suit is unremarkable. On the street, walking toward the complex of Brooklyn court buildings a few hundred yards away, he would not be noticed: someone in the civil service, perhaps, or a senior accountant for a large corporation. When he arrives in Family Court, however, something happens—not to him, but to the familiars of the court. Schinitsky's authority is of the kind that is visible primarily in the responses of others: social workers, lawyers, even judges are pleased to attract his attention for a moment.

Now, in his modest office in the even more modest quarters of the Legal Aid Society's Juvenile Rights Division, Schinitsky recalls the rumblings of discontent these courts provoked in the late 1950s. "Throughout the years, facilities were lacking. The hope was that with these new courts, resources and facilities would be developed to help the kids become useful citizens. It was a good concept, except these kinds of resources require a great deal of money. The money wasn't there. The people responsible for treating kids, even today, are thinking mainly about pensions, hours, perquisites. Unions are very strong in the agencies. The courts couldn't compel private agencies to take a kid, so the kids who most desperately need help, the ones who are seriously disturbed and acting out, aren't accepted anywhere. Nothing was being done, is being done now. There were many instances where kids who were dealt with in a juvenile court ended up in a correctional facility. There's a question even now if there aren't some states that mix kids with adults in jails.

"And of course there was the concept that a kid is not a full individual with constitutional rights. You did with him what you wanted because he was a kid. Toward the end of the '50s you could hear a little rumbling going on. In New York, the Citizens' Committee for Children was concerned with what was seeping out of the court. They decided to take a look—to make a study, a very narrow study, of whether there was a need for a lawyer in the court. And so they asked the New York City Bar Association and the old Domestic Relations Court Committee to pull it together. They asked Legal Aid to do the study, and they said yes."

Over the years, the Legal Aid Society, which employs nearly seven hundred attorneys, has been fond of saying that it is the largest private law firm in the world. Recently, it has been surpassed: A.T.&T., with nine hundred lawyers on its staff, is now the largest, leaving Legal Aid preeminent only among law firms representing the indigent. Each year, this nonprofit agency speaks for more than 200,000 New York City residents who cannot afford lawyers—not only in trial courts and civil courts but in state and federal appellate courts and the U.S. Supreme Court as well.

In 1960, Legal Aid asked Schinitsky if he would be willing to undertake the job. Schinitsky, who was graduated from St. John's University and St. John's Law School, had worked in Legal Aid's Criminal Division from 1947 to 1954, but thereafter he had tended to his own private practice. Excepting five years in the service, Schinitsky had been a lawyer for twenty years, and he was tired of running around, but at the same time this offer represented a challenge to do something new. He agreed to take it on. "It wasn't to be a full-time thing, so I could take care of my own practice. Well, I got involved and spent most of my time there. I found myself calling my colleagues and getting most of my cases put over."

He spent ten months in Children's Court, taking with him several

members of the Young Lawyers Committee of the Association of the
Bar. The first lawyers ever to take a long look at this court, they
observed more than a thousand cases, and because lawyers were not
actually barred from Children's Court (8 percent of the respondents
were even then represented by private counsel), they participated in
the defense of more than a hundred of them. "What we saw," Schinitsky said later, "was an abundance of practices which were not
consonant with notions of fundamental fairness." Fairness, for example, requires that the court decide a case on its merits, untainted (as
lawyers say) by prejudicial matter, yet the judges in Children's Court
were presented with a child's previous records *before* his case was
heard, and most of the judges made full use of these unedited antholo-
gies of rumor and unproved allegations. The result, as a study published in the *Syracuse Law Review* put it, was that "the youngster
actually has the disadvantage of disproving testimony he has not even
heard. . . . His character has been put in issue and it may be overlooked that the proceeding was initially instituted to discover whether
or not the youth has committed a specific wrong."

To make matters worse, petitions were so vague, containing conclu-
sions and prejudicial allegations, that even a lawyer often could not
determine how to formulate a response. The nature of the hearings
and the purpose of the judgments were rarely explained to the children, who sometimes realized the seriousness of their situation only
when they were placed in detention, and who had no way of knowing
whether the testimony offered against them was legal. In only one case
that Schinitsky observed did an unrepresented child ever object to any
testimony on any grounds. When parents appeared, they often could
not understand why their children were being taken away from them.
Parents and children alike had to rely on the court for protection of
their rights, and since there was no effective review of the courts'
operations, little protection was forthcoming.

"I saw a youngster come in," Schinitsky says. "The judge says,
'Look, son, we're not trying to hurt you, we want to help you and talk
to you.' The kid may have been charged with a burglary. The only
other person in court is a police officer. So the police officer testifies
that he got a call to go to a place and the window was broken and
this kid was out on the sidewalk. A lady told him that another lady

had told her that this kid had thrown a brick through the window. Neither lady is there. Triple hearsay. The judge says, 'Did you do it?' The kid says, 'No.' 'Well, were you there?' 'Well, I was there.' And the judge says, 'At eleven at *night?* Well, look, I want to help you.' Three weeks later, at the disposition, I walk in the door and I hear the judge say, 'Well, we tried many places and we can't get you in anywhere. So I think I'm going to send you to a state training school' —which is, of course, a jail for kids."

In those days, when the power of judges in Children's Court went unchallenged by lawyers or by the appellate courts, children were locked away with a fine indifference to determining the facts. Particularly vulnerable were children who appeared before these courts without a parent or a friend, let alone a lawyer, to speak up for them. A judge would appoint such a child a "guardian *ad litem*"—usually a Probation officer or a court attendant—to look out for his interests, but such temporary "guardians" had no intention of ruffling the court's tranquillity. They rarely questioned witnesses and almost never made a statement on behalf of the child.

Schinitsky addressed this problem in a groundbreaking article, "The Role of the Lawyer in the Children's Court," that he wrote during the summer of 1961 for publication the following January in *The Record of the Association of the Bar of the City of New York.* There he related the following story:

> . . . a young girl, twelve to fourteen years of age . . . was charged, in a petition obtained by her father, with being a delinquent. Her mother and the petitioner had been divorced, and because the child's mother resided in Washington, she was not at the hearing. A probation officer was appointed guardian ad litem of the child and after two or three minutes of consultation with her, waived counsel. The father's testimony was: that he had remarried and the child had been living with him. . . . She had paid no attention to him unless he scolded her and on two occasions had left home, staying away overnight each time. He was also permitted to testify that the child's mother did not want her back. No questions were asked of the father by the guardian ad litem and testimony by the girl was waived. The guardian ad

litem then suggested clinical observation of the child at a hospital. The judge remanded her to Kings County Hospital. As soon as the remand was ordered, the girl spoke up in an angry voice. She stated to the Court that she wanted to go to her mother and then asked why her father was believed. The judge reopened the case and permitted the child to tell her story. She claimed her father had often beaten her and now wanted her put away because of his new wife; that her father had threatened to kill her and when she had told him she would go to the police, he replied they would not believe her. The father was recalled and stated that while he did make the threat to kill her if she ran away again, this was done only to impress upon her that what she had done was wrong. The judge again remanded her to Kings County Hospital. The child protested. The judge told her he would send her to Youth House. Again she protested, whereupon, for the third and final time, he committed her for observation.

The guardian ad litem procedure of the court illustrates in some measure the helplessness of respondents in the Children's Court. The right of a child to refuse a guardian ad litem is ignored. The child has foisted upon him by the Court a person whose snap judgment of the child and his problems may be completely unreliable. The young girl may have fared better without her guardian. His sole role in the proceedings was to waive counsel and suggest observation at a mental hospital, a suggestion accepted by the Court. The guardian had no right to waive counsel without asking for an adjournment to contact the girl's mother. He knew of the girl's denial of some of the charges, yet asked no questions of the father. When the girl finally did testify she received no help from him in telling her story. When the father was recalled and admitted threatening the girl, the guardian remained silent. During the girl's protestations against being committed to a hospital, he said nothing. This kind of representation demeans a court of law.

The year that Schinitsky was in the Children's Court saw the beginning of a recognition that cases involving a child's potential loss of liberty were by their very nature adversary proceedings. This issue, the second most important in modern juvenile justice theory (the first is that children must receive the services and treatment to which they are entitled by law), is still a matter of occasional debate. The debate began in 1932, when New York's Court of Appeals in *People* v. *Lewis* reaffirmed the notion that because no criminal proceedings were involved in a juvenile case, no procedural protections were due a child. Nevertheless, a sharply worded minority opinion had warned that despite the court's commendable motives it was necessary to "minimize the chance of abuse and place limitations even upon those who have the best purposes and the most benevolent dispositions." For nearly thirty years the warning went unheeded. Then, in 1961, in a similar case, *People* v. *James*, the Court of Appeals declared that "regardless of the technical classification of the proceeding . . . there is some ground for the assertion that it was criminal in nature. . . ." The court went on to say that where there is a denial of charges by a youth in a proceeding whose sanctions are penal in nature, the proceeding becomes an adversary one, calling for cross-examination of witnesses with the aid of counsel. Good motives, the court added, are no substitute for principle.

The most eloquent affirmation of this idea was expressed five years later by Supreme Court Justice Abe Fortas in *Kent* v. *United States*. The original case, like most that reach the Supreme Court, was a dismal one. A sixteen-year-old boy accused of rape and burglary appeared before a Family Court judge who turned him over for trial in adult court without holding hearings, without ruling on motions made in the boy's behalf, without conferring with the boy, his parents or his lawyer, and without giving reasons for his action. Fortas, speaking for the majority, declared that the concept of *parens patriae* was not unlimited. "The admonition to function in a 'parental' relationship is not an invitation to procedural arbitrariness. . . . The hearing must measure up to the essentials of due process and fair treatment. . . . There is no place in our system of law for reaching a result of such tremendous consequences without ceremony—without hearing, without effective assistance of counsel, without a statement of reasons." Fortas then said, in words that have been often quoted, "There is evidence, in fact, that there may be grounds for concern that the child receives the worst of both worlds: that he gets neither the protections accorded to adults nor the solicitous care and regenerative treatment postulated for children."

Some of this concern had been evident five years earlier when the New York State legislature decided to reorganize the state courts. Prior to the creation of the Family Court in September 1962, cases relating to family life were dispersed among numerous jurisdictions. The Children's Court dealt primarily with delinquents and neglected children. The Domestic Relations Court dealt with support cases. If a husband beat his wife, he was pulled into Criminal Court. If there was a paternity proceeding, for some reason that was also heard in Criminal Court. Custody matters were brought to the Supreme Court. Adoption matters were heard in the Surrogate's Court. Once a court intervenes in one aspect of a family's life, other courts tend to intervene in others, so families in New York were running about from one court to another. What was needed, the legislature decided, was a single court to assimilate all these proceedings, with special emphasis on juvenile matters. It decided, too, on the basis of Schinitsky's article, that children in this new court must be represented by counsel.

"They did a marvelous thing," Schinitsky says this winter afternoon in his office. "It was a radical thing for juvenile courts. They actually talked about due process for *kids,* as a recognition that they weren't chattel, that they had some rights in what happens in their lives. They wrote the due process into the Family Court Act. And they wrote into the act a mandate for the assignment of counsel to youngsters who couldn't afford counsel. It gave the kid the right to be silent—the first time ever. They did that because if a lawyer is to be effective a judge ought not to be able to reach over and start talking to a kid whenever he felt like it: 'Did you do *this?* ' "

The right to counsel would also mean that for the first time the operations of a juvenile court would be subject to higher review. In his influential article, Schinitsky had reported that some twenty thousand children had been adjudicated delinquent or neglected in 1959 and 1960, but of all these cases only four had been appealed and reviewed by the appellate courts. "There is not," Schinitsky wrote, "nor could there be, effective review of the Children's Court under its present operation. That the great majority of respondents and their families cannot afford counsel is reflected in the 92 percent figure of respondents not represented by counsel in 1959. A considerable number do not speak or understand the English language and many who do speak English are of such limited intelligence or education that they have great difficulty in expressing themselves. The right to appeal is meaningless to these people; without funds and incapable of understanding, they are virtually prohibited from exercising this right."

With the restructuring of the state courts, the legislature asked the Legal Aid Society in New York City to provide the representation. "We started," Schinitsky remembers, "on September 3, 1962. We started with two or three people. And the first thing we had to do was adopt policy, because there was nowhere you could really look to be guided by. No other operation provided counsel to kids in Family Court. Now there were two ways in which we could operate. One was to decide the best interests of the child. We took a look at that and we quickly discarded it. For two reasons. First, the legislature was clearly not happy with that theory. It hadn't worked for sixty years. Second, when it comes to determining what really *is* a child's 'best interest,' everyone's an expert. If you have a child, *you're* an expert. If you have fifteen different people in a courtroom, you have fifteen opposing expert points of view. I thought, with a room full of experts there ought to be one person who would stand up and say, 'I don't have any idea what the best interest of this child is. I'm here to tell you what *he* wants. I'm here to look out for his rights.' "

In June 1976, Schinitsky was to press this point in more formal language in testimony given before the Temporary State Commission on Child Welfare. Fourteen years after the Family Court Act legislated counsel for children, and nine years after the U.S. Supreme Court made it a matter of constitutional law, Schinitsky must continually defend the principle: "The attorney has been injected into the system not primarily because of expertise in the behavioral sciences but because he is trained in law. Counsel for the child provides the primary check on abuse of judicial power. If counsel adopts a 'best interests' posture, he undercuts that check and denies to his client his statutorily and constitutionally mandated right to have someone to

protect his legal interests and articulate his side of the case as persua-
sively as possible. Those few children who are able to retain private
counsel do so for this precise reason. They would fire an attorney who
abrogated his duties in this regard and replace him with one who
would not. If assigned counsel"—that is, a lawyer assigned to a child
who cannot afford his own counsel—"failed to assert a child's rights,
in the common effort to advance the child's best interests, he would
be in essence participating in the creation of a separate class of youthful citizens—second-class citizens. . . . Counsel cannot ethically ignore
the law that exists. Nor can he evade his statutory mandate to guard
against invasions of his client's rights. . . .

"Another reason why the attorney should not be coopted into the
system is that the assumption that the court can serve both the child's
best interests and those of the state has proved to be faulty. There are
times when the child's and the state's interests conflict, and there are
times when the court can serve neither interest."

Here Schinitsky is delicately alluding to the failure of juvenile
courts to do what they were set up to do. In 1966, the President's Task
Force on Juvenile Delinquency and Youth Crime concluded that the
"failure of the juvenile court to fulfill its rehabilitative and preventive
promise stems in important measure from a grossly overoptimistic
view of what is known about the phenomenon of juvenile criminality
and what even a fully equipped juvenile court could do about it."
Court action, Schinitsky believes, may well do more harm than good.
A report prepared in 1972 by Justine Wise Polier, the most revered
of former Family Court judges, found that "the fragmented, fraction-
alized and inadequate psychiatric, psychological and casework services made available by [this] state for the training schools cannot
possibly provide even a modicum of the treatment services" required
by law, despite the fact that the children sent to these courts "are the
most deprived, those with the most intense problems, those who have
been rejected by society."

Schinitsky has always insisted that he is not opposed to the Family
Court's mission. "The court can do what it wants with a kid once a
finding has been reached. We want to be sure that the court has the
right child. That this child has done what he is accused of doing."
Nevertheless, he is pessimistic about this child's future, once the court

has made its disposition. "It is apparent that it would be less harmful for many children now processed by the court not to be burdened whenever possible with the weight of its helping hand." These two statements differ strikingly in kind: in one, a lawyer speaks; in the other, a man who is disenchanted with the law, who looks to the fate of children who have been worked over by the law. Schinitsky and his staff are accustomed to hearing that they don't care about the child's "best interests." And yet, rejecting the "best interests" principle from the moment he entered the Family Court, Schinitsky has labored mightily in behalf of that principle. He and his attorneys believe that if they are skillful enough to free their clients from the court's helping hand—or even if they are not—it behooves them to try to help their clients obtain the services they so desperately require.

They know they must do this even when the court defaults. For this reason, Schinitsky expects his lawyers to become concerned with their clients in extralegal ways. He expects them to suggest to the court appropriate treatment and when the court, through a failure of will or capacity, balks, to ride herd on it until that treatment is provided. To protect the child from the court's short-term failures, Schinitsky set up first an Appeals Unit and then a Writ and Stay Unit. To protect the child from the court's long-term lack of interest, he set up a Special Litigation Unit to argue class-action suits in superior courts, and then he set up a Juvenile Services Unit, comprising social workers with master's degrees whose job it is to counsel children and their families, and to look for services that the court cannot seem to find. All this took a lot of money, which Schinitsky had to hustle from federal grants.

All this, too, came later, as an extension of what he was asked to do by the state in 1962. "It's the court's responsibility to come up with the right kind of dispositional hearing to give a kid approximately what he needs," Schinitsky says. But some judges object. It's not our business, they say, and anyway, we have no time. Schinitsky's contempt for these judges, as cold to the touch as iron in winter, is purely legal. "They are ignorant of the law and of the appellate process," he says. "You can cite a Supreme Court decision to them and they will say they don't care." He remembers attending a conference of Family Court judges in Philadelphia in 1968, the year after the Supreme Court had mandated for children nearly all the protections afforded adults. One judge stood up and said, "I don't mind if the Supreme Court overrules me from time to time. I overrule the Supreme Court in my courtroom every day." General laughter followed.

"They're political hacks," Schinitsky says, though there are some judges he respects. "They come up by the clubhouse route. They're lawyers, but not distinguished lawyers. They used to be somebody's secretary." It is, for instance, widely believed that Mayor Abraham Beame appointed to the Family Court bench his wife's mahjong partner. As 1977 and his term as mayor expired, Beame filled eight longstanding vacancies on the Family Court bench with people so manifestly unsuited to such a sensitive post that the press and Mayor-elect Edward Koch let out a cry of rage. Koch called the appointments "abominations." Justine Wise Polier, in a letter to the *Times,* agreed and said that "they demonstrated once more the lack of concern for justice to the poor and minority groups whose lives are disposed of in these courts."

"It shows the kind of regard in which this court is held," Schinitsky says. "It has no prestige at all. Nobody cares." No one seriously thinks that the judges have all bought their positions, but there is general agreement that many did. Half a year's salary—the judges make $48,603 a year—is thought to be the going rate. "You have to understand," says one attorney, "that forty-eight thousand a year is good money for that kind of lawyer. It's not good money, of course, for a competent lawyer."* Another attorney, with impeccable connections to the Family Court, was offered a judgeship a number of years ago, when judges' salaries were smaller. Flattered, he accepted. Then he was told by the party boss who offered him the job that the price was $10,000. The lawyer visibly winced. "Don't worry," he was told. "We've got it all arranged. Nobody can tell. You buy a number of tables when we give fund-raising dinners. A thousand dollars a table." The lawyer now practices in Connecticut.

In 1969, Schinitsky himself was proposed for a judgeship in the Family Court, but he discouraged his supporters' attempts to have him appointed. "I'm not political," he says. "I have a good base here.

---

*As of October 1980, the judges earn $51,000 a year.

I can get more done here." Schinitsky is admired for his skills as a negotiator, and part of what he tries to do is to keep the more outrageous judges in line. "We used to have a judge who was the most foul-mouthed person I ever knew. He would say things—off the record, but in the presence of court personnel and my women lawyers —things like, 'All that woman needs is a good screwing.' I went up to see him. Someone in his court said, 'That's Mr. Schinitsky,' and he asked if I wanted to talk to him. He took me into his robing room, where there were two other judges. I waited, but he made no motion for them to leave. He said, 'Well, what did you want to see me about?' I said, 'Judge, you are the most foul-mouthed man I've ever heard of. You say these outrageous things in court.' Well, about now the other two judges were backing out of the room. I said, 'You're no judge. You're no lawyer. You should be selling fish so you could use that language to your colleagues. If you ever use that language in court again I'm going to file a grievance. In fact, I think I may file a grievance anyway.' Well, I did file one, and he was transferred out somewhere in Queens. One of my lawyers heard him say, 'That bastard Schinitsky. I'd like to get him alone in an alley sometime.' "

Schinitsky laughs and tells a story of a local television reporter who followed one of the state's administrative judges around for a year, trying to get him to comment on the Family Courts. "All that the judge would say for this guy's camera was 'Fuck you.' That's all, for a year. It's all on film, you can see the seasons change behind him." Improper language appears to be an occupational hazard of the Family Court bench. Recently a judge was denied reappointment (a judge's term runs for ten years) because of his willingness to allow his abuse to become part of the record. "You bastard," he would say to small black boys appearing before him. The word could hardly have shocked the boys—indeed, it may have been technically correct—but to put it repeatedly on the record was an impropriety that could not be overlooked.

"The courts are worse now than they were a year ago, in 1975," Schinitsky says. "Nothing moves. The story is, the best way to lose papers is to file a motion. Nobody knows what to do." He remembers times when he has lost his temper, sometimes in court. "Now I've learned to internalize it. You have to strike a balance, to get something done. I file suits a lot now, just to get something done. But now my rage is all inside."

And so, given the assorted incapacities of the juvenile court, many of which they could hardly have foreseen, Schinitsky and his two or three colleagues decided in 1962 to go into the new Family Court on the basis of a regular lawyer-client relationship. "Family Court is not a 'junior criminal court,' " Schinitsky says. "Far from it. But since loss of liberty may be involved, in some cases up to eighteen months, there ought to be a recognition of safeguards of procedure. Innocent kids need to be protected." The adversary process, historically the surest method of establishing facts and responsibility, is necessary; it need be neither combative nor contentious, Schinitsky insists, though it is often both. Yet the judges, many of them, still think of the law guardians as obstacles. "They'd prefer to proceed alone: the paternalistic despotism they enjoyed for sixty years."

They do indeed. Fifteen years after the Family Court Act, Schinitsky's lawyers are used to coping daily with situations like this:

Judge Nanette Dembitz: "Where have you *been*, Mr. Pokart? Aren't you the law guardian assigned to this case?"

Stephen Pokart: "Yes, your honor."

Dembitz: "Well, this case began twenty minutes ago."

Pokart: "It began without *me?*"

Dembitz: "It certainly did. You weren't here."

Pokart: "Your honor, I didn't know the case had been called."

Dembitz: "You're supposed to be here, counselor."

Pokart: "I was trying another case, your honor. May I have a few minutes to confer with my client?"

Dembitz: "No."

Pokart: "But I don't know what's going on."

Dembitz: "What's going on is what you see is going on."

Or with situations like this:

Judge Paul T. E. Bookson: "Where's the law guardian for this case?"

Nanette Kripke (a law guardian): "She's on another case, judge."

Bookson: "Well, you stand in for her, please."

Kripke: "I don't know anything about the case, your honor."
Bookson: "You don't need to know anything."
Kripke: "How can I represent the respondent?"
Bookson: "I'll coach you. I'll hum the tune."
Kripke: "Your honor—"
Bookson: "There's nothing to know. The kid ran away from Hill-crest, that's all."
Kripke yields, and the case is settled in the judge's chambers.

For five years, Schinitsky worried that the legislature would reverse itself: these lawyers cause so many problems; let's throw them out the door. Then in 1967 the U.S. Supreme Court made into constitutional law the reforms that Schinitsky had induced the state legislature to put into effect in New York in 1962. Anyone familiar with our judicial history has heard of the great cases involving the rights of adult criminals—the Gideon and Miranda cases, for example—but virtually no one not affected by them has heard of the great cases involving the rights of juvenile offenders. Nevertheless, *In Re Gault,* the most important juvenile case ever heard by the Supreme Court, has had a profound effect upon the fabric of American life.

The effect could not have been so sweeping had not the original case been such a model of judicial malpractice. In 1964, a fifteen-year-old boy, Gerald Francis Gault, was arrested by the sheriff of Gila County, Arizona, on the complaint of a woman neighbor who accused Gerald of making an indecent phone call. "Do you give any?" Gerald was said to have asked. "Are your cherries ripe today? Do you have big bombers?" Adolescent stuff, to be sure, and the kind of offense that would have netted an adult a fine of $50 or two months in jail. Gerald, however, got six years' incarceration. Between the offense and the sentence nothing seemed to work as decency and simple good judgment would require. Gerald's parents were not notified of his arrest. The petition filed in court against Gerald did not refer to any facts, nor was a copy of the petition served on the Gaults. At the hearing, the complainant did not appear, nor was sworn testimony taken, nor was any record of what took place prepared. When the Gaults filed habeas corpus proceedings, they learned that another boy may have made the call, though the judge said Gerald had confessed. The judge never spoke to the complainant, and told the Gaults that she was not required to appear in court. At this point, the judge committed Gerald as a juvenile delinquent to the state industrial school "for the period of his minority"—that is, until he became twenty-one.

Arizona permitted no appeal in juvenile cases, but the Gaults pursued the case through their state habeas corpus proceeding. At a hearing, the judge was asked, "Under what section of the code [did] you find the boy delinquent?" The judge replied, "Well, there is a— I think it amounts to disturbing the peace. I can't give you the section, but I can tell you the law, that when one person uses lewd language in the presence of another person, that it can amount to—and I consider that when a person makes it over the phone, that it is considered in the presence, I might be wrong, that is one section. The other section upon which I consider the boy delinquent is section 8-201, subsection (d), habitually involved in immoral matters." Challenged as to why he thought the boy habitually immoral, the judge said something about having heard that Gerald had stolen a baseball glove and lied to the police about it. There had been, the judge admitted, no hearing, no accusation relating to this matter of the glove, "because of lack of material foundation."

Satisfied by what it had heard, the Superior Court dismissed the Gaults' application, telling them that they were wrong to think that parents and children should be apprised of the specific charges, or that they should be properly notified of the hearing, or that they had any right of appeal. They were also wrong to think that the court was obliged to notify them of their rights to counsel, to confront their son's accuser, to refuse self-incrimination. Nor could the Gaults legally object to the use of unsworn hearsay testimony, or to the court's failure to keep a record of its proceedings. Arizona's Supreme Court agreed, adding that confession was good for the child, evidence that his therapy had begun and instrumental in his assuming an attitude of trust and confidence in the officials who would be in charge of his life for the next six years.

The U.S. Supreme Court, however, no longer had faith in such sentiments. Justice Abe Fortas, speaking again for the majority (as he had in *Kent* v. *United States* the year before), remarked that when the state intervenes in a child's life it does not deprive him of his rights, because he has none. Such a situation could no longer endure. "The history of American freedom," Fortas said, "is, in no small measure, the history of procedure." He cited the statistics of recidivism among juvenile offenders in the District of Columbia in 1966: 66 percent of sixteen- and seventeen-year-old children referred to the court had been before the court on previous charges. From this, the Court concluded that the absence of constitutional procedures in juvenile courts did not greatly enhance the child's chance of rehabilitation. Fortas observed that the term "juvenile delinquent" involved only slightly less stigma than the term "criminal" as applied to adults; as for the much-vaunted claim of secrecy in juvenile proceedings, he pointed out that juvenile courts routinely furnish their records to the FBI, to the military, even to private employers. Declaring that "under our Constitution the condition of being a boy does not justify a kangaroo court," he suggested that the child's perception of due process being afforded him might be more therapeutic, more conducive to respect for the law, than the old idea of a fatherly judge touching "the heart and conscience of the erring youth by talking over his problems."

Fortas then proceeded to award to children in trouble with the law six fundamental rights already possessed by adults (and by children in New York): the right to notice of charges; the right to counsel; the right to confront and cross-examine sworn witnesses; the privilege against self-incrimination; the right to a transcript of the proceedings; the right to appellate review. On the subject of induced confessions he was tersely eloquent: "It would indeed be surprising if the privilege against self-incrimination were available to hardened criminals but not to children." Admissions made by children unrepresented by counsel in court might well be "the product of ignorance of rights or of adolescent fantasy, fright or despair."

The Gault case was decided by a majority of five to four. Justice Potter Stewart, in dissent, expressed fear that the ruling would restrict or destroy the juvenile court's humanitarian and social qualities, would indeed make the juvenile court a criminal court. "To impose the Court's long catalogue of requirements upon juvenile proceedings in every area of the country is to invite a long step backwards into the nineteenth century. In that era there were no juvenile proceedings, and a child was tried in a conventional criminal court with all the trappings of a conventional criminal trial. So it was that a 12-year-old boy named James Guild was tried in New Jersey for killing Catharine Beakes. A jury found him guilty of murder, and he was sentenced to death by hanging. The sentence was executed. It was all very constitutional."

Nevertheless, the Supreme Court, however narrowly, had committed itself to constitutional reform of the juvenile judicial process, though it sometimes seemed unhappy with what it was doing. In 1970, in *In Re Winship*, a case developed by Charles Schinitsky's Appeals Unit, the Court declared that the old civil court requirement of a "preponderance of the evidence" was no longer sufficient to convict a child; delinquency findings must be proved beyond a reasonable doubt. But in dissent, Chief Justice Warren Burger seemed to hanker still for the old ways: "What the juvenile court system needs is not more but less of the trappings of legal procedure and judicial formalism. The juvenile court system requires breathing room and flexibility in order to survive." And in 1971, in *McKeiver* v. *Pennsylvania,* the Court retreated, declaring that children were not entitled to jury trials. Justice Harry Blackmun, speaking for the majority, implied that enough was enough: the Court had gone far to determine that juvenile hearings should involve "procedural orderliness" in the interest of "fundamental fairness," but jury trials were not constitutionally required for children because they would not strengthen the court's fact-finding function or remedy the defects of the system.*

What remained was to see what effect the *Gault* decision would

*There have been other cases which have further defined the rights of children. Among these are *Ivan V.* v. *City of New York,* 407 U.S. 203 (1972), which held that the "beyond a reasonable doubt" standard must be retroactive; *In re Daisy H.,* 337 N.Y.S. 2d 938 (1968), which held that juveniles are entitled to Miranda warnings; *In re Steven B.,* 292 N.Y.S. 2d 986 (1968), which held that the unsworn testimony of a minor must be corroborated; *In re Gary C.,* 346 N.Y.S. 2d 212 (1972), which held that a juvenile has the right to voir dire examination to suppress evidence; and *People ex rel. F.* v. *Hill,* 319 N.Y.S. 2d 961 (1971), which held that a juvenile has the right to notice and hearing in a proceeding to terminate or extend placement. The basic rights of adults not yet possessed by children tried in Family Court are three: the right to a jury trial, the right to bail, the right to a public hearing.

have in juvenile courts around the country. Like the Pope, the Supreme Court has no battalions, and in 1969 a large-scale study of juvenile proceedings in three cities indicated that many judges, accustomed to the old socialized court procedures, were ignoring the provisions of *Gault,* particularly in regard to the troublesome right to counsel. Implementation of the second revolution in juvenile justice philosophy would take time to accomplish, but Charles Schinitsky's efforts had been vindicated. He need no longer fear that the vagaries of a politically minded legislature could entirely reverse what he had accomplished. By the mid-1970s his original staff of "two or three" had grown to seventy attorneys and more than thirty social workers. Many of the lawyers work in specialized units—Appeals, Writs and Stays, Special Litigation—but forty-four are trial attorneys who represent 90 percent of the children brought into the city's Family Courts. For the chance to do this work, they accept salaries starting at $19,000—far lower than most of them could obtain elsewhere—and each must juggle between 300 and 350 cases at a time. Some are drawn to the Legal Aid Society for the chance to do trial work, others for idealistic reasons. Few have heard of Schinitsky when they arrive, but many remain because they admire him, what he has accomplished, his continuing attempts to ameliorate the lives of children in trouble.

III

The Black Hole
of the Bronx

Q: "Do you feel these children do need supervision
or they do not?"
A: "I can make a real general statement and say the
whole society needs supervision. But I don't think
that would be the question you are asking me."

Cross-examination in *Martarella* v. *Kelley* (1971)

Still, there were days, even months, in which these young attorneys
wondered what, if anything, had been accomplished by way of bringing some semblance of order, let alone law, into the juvenile courts.
The lack of order, perhaps, might be tolerable. One morning Judge
Bookson entered his courtroom and did not tell those assembled there
—a black family with their lawyers, assorted employees of the Bureau
of Child Welfare—to be seated. Kept standing, a BCW case worker
began to squeeze drops from a bottle into his eyes, thereby provoking
Bookson's curiosity: Family Court is meant to be informal, but not
that informal. And so, while everyone stood, the seated Bookson held
forth for a time on the merits of competing brands of eyedrops—
Visine, in the judge's opinion, is bad for the eyes over the long haul,
whereas Murine, though not harmful, is perhaps ineffective—and
then he launched into a bit of autobiography: the time he got conjunc-
tivitis while traveling abroad, the infection settling first in his eye and

then developing into a fever of 104 degrees as he climbed a mountain. All this went down very well with his standing congregation, including (it seemed) the father and mother who had come to learn whether their child would be returned to them.

The lack of law, however, was not tolerable. Not a few of the Family Court judges appear to agree with Judge Phillip D. Roache, who once remarked to his clerk, "If you do it the way the law says, forget it." Nearly every day the young attorneys saw judges dispose of cases in patently illegal fashion. By the evidence of their actions, if not of their words, presumption of innocence is not a popular attitude among the judges in these courts. Even though the whole philosophy behind the Family Court Act is aimed at *releasing* the child, at sending him back to his family, community and treatment, the judges clearly favor *detention:* the child must be held, usually securely, until a determination of his guilt is made, until the court can figure out what to do with him.

On the day after the great citywide blackout in July 1977, Judge Blossom Heller, presiding over Intake A of the Manhattan Court, announced that all children brought before her that day would be remanded, period. That included one boy with no previous record who had been charged with looting. Probation recommended parole, which Heller refused as she launched into what can only be called a legal voluntary: "In a dire emergency that the City of New York has been in since 9:30 in the evening of July 13th, at 4:15 in the morning when the lawful people were trying to help each other, lawlessness was rampant throughout the streets of the City of New York. This has been—this City has been devastated beyond words that it will take at least ten years before the wounds that have been inflicted upon us will alleviate. The City of New York and certain sections thereof for sure were in bad shape before and little people who are trying to maintain businesses had their places ransacked, devastated, destroyed, being put out of business, God knows it, the amount of money which has been lost or the people that are being forced to give up their businesses because of acts such as this respondent and others have done who think they had the right for whatever reasons that they give to become part of a mob scene. Here the streets of the City of New York were blackened for almost twenty-four hours and more in most areas. This

Court must consider the needs of the community and now in the summer months with this hot humid weather and with the power failures that this City is subjected to, this Court believes that this respondent would commit the same crime again given that opportunity and/or also not appear within the confines of this Court. This is not just the ordinary time or ordinary case when this Court would consider parole since it would be the respondent's first case before the Court but because of the emergency situation and because of what occurred and animals would not do what these people have done and inflicted upon the City and I am constrained to remand this respondent for a hearing. You have your exception. If you wish to be heard you may."

Steven Hiltz, attorney-in-charge of the law guardians in Manhattan, filed a writ against her. It took him only fifteen minutes to persuade another judge of Heller's illegal maneuver: that there was no reason to believe the boy would not appear at his hearing, or that he would commit another crime, and that Heller's remarks on the record were clearly prejudicial.

What most depressed the law guardians (for they could always slap a writ on a judge, or seek to have his decision reversed on appeal, even though they knew that same judge would be doing the same illegal thing the very next day) was what they took to be a negative attitude on the part of many judges toward the children who came before them. Out of court, law guardians will agree with Corporation Counsel that 90 percent of the kids brought into court are guilty, but such a low probability of innocence should not affect judicial equanimity in a court charged with attending to the best interests of these children. What is a thirteen-year-old girl who keeps running away from home to think of the law when on her first appearance in court she hears from Judge Roache, "Now I don't know you, right? To me you are just one more piece of paper. I can send you home or put you in jail; it makes no difference to me at all"? What effect has a judge like Harold A. Felix on a small child whom he cannot by law confine when he says to that child, "I think it would be good for you to experience a loss of liberty. In my opinion, that's therapy"? Felix, now retired, enjoyed lengthy coffee breaks with his staff in his robing room, and there he would summarize what he had learned from his years on the bench: "Some of these kids need a kick in the ass." He would do away with hearings in their present form. "When a kid is a delinquent, I wouldn't wait for disposition. And all those reports from social workers and psychiatrists. All this time the kid is back on the street collecting more delinquency petitions. I'd send him for a short and sweet period to some place like Parris Island. Not a rock pile, but the kid would work himself to exhaustion every night. I think if a boy has done an antisocial act he has to pay for it. I think the community is demanding it."

He is almost certainly right. Not long after Judge Felix's pronouncement, a prominent member of the New York community told an observer that he had a solution to the juvenile delinquency problem. "I'm a horse breeder," he said, "and one of the facts in my life is that some of the colts I breed aren't quite right. I shoot them. The Winchester is a very effective tool." Sensing his listener's alarm, he offered reassurance: "You'd be surprised how few you actually have to shoot." At about the same time, a suburban matron who had heard that 90 percent of those brought before the courts are blacks and Hispanics was moved to a reconsideration of history: "I know I'm not supposed to say this," she said, "but are you sure they weren't better off under slavery?"

Even Charles Schinitsky, in 1976, had become pessimistic. He feels nothing is being done. "Probably nothing *can* be done in our society. Not enough money is voted." Many disagree with him, arguing that the injection of more money into an intolerable system only makes that system work more intolerably, but Schinitsky is very good at raising money. The budget for the Juvenile Rights Division's first year was $35,000; by 1976, it had burgeoned to $2.7 million. For the following fiscal year, Schinitsky asked the state's Office of Court Administration for $4.2 million—an increase of 30 percent which he did not get because the OCA, the governor and the legislature's Ways and Means Committee all whittled away at it. He also obtained $250,000 in federal funds for a pilot project in cases involving neglect and abuse. Through the Law Enforcement Assistance Act, the federal government at that time dispersed annually to the states between $40 million and $50 million for work in juvenile justice, the idea being to encourage the creation of innovative programs which must, after three years, be funded by the states themselves. Of this amount, the state of New York pulled down $11 million, and of *that,* Schinitsky secured $750,-000 for his Juvenile Rights Division.*

What, in the long run, this money buys is problematical. "Fifty thousand cases of the most sensitive kind are called before the city's Family Courts each year," Schinitsky says. "The courts are over-crowded, the waiting rooms are terrible places, each case involves a minimum of three to four people, not counting lawyers and court personnel, and they sit there all day with no notification of when their cases will be called. In many cases, jobs have been lost. Two to three million people in this city have passed through these courts, more than a hundred thousand last year, and every one of them has left with a terrible impression of the law, of the judges." For reasons of its own, the Family Court has recently refused funds it could have obtained from the LEAA. "The administration of the court is incompetent," Schinitsky says. "They had some programs and let them drop. They could have two million, three million. In fact, *we* would have given it to them—for proposals for what to do with kids after fact-finding, for programs for these kids."

What's worse, "the court has washed its hands of its responsibility for placing a kid where that child belongs." Opinion on this responsi-bility is hotly disputed among the judges, but one said in court, "I'm not in the child-care business," whereupon the law guardian shot back, "Then what are we *doing* here?" Schinitsky has no use for the court's psychologists, most of whom are of the behaviorist persuasion and upon whom the judges rely. "I think it's all bullshit. We can get psychologists to say anything at all." The state's Division for Youth, which assumes charge of children involved in the more serious offenses, is even more exasperating because, for no better reason than its own convenience, it won't specify the institution to which a child will be sent. "We don't know where they are. We can't stay in touch with them. There's uncertainty everywhere. The DFY moves them

---

*For the fiscal year beginning on April 1, 1979, Schinitsky requested from the state a budget of $5,503,551. The Juvenile Rights Division received $4,629,062: enough, his office says, to maintain the "status quo"—which is to say that no personnel had to be laid off, but no one could be hired and none of the programs that the Division wants to pursue could be advanced.

around. The court doesn't know if the kids are getting the treatment the law requires. *We* don't know. We want to make sure our kids know where they're going, we know where they're going, because they're still our clients after disposition. We can't contest a placement, but we can suggest alternatives. That's what our Juvenile Services Unit is for. If we argue in court we don't want the judge to say, 'It's not my business, argue with the commissioner for social services.'

"Nobody cares primarily for these kids. They want to see them swept out of sight. We're raising an entire generation of blacks, they're now between seventeen and twenty, who have nothing to do: no jobs, no education. Work imposes a structure on life; they don't have this. They get up, get dressed, go down to the street and hang around. Trouble follows." Trouble follows because many of these young people have no sense of a stake in our society. What they *do* have is a television set which provides them, night and day, with a brightly colored vision of the good life in America. Wide, glossy cars. Silk suits and dresses. Elegant kitchens, expensively glassed and plated. Never mind that according to the gospels of ABC, CBS and NBC these cars will crash into each other, the silk suits and dresses will be punctured by bullets, and in the kitchens white folk will shriek a lot and throw the glasses and plates about. Television's message to those who are uneducated, unemployed and unencumbered by routine family concerns is that this brightly colored world *exists*—not just in Wonderland, or in California, but forty blocks down the street. A subway ride will get you there, but still—you are not there.

"Perhaps," says Schinitsky, speaking only of the courts, "the whole system should be scrapped."

In the summer of 1976, anyone who had a mind to scrap the system would have begun by scrapping the Family Court in the Bronx. Plans to do just that were well advanced. More accurately, work on a glistening new court building was so near completion that rumblings could be heard at every hand. Translated, these rumblings read: *Why in God's name do they expect us to sweat through another summer here?* "Here," like most places in the Bronx, is *terra incognita* to most

New Yorkers: half an hour by air-conditioned D train from midtown Manhattan to 167th Street. Disembarking, the visitor walks briskly toward the exit, alert for irregular movements from his fellow passengers. Ascending to the street, he discovers a neighborhood quite at odds with the images of the South Bronx familiar to all who watch television news—images that remind him of other pictures of the outskirts of Hamburg and Dresden as they looked in the summer of 1945. This area has gone to seed, no doubt—the middle-class Jews who once inhabited it have receded before the Hispanic tide—but the Grand Concourse, the community's most prepossessing feature, suggests still a faded nineteenth-century vision of orderly expansiveness. Here there is a graffiti-covered fountain erected in honor of the German-Jewish poet Heine, and here, too, stand a number of remarkably solid buildings, homes for the aged and the indigent, which in a more prosperous age were endowed with elaborate friezes, cornices, even a Roman colonnade.

Behind this facade of deteriorating elegance, the deterioration rapidly accelerates. In the heat of July, the side streets intersecting the Grand Concourse—McClellan Street is one—smell of urine. Across from the Legal Aid Society's storefront office (the store's owner, having been repeatedly burglarized, removed his business elsewhere) both the Perfect Cleaners and Tailors shop and the Elite Beauty Salon have grilles pulled over their fronts at noon. The Head Shop, Legal Aid's next-door neighbor, is also grilled, but a Chinese laundry remains open. At one end of this narrow street where cars are constantly double-parked there is a coffee shop in which, one morning this July, a woman collapsed bleeding to the floor. A miscarriage? A stabbing? No one knew or cared to look, but after the cops were called (they were a long time coming) business proceeded around her. Off McClellan Street, at 1109 Carroll Place, is the side entrance to the Bronx Family Court. Each morning at 10:00 or thereabouts, the bus from Spofford, containing children held in secure detention, runs up over the curb to make a V with the wall of the courthouse; a guard jumps out to stand in the throat of the V, thus making it impossible for the kids to escape as they disembark. A few feet away, neighborhood children shoot craps against the Family Court wall, and above them towers a rusty fire escape that concludes in a locked door and a flourish of barbed wire: the need to prevent children from escaping apparently supersedes their need to leave a burning building safely.

The Family Court that summer occupied two adjoining dilapidated buildings, one opening to the Grand Concourse, the other to Carroll Place. Within, there is a variety of levels, a warren of corridors and stairs, hand-lettered signs with misleading arrows or stern injunctions not to enter a courtroom, not even to knock, until your name is called. Signs proliferate throughout the buildings. A No Smoking sign in a waiting room is widely disregarded; another, on a waiting-room window with broken panes that will not be replaced in anticipation of the court's removal, reads: "Please keep window closed. A kid almost fell out window." Graffiti obscure the doors and flaking walls. Unidentifiable fluids stand upon the floors. There is no air conditioning; indeed, there is very little air on a summer afternoon: wherever a window is open a crowd congregates to breathe. The waiting room at the ground-floor Probation Intake is so small that more people must stand than can be seated; the overflow lines the corridors and stairs, obliging lawyers and court personnel to scuttle sideways from here to there. Whenever the men's-room door opens on a corridor by the waiting room, men standing at the urinals are displayed. The toilets in this men's room are clogged; there is no sign of toilet paper. In the waiting rooms, in the halls and on the stairs, children cry and scream, obliging the adults to raise their animated chatter to a level that makes proceedings in the courtrooms impossible to follow. Judges constantly interrupt their cases to send court officers out in an attempt to suppress the din.

Several of the signs tacked here and there announce that Part IV is closed, as well it might be, for Part IV was designed as a judge's robing room. When it is in session, as it will be next month, the judge sits wedged in a corner by a filthy flag and an inoperable air conditioner. "You get fourteen or eighteen people packed in here," says one of the attorneys, "and you can only breathe through your mouth. The stink is terrific." Once a judge was assaulted right here; only one Part in this court has room for a proper, protective judge's bench—the others sit behind tables—and this judge had no room to get away. Perhaps to prevent a recurrence, or perhaps only to emphasize the distance between the law and the putative felon, respondents in the

Bronx now face the judge across the length of a table placed at a right
angle to his own.

Under these conditions, on a sweltering July 13, Judge George Bundy
Smith settles in for a day of justice in the Bronx. Young, black, very
quiet and methodical, Smith is not to be rushed, although today,
because another judge is absent, he must cover both Part II and Part
III. He begins by assembling the entire cast of his first case—complainant, cop, respondent, respondent's mother, two lawyers—and
since everybody is here and set to go, he explains that he will hear the
case "at the end of the calendar." The cast is dismissed—remanded,
as it were, to the waiting room, where they must stew for the rest of
the day. This procedure took hardly any time at all.

After such a brisk start, Judge Smith attends briefly to the following:

• An aged couple arrive to demand that their great-great-grand-
daughter, now sixteen, be put in jail. "I have to lock up the food," the
aged woman says. "I have to sleep with the door locked." Her husband has a bruise next to his ear. "Look where she hit him upside the
head." The girl has often been before the Court as a PINS—a Person
in Need of Supervision, which means that although she has committed no crimes, her behavior hasn't met with the approval of her
great-great-grandparents—and she has had a baby. The judge gives
the aged couple an Order of Protection, which means that when this
girl hits the old man again, as she surely will, she can get six months
in the adult prison on Rikers Island.

• A woman with ten children wants to retrieve "Child Number
10," as she is known to the Court, from the foster home to which she
has been remanded since birth. The mother is not married. To house
her family, she needs two apartments. Children 1 through 9 have so
far broken up every apartment she has had. Still, she feeds her kids,
dresses them adequately for court appearances and wants to keep
them. Child Number 10 must be returned to her soon, says a law
guardian, because there is no legal reason to keep her away and
because the child now assumes her foster mother is her real one; the
break is going to be very hard.

• A fat young woman wearing the peculiar smile of entrenched stupidity and the tight stretch pants favored by the mothers who appear in this court listens vacantly to plans for the dispersal of her children. What this woman does, says a lawyer from the Bureau of Child Welfare, is breed children for the agencies to take over. Her lawyer and a nun talk across her; she has no comprehension of what is happening. From time to time, Judge Smith, just to keep her abreast of events, asks her a slow, monosyllabic question, to which she replies only yes or no. Her fixed smile is an embarrassed confession that she cannot be expected to grasp what is required of her.

• Another mother of a PINS girl, fifteen, is a deaf-mute. She cannot communicate with a deaf-mute interpreter; she has never learned how the flashing fingers work. Over the years, however, she has managed to communicate with precisely one person, a neighbor who accompanies her to court. Intrigued, Judge Smith asks the neighbor how she can "talk" to her deaf-mute friend, but the woman just shrugs: "You know."

• Still another mother demands that the judge arrest her son. She wants only to get him back; he disappeared over a month ago in the company of a homosexual.

After a lot more of this kind of thing, the court recesses for the 1:00 P.M. lunch break. Little, if anything, has been decided this morning; virtually every case has had to be adjourned because someone or other did not show. A woman, for instance, wanted the court to prevent her estranged husband from taking their child away from school and putting her in schools unknown to her, but the husband didn't show. A boy appeared who had been held at Spofford for two weeks—far longer than the law allows. His mother knew he was there, but never communicated with him and failed to show for this morning's hearing. The boy has several petitions filed against him and is very much on his own.

Throughout the morning, the court personnel have resisted as well as they can this flow of incompetence and indifference. One court officer perpetually frowns, shaking his head in mute consternation at so much exposure to human fallibility. The court clerk, arrogant and disdainful, speaks as little as possible as if in fear of contamination. When he must speak, his tone is dry and contemptuous, his words chopped short: the burden of dealing with these people and their problems! "I've been here two years," a court officer remarks. "Two years too long. But once you're assigned to Family Court, you're stuck because no one wants to come here."

The afternoon is indistinguishable from the morning, but hotter.

• In an abuse case—a child has been battered by her father—the child enters the courtroom with her mother; there is no one to wait with her outside. Her presence disturbs the judge, who does not want her to hear the particulars of the case in which she was the victim, so nothing much is done.

• A woman appears to say she must drop her complaint against a boy who assaulted her daughter in the school playground; she can't take time off from her job to appear in court. Because the boy has failed to appear for his hearing, Judge Smith is very sympathetic, orders a warrant for the boy's arrest and offers the mother as long an adjournment as she requires.

• A mother enters with her surly son.

Judge Smith (to boy): "Why weren't you here this morning?"

Boy: "I was sleeping."

Smith (to mother): "Why weren't *you* here this morning?"

Mother: "I was waiting for him to wake up."

A court officer rolls his eyes to the ceiling. Judge Smith makes no comment.

• A dapper black man in a white-on-white suit, carrying a silver-headed cane, appears to answer his wife's charge that he has had sexual relations with one of his daughters, who is eight. As he enters, his cane is confiscated by a court officer who has, throughout the day, told various children to remove their gum, their hats, their hands from their pockets, the cigarettes perched behind their ears. The father, all amiability, nods, smiles, brushes aside his wife's unpleasant suggestion regarding his conduct. Maintaining his calm, Judge Smith summons the entire family into the courtroom. He wants to look at this man's children. Are they alive? Do they look all right? How are they dressed? He asks them their names and sends them out again. The children's mother looks about sixteen, though that is hardly possible, and is hugely pregnant. By the father? If so, her condition doesn't help her case.

Toward the end of the afternoon, Judge Smith recalls the case with which he began the morning, the case that was ready to proceed but which he deferred in order to deal with less time-consuming matters. He's sorry, the judge explains to the crew that has spent the day outside his door, but there is no time remaining. The case must be adjourned until October. Will they all appear again? No one seems to think so, but then this has been something of a model day in court: no hearings or dispositions have been accomplished at all.

So inconclusive a day in court cannot be achieved without preparation. Judge Smith, says Irving Cohen, "is becoming good," but the judges as a whole "aren't playing the role they should. Strong judges get hearings. I've seen judges overwhelmed, immobilized by the role they think they have to play. They're not evil, they're just stupid." Cohen, who is in his thirties, has for three years been chief of Probation for all the Bronx courts. His juvenile branch at the Family Court has nothing to do with neglect and abuse cases—these fall to the Bureau of Child Welfare—but it must decide which of the 7,800 new delinquency and PINS applications that are presented each year are sufficiently serious to be sent to the judge in Intake A. The task is not unlike that which Hercules confronted at the Augean stables. To accomplish it, nine officers at Probation Intake screen every case, conferring for thirty minutes or an hour with the parties involved, gathering information—what were the circumstances of the crime? what property damage? was there a weapon?—before making a decision. In theory, the information Probation derives from the child or his parents is confidential—it may not be sent to the court—but among law guardians there is widespread belief that any confession a child makes will shortly be presented to the judge.

With the exception of homicides that are really accidents, all serious felonies must be sent to the court. To make room for them, a distraught merchant who has nabbed a kid in the act of shoplifting, or a woman who has been roughed up on the subway by a large boy, will find themselves under pressure not to proceed with their complaints. Most people who appear in Family Court are unaware that although Probation operates within the court, it is not part of it. The

Family Court is a creature of the state; Probation is responsible to the city's mayoral department. Probation's operating philosophy is to divert as many cases as it can from going to court. Fully 60 percent of the cases it reviews never go before a judge. The merchant may be told that shoplifting is so common that most judges perceive it as less of a crime than a signal that a child is unloved. The woman will be shocked to find that she is treated as if she, not the large boy, were the cause of the problem Probation faces today. In fact, Probation cannot stop a complainant from taking his case to court, but the injured party's tenacity will get him nowhere: his case, when presented, will be accompanied by Probation's recommendation to dismiss.

Cohen, who in his tiny office at Family Court sits beneath a poster of cacti on a desert with the caption *"No te prometemos un jardin de rosas,"* believes his department's diversion philosophy works. More than two-thirds of these "adjusted" cases—meaning cases that are not sent to court on condition that the offender accept some kind of guidance—do not return. Some of the more fiery law guardians resent the idea of requiring a kid who has been found guilty of nothing to report to a Probation officer, but most will settle for any means of escaping the court and its dread sanctions. Besides, Probation counseling is but another of the system's dismal inadequacies. An initial hour-long interview will be followed by fifteen-minute sessions once a week, then once a month, if ever. Cohen's field workers juggle more than eighty cases at a time ("More than forty or forty-five is crazy," Cohen says) and are sometimes embarrassed in court: *What* child, your honor? No, I don't seem to have a file on him.

Probation is represented in the courtrooms by court liaison officers, whose job it is to shuffle the files of respondents as their cases are called and to advise the judge when he asks for background material on which to base a decision whether to parole or remand. When, after a hearing, a finding is made against a child, the judge will generally ask Probation for an "I&R," an Investigation and Report on the circumstances of the child and his family and a prognosis of his future adjustment. This will be presented at the disposition by Probation, which here plays the role of prosecutor, parrying the wily moves of the law guardians, because Corporation Counsel lacks the staff to see its cases through to the end.

Like everyone connected with Family Court, Irving Cohen believes
the system doesn't work. Although his department, in both adult and
juvenile courts, is understaffed, this past year cost him 30 percent of
his staff—through layoffs and forced retirements. He needs four or
five more officers in Probation Intake here at Family Court, another
for investigations, another court liaison officer. It would help if he
could get people with master's degrees in social work.

Cohen's deputy in the Bronx Family Court, Hubert Benjamin, Jr.,
agrees: "If one person calls in sick, we're overwhelmed. We can't
cover all the Parts now. The people here are constantly making decisions, decisions, right then and there. It takes its toll. We need more
officers, more time to get really into a family's situation. We need to
provide more services instead of referring so many people to other
agencies. We need more time to get out into the community, to see
what the resources are for youngsters." Benjamin, who wanted to be
a doctor "until I saw the terminal cases," is skeptical about what
Probation or the Family Court can do for children. He is proud of his
officers' ability to drag the truth from the children more efficiently
than do judges and lawyers—"We have our ways"—and is impressed
by the kids' sophistication. "You can hear them predicting precisely
what movements Legal Aid will make for them, what the judge will
say, what will be done about them." But he is depressed that there is
no computerization or data processing of the files that flow through
Probation. "If a child is known to Manhattan or Brooklyn, we have
no way of finding out. We need a better means of establishing identification of children. Kids can be photographed and fingerprinted only
after fact-finding. Pictures should be taken at the arrest. I've seen kids
posing as their older brothers to get a case into Family Court when
it should have gone to Criminal Court. Parents bring in erroneous
birth certificates. We have kids here with four or five identifications
on file." Benjamin would also like to see the courts opened to the
press. Then, he believes, the public would rise in fury at Legal Aid
for getting these junior felons off "on technicalities."

"The whole setup is dysfunctional," Irving Cohen says. "Justice is
not happening. Few findings are made. There are not enough hearings. We have cases pending over a year; the average is six months.
There's a shocking number of dismissals on failure to prosecute, often
very serious felonies, because Corporation Counsel is overloaded. The

BCW lawyers are overloaded, too: even in neglect and abuse cases a high percentage are dismissed or withdrawn. Now we see kids convicted for offenses so old they've forgotten them. The judges are a lot of shnooks, they have no business being lawyers, let alone judges." Cohen believes adult and juvenile cases should be heard in separate Parts and that many cases could be sent to a referee for mediation. "The problem is, the judges don't want to let them go. Then you'd need fewer judges.

"Last June was a monster month. We got three hundred more cases than usual in Probation. Because of our overload, more cases went up to court. We didn't have time to sort through them. No one cares about Probation because we have no constituency. When cutbacks are made, they're made in social services, which means here. But for two or three days there we came very close to a total breakdown. Everything nearly stopped. If we do have a breakdown, it might not be noticed, though crime would rise in the streets. The public doesn't want to know. It's just as happy to have kids in jail, let 'em go to court, who needs Probation? Maybe we need to have a total breakdown before anyone will care."

Children arriving at Probation Intake in the Bronx are sent first to two small registration rooms. Here, as elsewhere in this court, posters attempt to offset the grimness: "Safety First," says one; "Does Your Mother Know You're Here?" asks another; and a third, showing the famous cat hanging by its paws from a branch, strikes an optimistic note: "Hang In There, Baby, Friday's Coming." Parents arrive, and complainants, and sometimes cops—although the police are now allowed to fill in forms and disappear. This measure, a result of the economic crunch, saves thousands of police man-hours and irritates Probation officers who would rather question the policeman in person. The families are told they must appear by 9:30, but the Probation officers rarely begin hearing cases before 11:30. Police dispositions take a lot of time, and the Intake clerks hold up matters, too, trying to separate the PINS from the neglects.

From the small Probation waiting room, five doors open to the officers' cubicles. Some of these doors are decorated with articles from

The New York Times on wife beating and juvenile crime—something to read for those who must wait so long. Mrs. Elena Yeardon, who lives a block away from the court, arrives at 8:15 to catch up on writing reports. Her desk, each morning, is covered with files, each requiring action. She has been here four months, but has been seventeen years a Probation officer, three of those in a unit covering three Bronx police precincts, including the notorious Fort Apache. On particularly rough days, Yeardon, who is in her mid-forties, copes with seven or eight cases, but four or five is the usual load—between a thousand and fifteen hundred cases every year.

"I spend most of my time on the PINS. The parents feel they are threatened, they're failures. When they come here they're ready to place the children somewhere out of the home right away. They're angry. Their problem accompanies some crisis in the family: a welfare check didn't arrive, they have housing problems. It's difficult to get at the *real* problem. We get a lot of shouting and screaming. A PINS case can take two hours, especially when Puerto Rican parents are involved." Yeardon is Puerto Rican, the only Probation officer in this court who speaks Spanish. Two clerks speak it and are used as interpreters, "but it's not the same. The lack of Puerto Rican staff hurts us. It's not enough to understand the language, you have to understand the culture." Delinquency cases are relatively tranquil, because parents tell her the police are picking on their kids, but PINS cases require patience. "You have to let them ventilate their feelings here before you can work something out with them. Usually a boyfriend is around. The mother may want to keep her boyfriend, not her kid." To get the mother to admit to the boyfriend, Yeardon must explain she has nothing to do with welfare. Most of the children, PINS and delinquents, deny the charges against them, leaving Yeardon to work through instinct and experience. She has developed techniques she can't define. "I don't want to become immune to these people's problems. I still take some of them home with me."

On July 28, Yeardon begins with an attractive black woman and her infant who have waited nearly two and a half hours to *withdraw* a petition. A boy had slugged this woman's older child and stolen his bike, but the bike was recovered. The boy involved has other petitions outstanding—armed robbery and possession of weapons—but he turned sixteen two days ago, so Yeardon does not press the woman to proceed. Ordinarily she would have: "Sometimes, before a judge will do something for a child, he has to have five or six findings. So we feel it worthwhile to get the case into court."

Her next case involves Carlos Dyer, a fifteen-year-old boy with eight "priors"—among them five robberies adjusted at Probation and a shoplifting case, dismissed. Yeardon sees the complainant first, alone, and asks him immediately if he plans to go to court; if he doesn't show sufficient resolve, she won't take as many notes. The complainant, a strong young man who runs a shoe store, says: "I want this kid locked up." Carlos, he explains, entered his store one morning. Complainant, all sociability: "How ya doin'?" Carlos: "What you lookin' at, mothafucka?" Complainant orders Carlos from store. Carlos pulls a long knife: "I'm gonna cut your eyes out." He braces complainant against a wall, waves his knife about complainant's head. Complainant signals a security man, who fails to respond. Finally, one of complainant's employees pulls Carlos off and ejects him, but not before Carlos kicks down the door to the store. Cops are summoned, but before he is caught Carlos reappears, beats up the interfering employee with a billy club and threatens complainant again.

Yeardon dismisses the complainant and discovers she doesn't have the file she needs. Apparently, Carlos was paroled just last May 15, but there's no record of anything happening afterward. Carlos, a small, glistening boy with a huge mother, enters. Yeardon tells the mother that Carlos doesn't have to discuss his case with her, but she hopes he will so she can give the judge a report. The case, she explains, will go to court. Carlos is eager to tell his version:

Carlos: "My little brother was getting some socks in the store. I go in, that dude out there say somethin' to me. He always sayin' somethin' ever' time he see me. I ask him what he lookin' at. He get mad and try to throw me out of the store. He grab me by my collar here and we start to fight. I pull my knife out."

Yeardon: "What kind of knife?"

Carlos: "Double-oh-seven."

Carlos's mother is confused. Yeardon explains that a 007 is a long-bladed knife that opens with a flick of the wrist. "It's illegal. What were you doing with the knife?"

Carlos: "It wasn't mine. I was holding it for someone."

Yeardon: "Did you kick down the door?"

Carlos: "No, the dude broke it when he chased me out."

Yeardon: "And did you come back? When?"

Carlos: "About fifteen minutes."

Yeardon: "What did you do then?"

Carlos: "I beat him up again."

Yeardon: "With a billy club?"

Carlos: "It fell outta my pocket and he picked it up."

Yeardon turns to the mother, a great lump of aggrieved, resigned flesh. "How is Carlos at home?"

"Better," the mother says. She had brought Carlos in on a PINS petition eighteen months earlier; the boy had been stealing stuff around the house and smoking marijuana. "I wanted help, some counseling. I came in twice. But the judge dismissed the case."

Later, Yeardon says, "I feel the law guardians here. That's why the case was dismissed." She believes the Legal Aid people don't care about the children, but only want to win cases. To the mother, she says, "You better get some lunch. Your case won't get to Intake until two." The mother replies, "We got no money for lunch. We'll just wait."

Another boy, thirteen, is involved in this case. Donny Williams bears his mother's maiden name. "I had him and several others before I got married," the mother says bluntly, as if expecting some kind of moral judgment from Yeardon, which she does not get. Donny was nabbed by the police for concealing Carlos's knife and billy club after the event. Carlos had tried to shield Donny, claiming he had the club. Donny, not having heard Carlos's story, admits easily that the club was his. Yeardon picks up the discrepancy but does not comment on it. When she knows a case is going to court, she doesn't point out to the kids where their stories diverge. She doesn't want to aid their collaboration, but she won't put the discrepancy in her report, either; it's really the judge's business to discover it. But because this mother is hostile, she doesn't tell her or Donny that they don't have to talk to her. Over the mother's resistance—she thinks all these questions an invasion of her privacy—Yeardon slowly adduces most of what she needs to know. Still, mother can't remember Donny's birthday

(Donny can), or his father's, and she falls into an easy trap, lying about her income. Yeardon just shrugs: when it comes to fielding lies, no one, certainly not the judges, gets as much practice as a Probation officer.

With this case ready to go to court, Yeardon turns to one that isn't. The case is an "in concert" involving four boys from three families. The complainant doesn't show, making matters tough for Yeardon, who doesn't know whether he means to pursue the matter. Nor does the mother of the two youngest boys appear. Their father is there, however, though he doesn't live at home. Yeardon begins with these boys. When dealing with "in concerts" she takes the youngest first, leaving the older boys, more experienced in lying, to wonder what their more naive colleagues have inadvertently revealed.

Edward, ten, and Ellery, eight, enter with their father.

Yeardon: "Does your wife work?"

Father: "No."

Ellery: "Yes she does!"

Father: "No. I said no, so it's no. Shut up."

To Yeardon this means that mother works and takes welfare too. That's not Yeardon's business, but it may mean that mother is away from home, neglecting the kids, and that *is* her business. The police report in front of her charges these boys and two others with attacking another boy and relieving him of $5. Edward and Ellery's stories coincide: they were innocent bystanders who got no proceeds from the heist. Freddy took the money, and the other boy, George, got twenty-five cents.

Yeardon: "How did George get only twenty-five cents?"

Edward: "That's what he always gets. This guy gives it to him."

Yeardon: "*Gives* it to George?"

Edward (brightly): "Every week."

Yeardon doesn't have to pursue this; she knows what protection money is.

Yeardon: "What were you two doing with Freddy?"

Edward: "Walking along. When he took the money, we ran."

Yeardon: "Why?"

Edward: "We get in trouble if we caught there."

Yeardon: "What *should* you have done?"

Ellery: "Run away."

Yeardon: "Shouldn't you have tried to stop Freddy?"

There's no reply to this. Such a maneuver is unheard of on the streets. In the next interview, George explains that Freddy took the money, that he, George, "never got no quarters," and that Edward and Ellery rifled the victim's pockets while Freddy held his arms behind his back.

Freddy and his mother enter next. Freddy is thirteen and wears an imitation jewel in his left ear. Mother is a lush woman, just over the hill. She explains that she married Freddy's father two years after Freddy was born and "lost" the father the same year. Four more children followed. Freddy says he has no idea why a boy should give George a quarter every week. As for himself, he had nothing to do with any robbery; he just picked up the $5 bill when it fell from the kid's pocket.

Now Yeardon brings everybody into her cubicle together. It is very crowded, very hot and uncomfortable. People crowd along the walls, and two of the boys have to share a seat, which is awkward when they're trading accusations. To each one Yeardon says, "Now tell me what you told me before." This is one of her techniques she can't define: it puts each boy in a bind. He's not being asked again to tell what happened, but to repeat a story he thought he told in confidence; if for his own later safety he varies it, he fears Yeardon will jump on him. Much shouting and cross-argument follows, with Yeardon interjecting: "Now let *him* talk!"

Finally, she's had enough. "Now somebody here is not telling the truth! This is *terrible,* for a kid to have to worry that when he's out on the street some other kid may take his money. I do not like this! If you do not tell me the truth, I promise you I will tell it before the judge. Because it's all right to make a mistake. Everybody's entitled to one mistake. But if I let you go, you will think you have got away with something. You're *not* going to get away with it! Now I am going to get this other boy in here and hear what *he* has to say. And I want Edward and Ellery's mother in here. She *must* come, so I can see how you two behave at home. And then I'm going to call you all back again!"

For the present, she has done what she can. Freddy, Yeardon

thinks, was the principal thief, the other boys just going along, but despite her promise to the four boys there will never be a case before a judge if the victim doesn't show up.

Later that afternoon, as she is working on her forms, a fifteen-year-old boy knocks on Yeardon's door and enters. Harold is small, smart-looking, waves a cigarette. His mother is an alcoholic, and he works at odd jobs—when he's not being arrested. Harold has been arrested ten times: "Four or five," he says when asked. He's in today on another charge and has just dropped by for a social call—to see how Mrs. Yeardon is doing. "One of my old customers," Yeardon says. "But you're trying, aren't you? You haven't been arrested in four or five months. That's a record for you."

Yeardon remembers the faces of the children she has worked with, but not their names. "This embarrasses me. They come by to see me, they want to show me their new baby, and they don't grasp that I see a thousand of them a year and can't remember names."

It is four o'clock, court closing time in the airless summer months, and Yeardon must leave, because when the court officers go she is left without protection.

"It's not all bad," she says. "There *are* small gratifications."

There were some in the Bronx Family Court that July who took wry satisfaction from evidence that their favorite metaphor for the court and all its works had been translated into a physical presence that no one could ignore. On Monday, July 19, a boy in the top-floor detention room deliberately clogged a toilet. Two inches of water, mixed with urine and feces, covered the floor.

In the best of times, these detention rooms—one for boys, another for girls—have a Dickensian quality about them. The boys' room, measuring about twenty by twenty feet, usually confines fifteen of the accused, who doze on hard wooden benches or gaze dully at a black-and-white television set installed to serve as a pacifier. The few windows are covered with locked grilles, and one is nailed shut for good measure. None affords a view of the Bronx scenery, for all are translucent with grime. Legal Aid's appeals to have these windows washed have been unavailing. So, too, have been Legal Aid's appeals to make drinking water available. One visitor appearing in this room is met first by a boy who asks him for water and then by a guard who attempts a joke: Is the visitor thirsty? Perhaps when he finds water he will bring the boy some. A thermometer, nailed to the wall, reads 87 degrees. Thomas Esposito, Legal Aid's assistant attorney-in-charge in the Bronx, hung it there—"for the record," he says, because his office plans to sue the city for water, knowing that the suit will take months to creep through the courts and will eventually be dismissed because, of course, the court is moving to better quarters.

Between the boys' and girls' detention rooms is an interview room, six feet by six, crowded with a table, a file cabinet and two chairs—one for a lawyer, the other for his client, pressed so close together that their corners touch. The room is dark, paint peels from the walls, the overhead light has been broken for months. "The right to counsel," Esposito says, "involves the right to be able to talk to your lawyer in decency."

In an alcove off the boys' room the boys' lunches—milk and peanut-butter sandwiches—are warmed in a refrigerator that hasn't worked within memory. There is a toilet here, too, with no basin, no seat on the toilet, and no toilet paper. The toilet paper is hoarded by the guards, who dole it out to the boys a few sheets at a time: "Otherwise the kids get angry and shove the whole roll down the bowl." Which, on July 19, was precisely what happened.

No one makes a move to mop up the mess that day, or the next. At 7:53 A.M. on Tuesday, July 20, America's Viking robot craft lands perfectly on Mars and begins to send back sharply defined photographs of a rocky, barren landscape (the landing module is, says astronomer Carl Sagan, "inexpensive—about a billion dollars"), but in the Bronx Family Court the previous day's colloidal mixture, not at all improved by the heat, has seeped into the girls' detention room. There is not so much of it here and the stench is not quite as bad, so the boys are crowded in with the girls and everybody spends the day sitting or lying upon benches and tables. The women guards, not normally a fastidious crew, do not respond in good humor. The day's conversation about lack of routine maintenance and superior conditions in the Bronx Zoo is punctuated by shouts: "Feces! You can see them! *There!*" and "Can you imagine this yellow stuff floating right here on our floor!" The guards—two men and two women—point out that their supervisor at Spofford has the right to bus the kids right out of this health hazard, "but he doesn't dare." Nor do *they* dare walk out with the kids themselves: "We'd lose our jobs." If they all stuck together, they agreed, they couldn't be fired; they might even clean the mess up themselves, though it isn't their job. These proposals of cooperative risk and remedial action progress no further. Tom Esposito is darkly angry: "The kids are probably breathing cholera germs. Which of them is ever going to give a damn, let alone have respect, for a system of law and justice that tolerates *this?*" Still, only the adults are exercised; the kids are comatose, dozing or gazing dully at the broken windows.

On Wednesday, the condition of the detention rooms having further deteriorated, eleven boys and one girl are confined in the minuscule courtroom, Part IV, that is not being used this month. Vague noises have circulated about a plumber imminently arriving, but he doesn't. Esposito has argued with the building's janitor to no avail. The janitor has a supervisor in Manhattan, but nobody can determine who he is and the janitor won't tell. Thursday brings no amelioration, and by now some of the judges are juggling their calendars in an attempt to get hearings for the children in detention out of the way in the mornings. Others maintain their imperturbability. "What's all the fuss?" asks Reginald Matthews. "What's this *raw sewage* talk? We had 'raw sewage' out front of this court for five days and no one made a fuss."

That week of the excremental flood, which was finally cleaned up on Friday, sees Judge Matthews at the top of his form. Matthews is black, about fifty, with grizzled graying hair. In court he speaks loudly for effect—often in a precise, formal style, but sometimes lapsing into street talk: "Ain't heard nothin' 'bout that." Some lawyers say Matthews lacks judicial temperament. Certainly his face registers impatience with lawyers: he grimaces when they waffle on too long; he clutches his head; he looks elaborately bored. Monday finds him back from a judicial conference in Rhode Island—"I've been wandering in the country instead of walking through the fields of crime"—commenting on his weight ("One hundred seventy-seven pounds today") and his blood pressure ("Stable, high edge of normal"). Because of the heat he is decked out in a lime-green blazer instead of the judicial robe the law requires, and on the blazer's lapel he sports a large button: "I'm Crazy About the Big Apple."

Matthews must cover Parts II and III this week, and all adoptions. Instead of covering both Parts in one courtroom, he strides briskly from one Part to the other. "It's like a cancer, spreading," says Eugene Riley, a BCW lawyer. "Really, it's a question of style." "I'm the Pied Piper of Hamlin," Matthews says as he bounces along the corridors and up the stairs, a small retinue behind him. "That makes me a rat, then," says a Corporation Counsel lawyer. "Or a child," adds Riley. "I'm beating my chops today," Matthews says. "No hearings today; I got too many cases." Later, seated behind the table that serves him as a bench, he reluctantly explains to a family involved in a child abuse matter filed last May that he simply has no time to hear the case today. The child's grandmother, who has offered to take the girl, has flown in from St. Croix just for this appearance, but the case must be adjourned even so. "Family Court is supposed to have thirty-nine judges," he says. "We have seven vacancies and the calendars get out of hand." Everyone knows that the appointment of Family Court judges is a political matter. It suits Mayor Beame's politics just now to keep seven vacancies on the Family Court; it also shows the contempt in which even the mayor holds the court. "We can't go on this way," Matthews says. "Nobody can go on like this. If any more vacancies come, you'll see judges resigning. I'd just as soon resign myself if I get a good offer elsewhere."

The day begins poorly. "Just what I need," Matthews observes. "An early-morning obstacle." The obstacle is a man who proves balky in a support case. The man says: "This is a democracy, your honor." Matthews says: "I truly hope so. That's what they've told me all these years." Immediately afterward, he confronts a sixteen-year-old boy whose placement with an agency has been extended another year. Matthews is cross. "The agency should have found an adoption for him long ago. This boy has been with agencies since he was born. It's almost too late now, he's not as attractive as he was."

At a disposition in a homicide case, Matthews considers the situation of a fifteen-year-old boy, whose gang, the Five Percenters, killed a younger boy. The respondent hit the victim on the head with a chair leg; someone else, old enough to be tried in Criminal Court, shot him in the back. The chaplain at Spofford has submitted a letter praising the boy—"he searches out the good"—and a Probation officer recommends parole. The boy, who has been held five weeks, has already been remanded more often than the law allows. Threats have been made to the boy's family; a rival gang promises to kill the boy if he is released. Matthews, however, has an option: he can send the boy on parole to his father, who lives in Manhattan. "You're at the beginning of your life," Matthews says to him. "But if I'm not mistaken, you could be at the end of it if I let you out."

To a PINS girl, sixteen, whose troubles are such that he is reluctant to let her go, Matthews says, "You know what they say: New York may be broke, but it's not poor. There *is* something we can do. If there wasn't, I wouldn't be here. I can make much more money someplace else. Still, there's only so much I can do. I got one thing to say to you: Think. *Think* before you do something get you into trouble. If everybody *think* first, they be no wars, no more crime. Everybody think first, I be out of a job in two months. You're an attractive girl. How did you do in school? Honor grades? You got looks, you got brains. Now you gotta ask yourself: where you gonna be five years from now, ten years from now?"

Paul McAllister, the girl's lawyer, takes a dim view of this kind of peroration: "It's ludicrous. She's not going to listen. It leaves her with a terrible idea of what a court is." Doubtless Matthews is great theater —to another boy he says, "I promise to do everything in my power, an' I got a *lot* of power"—but the question of suitability troubles the lawyers who appear before him. McAllister believes a judge should be formal, remote from the kids, certainly not discussing his finances; the child should feel the seriousness of the occasion.

Nevertheless, Matthews's concern for the children before him cannot be discounted. Late in the morning, he confronts a boy who has been found to be both a delinquent and a PINS; he is also up on a burglary charge in Criminal Court. The boy is sixteen; he cannot seem to close his mouth or look directly at the judge. Corporation Counsel moves to quash both petitions—an unusual move, but at sixteen the boy will not be taken by any private agency. "It's out of our jurisdiction," the lawyer says. "It's in the adult courts now."

The law guardian objects: "This is rotation justice, your honor! We put off the hearing until he's too old and then rotate him to the adult court."

Matthews explodes: "*Rotating!* We ain't rotating *him!* He rotated himself up to the adult court of his own free will."

Law guardian: "Your honor, we hope this boy can still be rehabilitated through some Family Court agency."

Matthews: "What's his other charge? Burglary?" To the boy he says: "Well, I keep a shotgun at home and I'm gonna shoot the first head that comes in." He pauses and then addresses the lawyers. "I know I can't do anything here. I'm talking out of practical experience now. We live in a society that wants to spend one billion dollars on a B-1 bomber the only purpose of which is annihilating human beings. Another one billion dollars on a Trident sub-ma-rine. That's *your* society, not mine. That's *our* society. Nothin' I can do about it. It's amazing our agencies can do anything at all, they have so little money. I sit here every day and see cases like this one and maybe, with an agency, there's a ten percent success rate. With the money they have, it ought to be two percent." He looks at the ceiling for a moment and then speaks to the boy. "Son, you have worked yourself into a whole mess of trouble. You may be about to be sent away. I can tell you where they'll probably send you: Stormville. You won't like that. Boy, you can't hustle in New York. You wanna hustle, you gotta go *outside* New York. Here it's so bad the hustlers are hustlin' the hustlers. But I can tell you, you got one thing goin' for you. You got your father sittin' there beside you. Not one boy in ten has got that. You gotta get your head together, son. Get your nose clean. You can do it, I know you can." He then dismisses both petitions: "Not because I don't care about you, son, but because there's nothing I can do."

During the lunch break, William Logan, attorney-in-charge of Legal Aid's Bronx office, runs into a panel lawyer in one of the corridors. Panel lawyers, or "18-B" lawyers, are private attorneys who put in their names for occasional work in the Family Court representing, for

$15 an hour,* the mothers of the children Legal Aid defends, and sometimes children whom Legal Aid cannot represent because of a conflict of interest. A few of these lawyers are idealistic men who consider such service, under such conditions, a pro bono obligation, but most of them are incompetents who need the money.

"You just lost a case," Logan tells this lawyer amiably.

"*What* case?"

"Iris Lamming."

"How could I *lose* it? I wasn't even there!"

"You failed to appear. Caputo found against you."

The panel lawyer shrugs. "I don't give a shit. I've already filed my voucher. I get paid for the day."

Logan, nine years on the job, is thirty-five, a tall man with bushy blond hair who describes himself as a "McGovern-Harris civil libertarian." A popular man in the court, he would make a good politician. He believes that children's rights are our first line of defense—"When they go, so will adults' rights"—but he also believes that when children are at odds with their parents, the parents should be well represented, too. Iris Lamming is a girl who was, that morning, separated from her mother; she will go to her aunt's, which is where she wanted to go. Legal Aid advanced her cause, and the mother never had a chance to keep her because this panel lawyer didn't show. "His attitude," Logan says, "is typical of so many lawyers. It's the attitude that brought us the Nixon gang."

In room 207 of the Bronx Family Court a sign faces the door: "Kids on Your Nerves? Don't Hit, Don't Scream . . . Call Parents Anonymous of New York: 765-2336." Richard Ruedger, the Bureau of Child Welfare's liaison to the court, and Eugene F. Riley, a young BCW attorney, reflect on their profession. "I'm not sure we're efficient at all," Ruedger says. "There aren't many success stories in this business. There's not much motivation among parents."

In the Family Court, the role of the BCW attorneys is analogous to the role of the DAs in Criminal Court: they prosecute cases against

*The fee has recently been raised to $25 an hour.

parents who abuse or neglect their children. The BCW office, however, is analogous to the Police Department: its function is investigations. In the Bronx, BCW operates some twenty-five field units, each
containing five case workers, a supervisor and some paraprofessionals.
The case workers, when they appear in court, are instantly identifiable: the women tend to be black and lumpy, wearing stretch pants and
nylon blouses; the men are more often white—young, with long hair
and mustaches, wearing jeans and holding paperback copies of R.D.
Laing's books. These people inquire into reported cases of neglect and
child abuse—the Article 10 cases, as they are called in court—working
as often as not from anonymous tips, because neighbors are reluctant
to inform on each other if their names will be made known.

"We have enormous snooping power," Ruedger says. "The state
encourages anonymous tips."

Riley: "The snooping works basically on poor people. They're almost all on welfare. We rarely get calls about Jewish families except
when a parent is crazy."

Ruedger: "We have to check them all. We have to contact the
family within twenty-four hours. Parents won't tell you anything and
sometimes won't even open the door, so if it's not in a housing
authority, where the superintendent will usually let you in, we have
to get a warrant and a policeman who will get the door open. If things
are really bad, we have four sections of law that allow us to remove
the kids on the spot. If there is 'imminent danger' to the kids, we have
to be in court in twenty-four hours."

Only 10 percent of these cases, however, reach the court. No case
can come to court unless a complainant steps forward.

Ruedger: "The court is the last resort. It can't do much. We try to
resolve cases through social work. You really shouldn't go to court
unless you want to remove the kids or compel a parent into therapy
for alcohol or drugs."

Riley: "A large part of parents under Article 10 are deranged.
Incredible emotional problems, character disorders."

Ruedger: "In neglects, the parents are dispirited, can't use money
properly. The children are left alone because the parents can't afford
a sitter."

Riley: "It's hard to get a finding on emotional neglect. There's no way to go before a judge and say this child is not being emotionally nurtured. The public likes flashy cases. One I had, a child was taken away from its family by the court, then returned—the parents were addicts—and the kid was found in the river. Give me a child in a hospital with broken bones, there you have a case. Anything else is a problem.''

Ruedger: "I've had heads bashed in, one with a hammer, one against a radiator. I had a fourteen-month-old girl raped. Very few cases have gory details. Mostly, they're lack of school attendance, lice, dirty, underfed. These cases tend to go on for generations. Many more neglects than abuses, the parents are resistant to change. We have a fairly sizable Albanian community in the Bronx. They carry guns, shoot each other, haven't caught on they have to send their kids to school or give them shots. It's cultural differences, really, not so much neglect. Even the white trash has left the Bronx. The Bronx gets hind tit in everything in New York.''

Riley: "A good BCW worker has to be deranged. The women are constantly being raped, robbed, they have to go into the worst parts of town alone.''

Ruedger: "The clients we deal with are basically hostile. It used to be the BCW was a revolving door. Case workers were quitting because it was so draining. You spend seven hours a day in a garbage pail and it's injurious to your physical and mental health. But now the job market is drying up. So the people stay. It's not so much dedication as being stuck.''

That afternoon, Judge Joseph D. Caputo presides over an auto-theft case in Part I. Part I, in this labyrinth of justice, is far removed from Part III, and Caputo, in style and temperament, is far removed from Judge Matthews. "I'm careful how I walk to the subways," he says. "I've had death threats. The kids have a two-word phrase for me: 'motherfuckin' judge.' '' An elderly man, seven-and-a-half years on the bench, Caputo finds the work exhausting. "By Wednesday I'm bushed. When I went on vacation, leaving on a Friday, I stayed in bed Saturday and Sunday, couldn't go away until the following Tuesday. That tired.''

Part I is the worst of the courtrooms operating this month. Antique air conditioners, long broken, deteriorate in the windows; the air is not noticeably moved by an electric fan. "It's so hot in here," Caputo says, "my shirt becomes soaked and dries three or four times a day." There is a filthy flag and the inevitable motto, "In God We Trust," stuck upon a wall. Part I's particular affliction, however, is the din of airplanes constantly descending, obliterating testimony and instructions from the bench; nobody pays them any mind.

In the auto-theft case, the manager of a secondhand car lot testifies that he looked out the window to see one of his cars, a Mercury double-parked in the street, pull out and immediately collide with another car. The Mercury didn't stop. The manager ran out and spied one of the owners sitting in his car, and the two of them pursued the Mercury down the street. The Mercury careered into a dead-end alley. A boy leaped from the driver's seat and jumped over a wall. Corporation Counsel's other witness is the driver of the car hit by the renegade vehicle. He testifies that he expected the Mercury to stop and chased it when it didn't. He signaled a cop to arrest the boy, which the cop obligingly did.

The boy, fifteen, is charged with grand larceny, possession of a stolen automobile and unauthorized use of a motor vehicle. The case against Jerrold seems open-and-shut. Nevertheless, Clara Bilmacz, the law guardian, constructs a defense that dovetails exactly with every fact adduced by Corporation Counsel while making Jerrold look like an Eagle Scout. Before launching into it, however, she tries to get the case dismissed on what she calls "technicals."

The complainant, Bilmacz insists, should be the owner of the car lot, but he has not appeared. "He sent another man instead." This move incenses Corporation Counsel: "This man will do." Caputo is unsure. "What about the right of the respondent to confront his accuser?" "There's nothing in the Family Court Act that says an accuser must be present," Corporation Counsel replies. "That's left to *our* discretion." Caputo agrees, so Bilmacz tries another attack. For the charge of grand larceny to stand, she says, the car involved must be worth more than $1,500, but there has been no testimony to this effect. This ploy fails as well. On cross-examination, Bilmacz persuades the manager to admit that he didn't see the boy in the car, never saw him until the arrest, and in fact didn't notice the theft until the accident occurred.

Bilmacz then asks for a recess to consult with her client. Unknown to Judge Caputo, Jerrold is a famous juvenile felon, one who has been written up in the *Daily News*. Judges fear children like Jerrold because they don't want to read in tomorrow's newspaper "JUDGE FREES TEENAGE MUGGER." Having been paroled by a judge in a mugging case, Jerrold mugged another man, touching off the traditional hue and cry for tougher laws about violent kids. There's an irony here, because Judge Caputo favors stiffer sentences for violent children, but at this point he doesn't know Jerrold's history. "Do you want to go on the stand?" Bilmacz asks her client. He does.

Jerrold is duly sworn and testifies that he noticed this double-parked Mercury, its nose sticking out at an angle, start to slide back toward a car parked against the curb. He jumped in to stop it and (having found the keys in the ignition) pulled it forward, thus accidentally striking the oncoming car. Fearing that the accident was his fault, he panicked—this is a nice touch, because everyone knows children are easily frightened. In fact, Jerrold's entire testimony is very nice, conflicting in no way with Corporation Counsel's witnesses. What he has offered is a new interpretation of events already established.

Bilmacz: "Did you intend to steal the car?"

Jerrold: "No."

Bilmacz: "Did you mean to go on a joy ride?"

Jerrold: "No."

Caputo doesn't look at the boy as he testifies; how then can he tell if Jerrold is lying? Nevertheless, he finds Jerrold guilty of the third charge, unauthorized use of a motor vehicle, reserving decision on the other two counts. This maneuver allows Probation to present the boy's history to the judge. Over the years, Jerrold has had twelve prior charges, ranging from marijuana use to robbery and attempted murder.

Bilmacz: "Your honor, it's outrageous that Probation should present all these allegations without any findings, if there were any."

Court liaison officer: "I don't have a record of the findings."

Caputo: "I'll put the attempted murder out of my mind."

The judge orders a new Investigation and Report. Jerrold's previous case worker says that he's still willing to work with the boy in a Title II situation—that is, a situation in which Jerrold agrees to voluntary placement with an agency—but Caputo wants to see whether Title III is in order. Title III means that Jerrold will be involuntarily placed in a training school by the state's Division for Youth.

Caputo's approach saddens Clara Bilmacz. She would prefer Jerrold to have a chance to work with someone who might help him. After her clever maneuvers, Caputo's even more clever stroke won the day: by finding Jerrold guilty of an inconsequential charge, he gained access to Probation's records before deciding the important charges. Jerrold no doubt is a bad kid, but on the basis of what was offered in court he could not have been convicted of anything serious. "Of course, I don't believe Jerrold's story," Bilmacz said later, but that's not the point. "I don't believe his story," Judge Caputo said later still, and that *is.*

That afternoon, the heat rises in Part III, a room that measures eighteen by fifteen feet. As many as twenty-two people at a time press in, those not involved with the cases intent upon filing documents, conferring with each other, gossiping (a man, it seems, jumped out of a lavatory window during the lunch break, landing on the sidewalk twenty feet below), poring over court records or staring into space. Despite this congregation, Judge Matthews attempts to work through his calendar. "I'm too weak to pick up the gavel," he says at one point, "but I don' wan' counsel talkin' among themselves." His clerk mentions that some Gatorade would taste good at the end of the day. Matthews rolls his eyes: "Gatorade! *Gatorade!* Gonna take a whole lot more'n Ga-tor-ade when this is done."

Despite the heat, or possibly because of it, one case draws Judge Matthews's anger. A separated couple living on different floors of the same building are contesting custody of their children. The father has one child, the mother the other two. Both parents have appeared in court many times on a variety of petitions.

Matthews: "This makes me angry. Your irresponsibility is hurting these kids, who should be together. In this court, the children come first. If you can't behave responsibly, I'll take them away from both of you." He makes a decision: all three children to go with the mother. Suddenly, the father weeps.

Matthews: "Don't cry in here, sir. Save your crying for outside. You want to cry, you go outside."

Father: "Judge, see the children, please."

Matthews: "That's not necessary."

Father: "Judge, I got no money. My wife gets welfare. She's rich, she can go wherever she wants and she leaves the three kids with me."

Confronted with this curious but not unappealing argument, Matthews relents and orders the children into the courtroom. Like most small children, they are cute, bright-eyed; unlike most in this court, they are well dressed. Matthews, irregularly dressed, introduces himself: "I'm the judge. My robe is in the other room." He appoints a law guardian to find out what the kids want, agrees that a Legal Aid social worker shall investigate the children's homes and adjourns the case pending reports.

As the afternoon advances, the pace quickens. Decisions are made, or more often postponed, so abruptly—with a wave of a rubber stamp and a burst of legal jargon—that parents and children have no idea what has happened. Sometimes, as the judge begins another case, the parties of the previous case are still standing by their chairs, numbly attempting to formulate a question; an interpreter or court officer hustles them through the door, muttering a few words of explanation. By 3:30, those who have waited all day for their "day in court," who know now that the phrase means a day in the court waiting room, find their cases being disposed of in 120 seconds. In this one week, while covering Parts II and III, Judge Matthews hears 238 cases—147 involving juveniles and 91 adults—an average of 47.6 cases a day.

Despair in this court assumes a variety of forms. A young woman, an attorney for Corporation Counsel, says she finds her work "very fulfilling, but the court is too depressing to endure." Joseph Napolitano, a Probation officer with many years' experience, finds refuge in cynicism. "Justice is very rare here," he says. "Legal Aid doesn't care about these kids. They have noble intentions, sure, but you know what the road to hell is paved with. The kids tell me Legal Aid is full of shit. The psychiatrists here give you nothing but Freudian bullshit. The kid's gun is his penis: I've actually heard *that*. Crime is caused by environment, that kind of thing. Whatever happened to individual responsibility? We're positively reinforcing negative behavior here. I tell you, if A. Hitler walked into this court, they'd parole him."

Arthur Trufelli, supervisor of the Corporation Counsel attorneys in the Bronx, believes "the system may collapse." Corporation Counsel assumed the prosecutor's role in Family Court only in 1971; before their arrival this duty was relegated to the judges. "We have only five trial attorneys here, and me: I have to go into court myself. One of my people is actually assigned to Staten Island, but he's here to replace an absentee. Another has had exactly one week's experience. A third has been admitted to the bar for six months. A fourth, for a year and a half. Our fifth lawyer is experienced. We have no clerk, no typist, no one to answer the phone. Our attorneys have to do their own clerical work. Not too long ago, we had eight lawyers, but one was transferred, another quit, and the third quit under less-than-honorable conditions. We cover three thousand delinquency cases a year in the Bronx, never mind the PINS. We also have four thousand support cases, which, because they're disputes between adults, Legal Aid doesn't get involved in."

In June, which Irving Cohen called the "monster month," the delinquency and PINS cases handled by Trufelli's office resulted in 445 adjournments, 93 dismissals, 12 withdrawals, 81 dismissals for failure to prosecute, and 94 findings—guilty verdicts—of which half were obtained through confessions. These figures indicate that Corporation Counsel's batting average is .125, or .0625 if you don't count confessions. And of course this rate of attrition is reached only *after* Probation has thrown out 60 percent of the cases. The children don't know these figures, but many have a vague sense of how the prosecutors perform, and this understanding contributes to the contempt in which they hold the court. To oppose Corporation Counsel's efforts, Legal Aid had at that time in the Bronx ten trial attorneys, two supervisors, a lawyer in charge of writs and stays, and eleven supporting staff—and these, of course, dealt only with juvenile cases. This imbalance caused tremors as far away as Albany. State Senator Donald H. Halperin, presiding in June over a Temporary State Commission on Child Welfare hearing into the role of the prosecutor in Family Court proceedings, remarked that "sending Corporation Counsel into court against Legal Aid is like sending the Lithuanians to fight the Russians."

"We have no money to serve summonses," Trufelli says. "If we can't get a warrant, we have to mail the summons, and with the way the mails work today, we can't be certain the summons will arrive in the three days the law requires. And if the summons doesn't work, we can't follow it with a warrant unless we can prove that the summons was served. This literally approaches malpractice. We can't bring in the respondents. A respondent can only be held on remand for three days. After that, if he decides not to come to court, if he misses just once, he won't be tried. The kids just don't come. If Legal Aid brings a habeas corpus, we have to answer it, and it takes a morning to do *that.* We don't have the personnel. If a kid is involved in a crime with someone sixteen or over—and these kids tend to run together—then we have to go to the grand jury to get the minutes involving the adult. These are hard to get. The DA feels that his case is more important. We have to file a motion, that takes another morning. We can lose a full man-week.

"We're trying cases right now with five minutes' preparation. We're trying cases without knowing what's supposed to happen. We can't contact people. We can't follow up. We haven't got the complainant's address. *We have no time.* And we get a lot of dismissals for this. Dismissals are almost always our fault. We have to take an ACD"—an adjournment in contemplation of dismissal, which means that if a kid doesn't get in more trouble within a specified period of time his case will be dismissed—"when we could have forced the issue. There are other kinds of dismissal. If a kid has a lot of petitions, we go for one—a delinquency finding—and let the others go, it makes no difference. If we can get a case to trial, we generally win; we're 80 percent sure of a finding. *If* we can get them to trial. A judge has, say, forty cases on his calendar any given day. Only two or three of these can be tried. Now if twelve of these cases, say, are ours, we may have ten ready for trial. That means we have in the waiting room nine cops, some medical examiners, witnesses, the complainants, parents, but the judge can't possibly hear these cases. Legal Aid knows that if ten cases are ready it can play them against each other before the judge. Maybe none will be tried. Each will be used to adjourn another. One day I saw six cases not tried, just through this maneuver. Everyone has so much to do that their combined hopes that some will be adjourned result in all being adjourned."

This year (and Trufelli stresses that is *only* for this year) his office has received a rare federal grant to fund a Serious Crimes Unit whose purpose is simply to demonstrate that juvenile justice can be more effective if the prosecutors have a larger staff. The unit, comprising an assistant attorney, a medical examiner and a paralegal worker, is supposed to work only on serious crimes, but (although Trufelli will not say so) it is clear to court observers that these people are being used for Corporation Counsel's routine work—just so Trufelli's office can stay afloat. The government is not getting what it paid for, and nothing about effective handling of serious crimes is being proved. When the grant expires next May, these lawyers may well quit rather than be mired in the everyday workload of Corporation Counsel.

"We could use more of these grants," Trufelli says. "Legal Aid is always getting them. We don't because our boss is not a strong administrator. We've never had a strong administrator. The job doesn't lead anywhere, so we've just not had them. We could use more support staff, too. We need access to a stenographer to take a statement from someone. We need an investigator to go to the scene. We could use a police car for two hours a week to bring in reluctant witnesses. The worst of it is that we have no administrative control. I do things my way, the guy in Queens does it another. We have no memos, no standard procedures for ordering evidence, no reliable statistics."

Trufelli speculates for a few minutes on his opposition. "You can see with the Legal Aid lawyers after a time the edges get worn off. They come in aggressive and idealistic, but it rarely lasts. Tom Esposito is still aggressive, but the system took care of him. He's no longer a trial lawyer, he's administration, so Legal Aid can't use his aggression. Beverly Massy, now, she's more like the old law guardians, not aggressive in court, but good with kids." Indeed, Massy, who

is older than most of the law guardians, presents a striking contrast
to Corporation Counsel's lawyers. She will look a boy she has just
been called upon to defend straight in the eye: "Who are you?" It's
not a challenge, but a question of human concern. For her, the children are distinctly human in a way they are not, possibly cannot be,
for Trufelli's attorneys. The Corporation Counsel lawyers see children
as abstractions, or a fleeting problem to be resolved. They are manila
folders with long sheets of yellow paper in them, and so they may be
to some of the male law guardians who may think of the children as
pawns in a game played against Corporation Counsel and the judges.
But for Beverly Massy, the law to be applied to these children is
second nature; it comes instinctively, leaving her time to think of them
as human beings.

The following May, Family Court was removed to a huge new building six blocks away at 900 Sheridan Avenue, which it shares with the
Criminal Court. The new building is equipped with such hitherto
unthinkable amenities as elevators and air conditioning, with large
waiting rooms containing glass-framed tapestries of some vaguely
modern design, with interview rooms, a nursery (seldom used for lack
of a supervisor), a Victim Services Agency, where complainants can
wait for their hearings without having to confront their assailants, and
larger courtrooms which, according to Bill Logan, "look like some
kind of goddam conference rooms." The new court really *is* an improvement, and Logan is pleased with it, though in retrospect he
misses "the camaraderie of the old building—those cramped quarters
certainly brought people together." The new building, he says in 1980,
"is falling apart already." Most of the furniture has been stolen from
the interview rooms—chairs, coatracks have gone; only the heavier
tables remain—and someone stole the stereo from the Victim Services
Agency. "We'll have it in the same condition as the old court in no
time," Logan says cheerfully. "You can take the boys out of the old
building, but you can't take the old building out of the boys."

Still, the tone of the place is different. Toward the end of July 1976,
a phone call came to the old court to the effect that a bomb had been
placed in a Probation office across the waiting room from Elena

Yeardon's cubicle. A leisurely evacuation of the entire court ensued; no one really believed in the bomb, but then considering the place's clientele it was not improbable. The day was rainy. The law guardians stood on the pavements, getting wet, cracking one-line jokes.

"If it went off, no one would know."

"There'd be no change."

"They couldn't find the damage."

"They'd think we were making repairs."

And that same evening, some men broke into Bill Logan's office, smashing a window to gain entry. They were caught piling stuff up on the street. "If it happens again, I'm going to put a board up," Logan said—which would make the office look like every other shop-front around. Logan sent Tom Esposito to Supreme Court to testify. "I told him: 'Get those bastards! No ACDs!' " But he doubts they'll weather the delay to see the prosecution through. "I know in principle we should. But we just don't have the time."

IV

Natural Families

On June 15, 1977, Stephen Pokart rises from behind his table in Part
II of the Manhattan Family Court to note his appearance in the
formal language required of all law guardians: "Charles Schinitsky,
Legal Aid Society, Stephen Pokart of counsel to the child, Kenneth
Dubartas." Nothing more formal than that introduction, unless it is
Pokart's vested white suit, will present itself to the court that day.
Pokart (Harvard '62, Harvard Law '65) is a slender, dapper man who
went first into the theater and then to Vietnam. His job with Schinitsky's Juvenile Rights Division is his first in law. "I came with a
sense I could change the world," he says, "or at least people's lives.
That didn't last long. I don't think I can change anything now. I don't
think I'm even doing anybody any good, except in neglects and
abuses." Pokart is Manhattan's scrappiest law guardian. In court, he
behaves like a terrier, incessantly barking objections while maintaining a courteous, almost serene expression—a combination that exas-
perates both his opposition and the judges. No one doubts that Pokart
is exceedingly able, but the mere mention of his name provokes wan
smiles from all who hear it.

Today he has an abuse case of the medium-terrible variety, which is to say that his client, Kenneth Dubartas, will probably not be permanently disabled from his experience. A police detective in the witness box describes Kenneth's appearance when he first encountered him: a nine-year-old boy whose body, from his neck to his knees, was a mass of bruises, edema and contusions, and whose hands were badly burned. "The mother had been bragging at a party that she had burned her boy's hands, but she insisted to me that she was only joking. The boy says his father held his hands over the stove while it was lit because he stole a piece of candy. He stole the candy because he was hungry."

This testimony brings a rash of objections from Isadore Bassof, a private attorney representing Kenneth's parents: "Hearsay, your honor! This is all inadmissible!" Judge Margaret Taylor reminds Bassof that Family Court law differs from any other court's law, and that while she deplores the present trend toward loosening the definition of what is admissible, hearsay testimony in a child abuse case *is* admissible under section 1046 of the Family Court Act. Because section 1046 causes more trouble in court than any other, everybody pauses to read it again. Article 10, section 1046 (vi) says: "Previous statements made by the child relating to any allegations of abuse or neglect shall be admissible in evidence; provided, however, that no such statement, if uncorroborated, shall be sufficient to make a fact-finding of abuse or neglect." In accordance with child abuse case tradition, Kenneth is not present in court. Bassof suggests that he must be cross-examined. Pokart, representing the absent child, is firm: he cannot allow this. Although Judge Taylor doesn't say so, she doesn't disagree with Bassof. She is opposed to section 1046 and believes in confrontation—"it may be a constitutional right, in spite of the Family Court Act"—even if this involves cross-examining a nine-year-old boy as his parents glare at him, the boy knowing that if he doesn't do in his parents properly this time, they will surely do him in in the hours and years to come. Traumatizing as the situation may be, Taylor believes that children who appear in this court have already been so traumatized that they cannot be further damaged here.

From the start, the only calm people in the court are Kenneth's parents: Lionel and Victoria Dubartas appear normal; their smooth black faces are expressionless. Both have crew cuts and wear identical gold-rimmed glasses. This case began in Supreme Court and was sent over here, though it could have been tried in either place; in fact, Lionel will almost certainly be tried in Supreme Court after (as is generally assumed) he loses his child here. Marvin Epstein, the Bureau of Child Welfare lawyer who is prosecuting this case, can almost taste his victory. "This is the one case I care about most. Boy, do I want this one! The DA has been bugging me; it should never have gone out of Criminal Court. This is the father of the year. He did it before, last year—he broke the kid's arm, but we had to let him go. No corroborative evidence." Steve Pokart thinks Epstein is simply "trying to cover his ass. He's guilt-ridden. He could have prosecuted last year from hospital records. The records show countless failures of BCW to follow up on this case. I'm thinking of getting a lawyer to sue the city—all this wouldn't have happened if the city had prosecuted."

To get the case into court at all, Pokart had to browbeat the telephone company to get the unlisted number of Kenneth's great-aunt, with whom he now lives. "I've never failed yet," Pokart says. The great-aunt is now on the stand. It was she who discovered Kenneth's condition: "Kenny told me he burnt his hands in a pot of French fries. I told him, 'You don't have to be afraid.' He said, 'Mommy held me and Lionel burned me.'" There is some doubt as to whether Lionel is Kenneth's father; Victoria Dubartas says he is. "I saw him undressed," the great-aunt continues, "his badly beaten and scarred body. He'd been whipped with ropes and chains."

Isadore Bassof objects again: "This is characterizing, your honor." The aunt's remarks are stricken from the record, but Bassof's move does him no good, for the aunt took snapshots of Kenneth's body. Marvin Epstein has some color slides as well, taken by the hospital —gruesome evidence that make Kenneth look like a victim of war atrocities.

"They tried to burn his privates with a newspaper before they burned his hands," the aunt testifies. "He showed me the burns on his thighs." Bassof, on cross-examination, inquires whether this great-aunt was living with anyone. No. Had she not been hospitalized by a man? No. Had she ever been convicted in a numbers game? For dealing drugs? No and no. Bassof is not quite convinced of these denials. The aunt, it seems, had been hospitalized, during which time "Victoria took the boy back, to get the welfare." To Steve Pokart, she offers a little background about Kenneth's life at home: "They'd lock him in the bedroom, not let him out to go to the bathroom. When he went in the bedroom, he was beaten. He was beaten when he tried to find food in the refrigerator.

"I think Lionel is a vicious person," she says. "I hate him with a passion. After what he did to Kenneth, I despise him."

"And your niece?" Pokart asks. "Victoria Dubartas?" Pokart, alone in the courtroom, pronounces this French name correctly; Bassof refers to his clients as "Dubartiss."

"Personally, I think she's insane."

Victoria's cousin, taking the stand, describes a scene at the Dubartas home in which Kenneth was obliged to hold out his burned hands while his mother demanded, "Tell her how many times you've lied to me!" "I felt ill," the cousin says, "and left. There were no bandages on that child's hands. His face was covered with bumps, knots on his head, like someone hit him upside the head and gave him the knots."

She is followed by a BCW case worker who testifies that the burns became infected, and that he has seen the scars that decorate Kenneth's torso and upper legs. This man, like many BCW workers, makes a bad witness: his heavy Spanish accent and mushy articulation slow up proceedings as everyone asks what it is he is trying to say. He is reluctant, too, to let his voluminous file be entered in evidence —possibly because it is disorderly, or possibly because it contains evidence of BCW's bungled attempts to prosecute the father, and of the father's long police record.

Bassof then asks Victoria Dubartas to take the stand. Marvin Epstein grins: "She's asking for it! She's asking!"

Judge Taylor, however, calls a recess for lunch. During the break, she knocks off four extension-of-placement cases.

"Why do you want to go to school?" she asks a fourteen-year-old boy. She knows the answer, but the boy, nonplussed, says nothing. "School's a difficult place, you know. Not much fun."

"I can live at home if I go to school." *That's* the reason: not the pleasures of the New York City school system, but the alternative to institutional placement.

"You're going to have to do it all yourself, you know," Taylor says. "The teachers aren't going to do it for you. Your mother can't do it for you." She is talking in her usual manner, very fast, asking the boy his advice; he just nods, probably just gets the gist of it. "I want you to go home for two weeks, work out a summer and fall program and come back and present it to me."

Moving rapidly now, Taylor knocks off a similar case, thanking the parties for waiting so long, and a third, telling a boy no, he can't go home, while giving him a friendly smile, and a fourth. "Sloppy judges," a law guardian remarks, "will go by what Probation or BCW says and has in his files; Taylor won't."

When the Dubartas case resumes in the afternoon, Victoria admits to Isadore Bassof that she is a reformed addict. "I used all kinds of drugs. I was evicted, I was sleeping in the streets, on rooftops. I gave Kenny to my aunt." The aunt, however, pushed cocaine. "She told me her man hit her with a bar stool and knocked her eye out of her head" —which is stricken from the record because hearsay evidence un-related to the child in question cannot be allowed. While on heroin, Victoria was convicted of theft and given three years' probation. As for Kenneth, when he was at home, "I talked to him about his problems, then punished him. Then I spanked him."

Bassof: "What did you spank him with?"

Victoria: "A little thin belt that came off a dress."

Kenneth's problems, it seems, had to do with stealing from stores —his mother had to reimburse them—and with unruliness in school. "I had to go there a couple of hundred times in three years." Bassof introduces as evidence letters from Kenneth's teachers, presumably to show reasons for beating the boy at home, and then, out of order, brings the school principal to the stand. Reginald F. Knox, of Manhattan's P.S. 192, testifies that Kenneth was involved in disciplinary problems: throwing food in the lunchroom, stealing from a store during school hours, disrupting classrooms.

Steve Pokart's objections arrive staccato, like machine-gun fire. He wants Knox's testimony thrown out on the ground that he wasn't present at the food-throwing, but Taylor can't be persuaded. He objects to hearsay testimony—everyone in this court objects to it, even the law guardians who most benefit from it—but Taylor allows it "not for truth, but to indicate the respondent's state of mind"—that is, what Victoria Dubartas believed to be the truth.

"I turned the stove jets on to scare him," Victoria says. "He struggled and we both fell on the flame." She is crying now. "He pulled the bandages off his own hands. I rewrapped them every day, put on salve." Not only that, but Kenneth "sleeps through the school hours. I found a reefer in his room, hidden. I took him to St. Luke hospital for psychiatric treatment and his behavior got worse."

Neither Pokart nor Epstein is pleased to see this woman taking the whole burden of guilt on herself. Convinced that the father is the villain of the piece, they think her confession must mean either that she is terrified of him or that, knowing his record and that he may be tried in Supreme Court, she must make him seem innocent here. During his wife's testimony, Lionel Dubartas shows no emotion whatever; in fact, he seems rather bored.

Bassof: "Do you love your child?"

Epstein: "Objection!"

Victoria: "Very much."

Pokart: "Irrelevant!"

Bassof: "Did you whip him?"

Victoria: "Not whip. I spanked him. Through his running away he was injured."

Bassof: "Please explain."

Victoria: "He try to get away from me and injure himself from running under the table, into the chair."

Under Pokart's cross-examination, she admits to whipping Kenneth with his father's thick belt and metal buckle. "I turned on two jets on the stove. I lift him up and explain to him I was just going to show him and punish him. He was kickin' up against the stove and sink. He threw us off balance."

Pokart: "How much do you weigh, Mrs. Dubartas?"

Victoria: "One hundred ninety-one pounds."

Pokart: "And how much does Kenneth weigh?"

Victoria: "Sixty, sixty-four pounds."

Pokart: "How could such a small boy throw you off balance?" Pokart is firm, swift, but not hostile.

Victoria: "I had the two front burners on full. When he pushed back with his feet he fell with his hands next to the fire. My weight was on top of him." She is weeping now, wiping tears from her cheeks. "Kenny was screaming."

Pokart: "When you turned on the flames? He was pretty scared, right?"

It is 4:05 in the afternoon, so Judge Taylor adjourns this case until 9:30 in the morning; she wants to settle a PINS case that has been waiting outside all day. Most people who are alert to the problems of Family Court agree that PINS cases should never appear here. The children involved have committed nothing which, in an adult court, would pass as a crime. At their worst, they are simply ungovernable children; at their best, they are victims of parents who need help in raising children, or who want the state to relieve them of their children. More often than not, the parents don't know what they want. In PINS cases, voices are usually raised.

Mother: "You're not helping me!"

Taylor: "We *are* helping you. We are going to place your son. He's not going to trouble you anymore. It's my understanding that most places are not very good. We are trying to put him in a halfway decent place."

Mother: "I don't want any of that."

Taylor: "What *do* you want? Do you want to take him home?"

Mother: "I may as well. Nothing doing here."

Taylor (with strain): "I have agreed to put him away!"

Mother: "I didn't come here to throw him away like a piece of garbage."

Taylor: "That's just fine! Do you want to put him in Spofford, then? *That's* a real nice place."

Mother *(sotto voce):* "He's fifteen, got a third-grade reading level, won't go to school. And she does what *he* wants! He's got himself a lawyer, big deal."

.   .   .

The next morning, riding the elevator to Part II, Lionel and Victoria Dubartas can read in the grime on the elevator door a message that someone has written with a finger: "LOVE ME."

Steve Pokart today urges Judge Taylor to see Kenneth in private, or failing that, in the presence of the attorneys only. The boy, he says, is frightened. In fact, the boy is now in Pokart's office; Pokart saw him for the first time just before court convened. Isadore Bassof insists that he must be allowed to cross-examine the child "in open court." He will need Kenneth's parents present to help him with his cross-examination.

Judge Taylor, reluctant to admit uncorroborated hearsay testimony even in an abuse case, agrees to call the boy as a witness. Only the parents, lawyers and court reporter will be present. Her decision is unusual—judges will often talk to children in chambers, but rarely allow them to be cross-examined in court—and it prompts her court reporter, an eccentric man whose facial expressions have provided an extensive commentary on the proceedings he has been recording, to storm from the courtroom. He objects to the exclusion of the court officers and their truncheons: "It's a matter of my personal safety." Delicate negotiations—how much harm can he expect from a frightened nine-year-old boy?—lure him back. The court officers try to lock the courtroom door; failing, they post a sign: "Do Not Enter: Closed Hearing in Progress." Kenneth enters at 10:55 and leaves at 12:05—a very long interview indeed.

Steve Pokart thinks Kenneth rather slow in his responses to Judge Taylor's careful voir dire. Because the boy is so young, he cannot simply be sworn in. Taylor asks him: "Do you know the difference between truth and falsehood? Do your parents tell you to tell the truth? Do you believe in God? Do you think you'll be punished if you don't tell the truth?" Taylor thinks Kenneth a good witness. He responds candidly to her questions: "Yes, I lied that time; this time I didn't."

This morning, in Pokart's office, Kenneth told his lawyer he would not testify against his parents: he was too scared. Pokart explained that Kenneth would have to "talk to the judge" if he wanted to stay with his great-aunt and offered some advice: "Don't look at your

parents. When you're in there, just don't ever look at them." For the
hour and ten minutes that Kenneth testifies, he never looks once in
their direction. He tells Judge Taylor that it was his father who burned
his hands. His mother had been in the next room. Once, he says, his
mother held a gun to his head because he had let his father into the
apartment when his mother had told him not to. Both parents had
also beaten him with chains and rods. Yes, he had seen "white powder" in his home. Where? "Next to the needle."

After the lunch recess, Pokart, who believes Victoria Dubartas's
story "is full of shit," resumes his cross-examination. "Are you afraid
of your husband?" No. "Has he ever beaten you?" No. She claims
their apartment was robbed, which is why she changed the locks—
not, as Kenneth said, to keep Lionel out. "He lies when he said that
thing about a gun; I don't know any gun." Kenneth lied, too, about
being beaten with a chain. "I burned him; Lionel didn't."

Lionel follows his wife to the stand. He appeared bored during her
testimony, but now he seems sincere and concerned. He confirms her
story: he did not burn Kenneth. "I spent quite a bit of my life in jail,"
he says. He has bought cocaine from his wife's aunt. He has "used"
heroin, cocaine, "both of them together in what they call a speedball,"
and opium. He kicked the habit in jail, then started again. "I kicked
it finally in '58 when I got diabetes, a mixture of sugar and poison goin'
into my system." He admits to spanking Kenneth: "I whipped him
with my belt in school in front of the principal. I told him, 'All my
life I been breakin' the law. You do better.' I got two girls, I don't
know where they are, the mother says they're mine. I spent a lot of
time talkin' to my boy so he might not walk in the life me and my
wife have walked in. So he might not go out and get killed out there.
I was tryin' to be correct. Trying to be a right father. I didn't lie to
him." Lionel now is trembling, suppressing tears. "I went to psychiatrist, I said, 'Help me.' I had to cling to this. I'm still clinging to it.
Otherwise, it's back to jail." Under Pokart's cross-examination, he
admits to taking welfare while working, and to picking a man's pocket
"last year when I promised Kenny I'd take him to Radio City. I didn't
want to lie to him."

Once his testimony is concluded, the day degenerates in squabbles
over the admissibility of hospital records and the scheduling of law-

yers' vacations. Both Pokart and Bassof plan to leave town tomorrow evening, but Taylor, furious over the delays caused by their interminable haggling, threatens to run the case into next week. Pokart's objections, Taylor believes, stem from his fear that she will throw the case out of court, but she has no intention of doing so: "Let's take three months to try this case," she says. Her irony failing, she urges Pokart toward moderation in his interruptions: "You can do what you want," she admits, "but what *good* will it do?" Rising, as if to adjourn the case, she stops before leaving to listen to argument, changes her mind, and orders memoranda filed by 1:00 tomorrow, then 1:00 on Monday, a vacation day for the two attorneys. The objections come at her like scatter shot. "I'm trying to be fair," she sighs. "I'm trying to accommodate you."

Marvin Epstein moves that the case be returned to Supreme Court, where it had begun as an assault case and where the DA wants it so he can get a crack at Lionel. Taylor denies him: "It doesn't solve this problem. Family Court does try; it does care." Epstein then asks for a finding of abuse against both parents. Bassof asks for the *intention* of the parents to be considered—their concern, their lack of education: "Within their lights they did everything they possibly could to see that their son does not follow in their footsteps." Finally, Taylor makes a decision of sorts: the boy is to go with his great-aunt under BCW supervision, pending disposition on July 29; whether he will see his parents is up to him. "He doesn't want parental visits," Pokart says.

The day is over, and so, except for the problem of the disputed hospital records, is the case. "The hospital records," Pokart says, "show that Lionel was beaten, too, when he was a kid in the Louisiana bayous. Probably Kenny will beat his kids when he grows up. This kind of chain you can't break easily; I've come to see the parents in these cases as victims, too." In time, both Lionel and Victoria Dubartas served prison sentences resulting from proceedings brought against them in Criminal Court for their abuse of their son. Kenneth Dubartas was put up for adoption. Pokart says: "I'm no longer angry at people—except judges and case workers."

· · ·

In abuse and neglect cases, the role of the law guardian is markedly different from other proceedings involving children in Family Court, and that difference has caused much concern. The children are not the accused and are often not present; although their welfare remains the court's principal obligation, the adversaries at the hearing are the parents and the City of New York, represented by the Bureau of Child Welfare. The law guardian plays an unaccustomed peripheral role; he does not—as he is bound to do in delinquency and PINS cases—necessarily argue for what his client wants. Often he can't speak to his client, who may be too young to speak at all. Sometimes the child, fascinated by his torturers, wants more, or cannot imagine any other way of life. Because these cases involve, more often than not, the interruption of the parent-child relationship that Legal Aid holds to be a fundamental right of the child, the law guardians find themselves in a delicate position: how to balance a child's right to safety and nurture against his right to live with his family—particularly when the child's wishes in such matters are unreliable.

The guidelines that Charles Schinitsky has established address the problem as a matter of law and are best expressed in an amicus curiae brief that his Juvenile Rights Division filed with the U.S. Supreme Court in 1980 in behalf of a Delaware couple who claimed that the state's determination that they were "not fitted to continue to exercise parental rights" over their five children was unconstitutional. Schinitsky made two fundamental points. First, by filing a petition to break up this particular family, the state had committed itself to a prosecutorial position and therefore could not also undertake to represent the rights of the children, who might wish to remain with their parents. The children, then, are entitled to separate counsel, which Delaware did not provide. Second, the old "preponderance of the evidence" rule, which still applies in abuse and neglect cases, is inadequate. "Clear and convincing evidence should be the standard of proof in termination proceedings. From the child's perspective, the right to family integrity is sufficiently fundamental that only when it has been proved by a more rigorous standard than preponderance of the evidence that his right to life and to freedom from harm are endangered, would the presumption be overcome that his best interests lie in being with his natural family." However wise these arguments in law may be, they do not ease the law guardian's burden. All too often, in the cases he sees in court, little remains of "family integrity," and what is left seems a clear and present danger to his client. Consequently, he frequently finds himself at odds with Legal Aid's two fundamental principles: arguing not his client's wishes, or even family inviolability, but what he takes to be the child's "best interests." His is a bind that Schinitsky could not have foreseen when he led his troops into the Court.

To determine what these "best interests" are, he relies to a cautious degree on recommendations made by Legal Aid's Juvenile Services Unit and its experimental arm, the Neglect and Abuse Bureau. These social workers—all of whom hold master's degrees—sense perhaps more clearly than others the mental instability that pervades Family Court, not only among its clients and respondents, who are often desperate, violent and obsessed, but among judges, lawyers, court personnel and the social workers themselves: the sense that everything the court works to patch together with Band-Aids may explode at any moment. The social workers are particularly vulnerable. Emily White, an NAB worker, who was graduated number one in her social work class at NYU in 1976, feels it in herself: "I'm traumatized by what I've seen." For six months after graduation she was on welfare, couldn't find a suitable job, refused help from her parents. "I slept for a month; that gives me a kind of perspective on the people I'm dealing with."

Nevertheless, Emily White's sensitivity to the people with whom she works provided the clue to another abuse case that lands in Margaret Taylor's court as she contends with the Dubartas muddle. A mother, Dolores Martin, is accused of lesbian practices with her four-year-old daughter, Lila. The case is odder than it sounds, for shocking as the allegation is, no one seriously thinks the child much damaged by these events; they must serve as an excuse to pry the girl away from a mother who is demonstrably mad.

Dolores Martin is short, squat, black and grotesquely fat; she dresses in a man's clothes, with a chain dangling against her hip. A case worker from Special Services for Children presents the evidence: the Martin home is filthy, without light. Until February, Lila was raised by her great-grandmother; since then, Lila has been neglected, given reefers to keep her quiet when her mother wants to get stoned. Although the mother beats Lila with a rope, she is a bright child, can spell her name.

Emily White is then called to interrupt this testimony. Pale and nervous, she describes how, on June 14, she interviewed Lila for half an hour in her Legal Aid office. "Lila's immediate response to me was to run up, push her hand against my mouth and shout, 'Don't tell! Don't tell!' I played several games with her, then I asked her again what had gone on between her and her mother. Lila cried, 'Don't tell! I fire you, you hurt me!' So I suggested we play a game: 'You be the mother and you do to me what she did to you.' She giggled and hit me about the head."

Peter Zeiler, a panel lawyer representing the mother, objects to this: "Only the sexual assault is relevant."

Morris Kaplan, the law guardian for Lila, supports White's testimony; he has, of course, coached her appearance. "It's a narrative that leads directly to relevant evidence." Taylor sustains the objection, so Kaplan, a quiet, reserved man of studious demeanor, argues that the testimony bears on the state of mind of the child. "The child's perceptions are relevant," Taylor agrees.

"Then," White continues, "she put my legs up on a chair, rolled up my pants, hit me about my feet, pinched and bit my calves. I stood up, she pulled up my blouse and kissed me on my chest and breasts. She said, 'Don't tell, don't tell mommy. I fire you, I fire you.' I said, 'Is that all?' She bent and kissed me on the crotch. I said, 'Is that all?' She went behind me and kissed me there, too."

Just to give this testimony has cost White a great effort. The scene in her office, though she takes pride in inventing the game that led this frightened child to reveal what she could not bring herself to say, was a shock from which she has not yet recovered.

"Lila is an extremely bright child," she tells the court. "Quick, sharp, witty, definitely based in reality."

When White steps down, the SSC case worker resumes her exposition of the case. Eleven days after White's interview, Lila admitted to this woman, "Dolores put her tongue on my tu-tu." While Dolores repeated, "I love you, I love you," Lila protested: "Mommy, don't do that." "Did it feel good?" the case worker asked. "Yes. I asked her to do it all over," and Lila pointed to "her back parts. Her mother did this to her two times."

Dolores Martin, interviewed immediately afterward, admitted, "I kissed her on the vagina because I love her and I don't think there's anything wrong with that." Martin went further: "I've been trained to be a homosexual." She belongs to a family homosexual group called "The Cloth," which meets regularly in her home and includes Lila's paternal grandmother. Though she is on welfare, Martin claims to play pro ball and expects to be paid $17,000 when, any day now, she is called to play for a team called the Nationals which is managed by Yogi Berra. Her skill in baseball has something to do with the "new eyes" she received as a child, after plastic surgery. "Then," says the case worker, "she cried for a long time."

When the case resumes that afternoon, Dolores Martin is brought in in handcuffs. During the recess, she occupied herself in the waiting room by carving a piece of wood with a three-inch knife. When a court officer asked her not to "litter," she exploded: "Get outta my space, mothafucka!" All around the waiting room desperate and disturbed people started to rise—a situation to set any court officer's nerves on edge. This one confiscated Martin's "weapon," and when she gave him the "mothafucka" routine again, arrested her. Judge Taylor closes her eyes and orders the cuffs removed. "I feel very calm," she says. "I'm probably going to yell at the lawyers, take it out on them."

The petitioner's case continues with Lila's great-grandmother on the stand. This imposing woman, who must be seventy and has straight red hair, is the very image of the legendary black matriarch who holds a family together through sheer force of will. Lila has been in her great-grandmother's custody off and on for three of her four years.

"One evenin', when I was givin' her her bath, Lila say to me, 'Nana, put your tongue in my tu-tu,' and she pointed to her vagina. I ask, 'What wrong with you? Where did you get *that* idea?' She say, 'My mommy always do it,' and kept on askin' me. And then I started cryin'.

"I called Dolores. I ask her, 'You mean you went down on Lila?' And she say, 'Yes, you know I'm a lesbian.' And I say, *'But you don' do lesbian on your own child!'* And she flung down the phone. I had to report her. I had no alternative."

Irving Kesselman (BCW attorney): "You knew your granddaughter was a lesbian?"

Grandmother: "I knew. I almost die when she told me that. She told me in my own house."

Kesselman's direct examination of his key witness proves a marvel of accommodation over preparation. He is constantly introducing salient material only to have it excluded because he had not properly laid a foundation for its introduction. Any law school student knows how to prepare a foundation. To establish the authority of a document, you must run through some routine dance steps: "I show you this . . . is this the paper that you signed . . . is it the kind of form you use in the normal course of business?" Kesselman, however, when stymied by objections, simply moves to another topic. Nor can he, when asking his witness questions, seem to remember her name.

Nevertheless, he is given a good deal of help by his adversary, Dolores Martin's attorney, on cross-examination. Somehow Peter Zeiler allows the great-grandmother, now in tears, to tell how his client appeared at her door one night, "foaming at the mouth. She say, 'I want my baby,' and she grab Lila, who was hidin' under the blankets, and brought out a double length of rope. And she say, 'If you don' come, I'm gonna beat you with this.' Lila was cryin': 'Nana, Nana, don't let her take me!' "

Forcing the door he has opened even wider, Zeiler asks: "Do you have any reason to think the respondent would beat her daughter?"

Great-grandmother: "I know she do. I see Lila once with a strap mark runnin' down her face to her chin, two inches wide. Dolores tell me, 'She jump in the way of the strap.' But I've *seen* her beat Lila. Sometimes you gotta use the strap a little, but not to brutalize. My mother did it to me."

Zeiler (retreating): "What did you do that night?"

Great-grandmother: "I say to myself, it was horrible, she's *killing* that child. I've got to get her out of here."

Zeiler: "Did you discuss her mother's lesbianism with Lila?"

Great-grandmother: "What kind of question is that? Of *course* I never. I don't tell nobody. I'm ashamed of it."

Zeiler, heedless that he should have abandoned this witness many minutes ago, plugs along, accomplishing what the BCW attorney could not. Great-grandmother tells him that Lila's father, never married to Dolores, was a wino who had once attempted suicide, and that Lila was made sick from the reefers and beers her mother pressed upon her. "When Dolores is high she's very nasty."

Zeiler tries a technical attack. "Have you the competence to tell when the respondent is high?"

Great-grandmother: "Common sense tells me that."

Zeiler: "Are you on welfare? What do you live on?"

Great-grandmother: "Social security and my pension from the Ladies Undergarment Workers Union."

Zeiler retires in disarray, but not before Great-grandmother volunteers a parting shot: "Dolores has no friends. She regularly goes berserk."

The question before Judge Taylor now is whether Lila herself must testify. Morris Kaplan vigorously opposes bringing this four-year-old into court and persuades Taylor to see her first in chambers. In chambers, Zeiler is again surprised: he had expected Taylor to interview Lila only to determine her fitness to testify in court; instead, Taylor asks Lila about the events adduced in court and Lila confirms them. Zeiler agrees to an adjournment during which he will try to get a psychiatric report on the mother. Nobody wants an adjournment— in these most sensitive of cases to appear before Family Court, the judicial process is supposed to move swiftly—but abuse cases are inevitably plagued by adjournments. In 1979, the Citizens' Committee for Children of New York published a study revealing that the majority of abuse cases remained in court at least six months—26 percent from six months to a year, and another 42 percent from one to two years and more. A single case may easily involve ten different judges and twenty-two adjournments. Children already traumatized by their parents find that they lose a year or more of their lives while the court diddles around; fortunately, they are too young to object.

Kaplan, however, is sanguine about a speedy resolution of Lila's case. He believes that the psychiatric report will be so bad that Zeiler won't introduce it into the record. "If he puts Dolores on the stand, I'll just try to get her to say more crazy things. She claims to be rich, to own a lot of property around the country." When Kaplan first interviewed the mother, she had seemed reasonable enough ("Of course I touched Lila, but nothing sexual"), but as she continued to talk about how she had been abused by her mother, who had cut her eyes, necessitating eye transplants, about the baseball and the rest of her fantasies, Kaplan had become appalled. "I finally had to make an excuse to leave." He is astonished that Zeiler, who has heard all this, doesn't think the woman insane. "The way to represent this mother is to try to persuade her to get help. If she refuses, then you have to do what she wants, but you can ask to be relieved of the case. Many of these lawyers don't think of their clients as such, because they're paid by the state."

As it happened, Kaplan's projected strategy proved unnecessary. In time, the case of abuse filed on Lila's behalf was dropped when her father sued for custody, and won. From time to time, Dolores Martin has appeared in Family Court seeking a modification of visiting rights, but each time the judge has denied her application. There is no reason to think the case is finished. Such cases in Family Court tend to continue indefinitely.

Legal Aid's policy, which is Family Court's policy as well, of return-ing a child to its parents whenever possible is rudely shaken on June 24, 1977, when Legal Aid loses one of its clients: Miguel Fernandez, three-and-a-half months old, has been murdered by his father. The news reaches Legal Aid's ninth-floor office in the morning, when Miguel's father, Isidro, telephones Marcia Bernstein, a case worker in the Neglect and Abuse Bureau, to say the child is dead. Bernstein calls Columbia Presbyterian Medical Center and then goes out to the Fernandez apartment, a fourth-floor walkup in the Inwood section of upper Manhattan. Finding the baby's battered corpse, she takes it to the hospital. The police are called; Bernstein and Jane Krieger, then the Juvenile Rights Division's director of management and planning, spend twelve hours conferring with them and a district attorney; in time, a grand jury indicts Isidro Fernandez for murder.

In the weeks following, there are many conferences, questions asked, fingers pointed. Charles Schinitsky calls his Manhattan lawyers and social workers together one afternoon in July to review the case and the division's policy. Miguel, he observes, is not the first child they have represented who has died from injuries: "It's happened often." Indeed, of the more than five thousand reports of child abuse recorded by the city in 1976, forty-eight involved the death of a child. Reports of abuse are rising steeply: the five thousand for 1976 represent an increase of 18 percent over 1975, a 50 percent increase over 1974. It is generally assumed that most cases are never reported, and of those that are, nearly 80 percent never reach Family Court; instead, they are investigated and disposed of by the Protective Services Unit of Special Services for Children. "It's not easy to keep on doing what we're supposed to be doing when we're faced with that kind of problem," Schinitsky tells his people. "Our overall policy is to keep families together. Should it change? I still feel that wherever possible the child should be returned."

Nevertheless, everyone feels that this particular tragedy might have been avoided. Miguel had been born in March. His mother, a polio victim confined to a wheelchair, was not married to his father. Having refused prenatal care, she wheeled herself into Bellevue the day of the delivery, which was by Caesarean section. The doctors discovered her uterus was ruptured and removed it; later she was to react bitterly to her involuntary hysterectomy. After three days in intensive care, she was examined by a psychiatrist who found her paranoid, self-destructive, "a grave threat to her baby's safety and life." Because she appeared to show no interest in Miguel and had made no plans for him, the Bureau of Child Welfare removed him temporarily. In April, however, Kathryn A. MacDonald—one of the newest Family Court judges, who had previously been the attorney-in-charge of Manhattan's Juvenile Rights Division—returned Miguel to his parents. In the days that followed, the baby was savagely beaten and burned by his father. His bones were fractured; every rib in his body had been broken one or more times; on one occasion Isidro put his son into a hot, empty pot on the stove, burning Miguel's feet and buttocks. These events occurred despite the presence of a homemaker—a woman employed by BCW not only to shop, cook and clean for families incapable of taking care of themselves, but to teach the mother these domestic skills—who claimed to have noticed nothing.

BCW had visited the home once, and so had Marcia Bernstein, who seemed to get along with the mother; telephone calls had been made. No one had any information that anything was wrong until the final call came through on June 24.

Later, Marcia Bernstein, who is thirty and new to her job, said: "I never knew it could affect me that way. I had to get away. I went shopping for some blouses. And then, I felt a scream rising in me. I looked around. I could hardly believe I had screamed. I thought if anybody heard, they'd take me away. It was the most horrible, most gruesome experience in my life."

At Schinitsky's conference, where the guilt is being pushed around, she says, "Perhaps if I had more time this would not have happened. In how many cases can we do the kind of work the proposal says we should do?" She is referring to the charter for the Neglect and Abuse Bureau, now in its initial year, which says that NAB is supposed to handle no more than four hundred cases—about 25 percent of Manhattan's child protective proceedings. Each of NAB's four social workers is supposed to deal with fifty families, but of course they were deluged with cases. "You want to do good work and you can't do good work with this many cases. It's impossible." Much of what she has to do is gather material for the attorneys to help them win their cases. "We run around after lawyers a lot. They're a different kind of person. They're very factual, concrete. Nice people, you know, but what we work on is intuition. It won't work in legalese."

Schinitsky admits that NAB mustn't be asked to overextend itself to the point where it doesn't do the job it wants to do: "A kind of guilt attaches itself." He himself is furious with BCW's lack of cooperation; he has read a memo sent to BCW workers telling them not to cooperate with NAB. "I can't understand the reasoning," Schinitsky says. "At one point the mother's wheelchair broke down. BCW wouldn't return Legal Aid's calls. We finally got her a new one through the Easter Seals people. We want to stop this kind of nonsense. We have a chance to double our effectiveness if we cooperate. We can try to cut down the element of risk. Learn to read the signs. Sometimes our clients are trying to tell us something. It may happen again, but it is not to deter us, really, from what we expect from you or from trying to help families to pull together again."

Jane Krieger confirms that BCW won't help Legal Aid with information. Probation, too, doesn't like the Juvenile Services Unit because it feels it alone knows what's good for the kids. "Perhaps we can get a court order for BCW's cooperation."

"To back off from services to a family because you're sore at your opponent," Schinitsky says, "is criminal. It's not only immature, it's outrageous. BCW must return our calls. We must exchange information. But then maybe *we*'re not willing to give all our information to BCW." Because BCW and Legal Aid are often antagonists in court, there's a real conflict of interest here.

Maura Dughi, a lawyer, observes that while everyone hates BCW, there's friction within BCW between its lawyers and its social workers. "The workers are contemptuous of the lawyers. BCW workers don't understand what our lawyers are up to in court."

Schinitsky: "Even their lawyers don't understand what goes on in court. No matter how you try, the response you get is: 'Don't you care about the kids?' "

Morris Kaplan: "You can't conduct a rigorous cross-examination of a BCW worker without destroying his case. We don't quite want to do that."

Dughi: "A BCW worker once said in court, 'Being in danger is a state of mind.' "

This is greeted by groans and a general shaking of heads. Schinitsky suggests that the lawyers throw the burden on the judge: "Tell 'em, 'You know as much about it as I do.' " But his lawyers disagree. "We really do try to take a position on every case," says Steve Hiltz, Manhattan's attorney-in-charge. "The judge insists on it. They are reading your objections. We have to maintain our credibility."

"I do hope," Schinitsky concludes, "you will continue to recommend children go home when you feel they should."

Later, Marcia Bernstein says: "Some of these kids should be behind bars. And they get let out again. I ain't no liberal no more. I can come across very idealistic: it's my cover, it's my defense. I was a radical once, but having too much faith is also a form of fanaticism. I have faith in a way that things could change, just a little bit. If only enough people had a similar idea! I had a fantasy of bringing my guitar in and singing to the people in the waiting room, of bringing magazines so they can do something while waiting to hear they're going to be adjourned. But we don't want Family Court to be too nice a place. It's the state intervening in the sanctity of the family, and that's very heavy.

"There's not much sanity around. It's very unhealthy. The lawyers contribute a lot to that feeling. According to them, *everything's* an emergency. They're running like chickens with no heads. But there's only so much energy to draw on. This is going to sound nuts, but when I'm feeling good I try to use my good energy to sort of transform the negativity I see in the waiting area, like smile at a lawyer from the other side. Just try to give off pleasant vibrations. Because it works. I can't do it very often because a lot of times I'm feeling very uptight myself. Quite often, I'm wasted at the end of the day, but luckily I have enough support systems in my life that I can build on that again.

"I look for little, little, tiny rewards, and they're all intrinsic because the money ain't that great. It's not enough for the amount of stress we're under. I feel like I'm always learning with the people I work with. Any good professional person gets off on that. What the hell would I be doing in child abuse if I wasn't getting some of that every day? Every work experience, every life experience, I see as a *learning* experience, so there's nothing I do just mindlessly unless I'm high."

The lawyers' Code of Professional Responsibility is unequivocally firm: a lawyer must represent the will of his client. Charles Schinitsky's younger lawyers tend to agree—none in the Manhattan office is over thirty-five and most grew up in a time when adamantine moral postures were in fashion—but Schinitsky himself has reservations. Someone to speak for the child—that is what brought Schinitsky into this messy court, but: "What do you do with a kid who has had both his arms broken, and who wants to return home? It's the most complex thing you can possibly imagine. On the one hand, you must argue for what the child wants; on the other, you have all this background material. Should the material be given to the judge? If you don't offer it, he has to make a decision in ignorance. But if the material is at odds with what the kid wants, then it's unethical to introduce it." Once again, the concept of a child's "best interests" muddies the law. Some people, the court's administrative judge among them, have told Schinitsky that his responsibility is different from a private lawyer's—which makes Schinitsky bridle because he insists that law guardians are not "second-class lawyers" and their clients deserve better than "second-class representation."

The issue flares again in October, when Schinitsky calls another conference to discuss a particularly thorny neglect case involving an extension of placement. Nina Valez, who has long been a client of Legal Aid, is sixteen and newly a mother. Her mother was a prostitute, which resulted in Nina's placement in a foster home, where her foster mother told her, "You're no good, you're going to be a hooker too." And so she is, whenever she runs away from her foster home these days; she picks up violent men to earn a little money. "These prophecies," Schinitsky observes, "tend to be self-fulfilling." Sometimes when she runs away, Nina takes younger children from the home for company. Sometimes when she doesn't run away, when she is just angry or bored, Nina sets fires in the home. She shows no remorse. "Her judgment is pretty wholly off," says Andrea Ostrum, a psychologist who works part-time for Legal Aid. Nina has been rejected by every agency and program that has heard of her problems, of her incarceration in a mental hospital; she is, they say, simply too disturbed.

What, Schinitsky asks, can we do for this girl? A new home must be found for her, which, given her incendiary, runaway history, will not be easy, and to complicate matters, she wants to keep her baby. BCW has filed a neglect suit against this neglected girl: Nina's history of psychiatric disorder and her lack of skills and education make her an unfit mother. Andrea Ostrum agrees with BCW's position: "If she keeps the baby, there's a real danger of gross physical neglect. She wouldn't know how to feed it." In fact, when Nina runs away she doesn't feed herself. Legal Aid is running through its usual reflexes here, thinking of the baby, but in this case it represents the mother and *her* wishes. An odd situation, but quite in keeping with Legal Aid policy: once a client, always a client; a panel lawyer will have to look after this baby. At the moment, Nina lives in a strictly religious home and is deeply attached to the woman who runs it, but now she wants to go to another place which has a mother-child program and which she mistakenly imagines to be less strict. If she is turned down, she is likely to bolt again.

Ostrum thinks Nina shouldn't have the baby: "She would have real problems and probably wouldn't make it." Nina's social worker wants Nina fitted with an IUD—she refuses oral contraceptives. Sandra Kaplan, a consulting psychiatrist to Legal Aid, describes Nina as "aggressive-passive. She herself was a premature baby, weighing four pounds. Hyperactive in school. Alienated all the other girls. Abnormal EEGs, reads at the second-grade level now. At Manhattan State" —the mental hospital—"she was given chemotherapy, psychotherapy, tranquilizers, anticonvulsive drugs. She suffers from personality disorder, learning disability, a conflict over roles at her foster home. She's not allowed outside there, but she wants to see men. She's a fuse about to go. She'll set a fire, or she'll run with her baby. She should have had intervention six years ago, but now she can act out sexually, too. She was in hospital for three years, all negative reports, but she's not psychotic and in-patient care is not called for. Her prognosis, psychiatrically, is very poor."

Denise Guggenheim, who is stunningly beautiful and Manhattan's newest law guardian, has no patience with any of this. Nina is her client. "Our role is to represent Nina as she wishes. I see no need for in-depth discussions like this." She is miffed that Ostrum interviewed Nina without consulting her. Schinitsky responds paternally: "I want to know everything about the case. *We* take responsibility. My responsibility is every bit as heavy as yours, probably heavier." For this reason, every law guardian presents himself in court as "Charles Schinitsky, Legal Aid Society, followed by his own name, of counsel."

Guggenheim: "I was kept in the dark."

Schinitsky: "My fault. But we must meet like this to consider these negative reports. We must ask what we should be doing. How do we meet her problems? If we decide to continue to represent her, we must try to work it out here. What can be done to keep mother and child together, our general policy? If we find that impossible, can we present something to her to make her realize it? There's no conflict in representation there. A lawyer does it all the time."

One of the ironies of neglect and abuse cases is that although it is the parent who misbehaves, it is the child who is packed away to an institution. Another irony is that the deterioration of the parties concerned seems contagious; during the court proceedings, invariably bitter and prolonged, one can see the judge and the attorneys appear to deteriorate as well.

In June of 1977, Judge Aileen Haas Schwartz has just such a case before her. Judge Schwartz is a spare, attractive woman who looks to be in her mid-forties; her hair is red, her expression severe, her demeanor somewhat neurasthenic. She has twenty-three cases on her calendar today, one a long neglect that may stretch into the following week, and she spends the early part of the morning sorting out priorities, putting little stars by the important cases and wondering how even they will be heard today. She adjourns a paternity case until September: "By statute, I must give priority to other cases," she tells the putative father. "Adjourning cases I do at great cost to myself." The man's lawyer objects, and Schwartz rebukes him: "Counselor, you are extending no courtesy to the Court. As long as I wear the *robe,* the robe demands it." A moment later: "I can barely call all the cases I have today in the courtroom." But she does, and when all the people have crowded against the wall and departed, she sighs. "You're judged by the number of cases. Sheer numbers, that's all. Not by an evaluation of the cases, what *kind* of cases they are. That's nonsense, isn't it?" Her unconscious use of the passive mode conceals the agency that judges judges. It, or rather he, is Joseph B. Williams, the administrative judge of the city's Family Courts, who has decreed that no case pending over ninety days without a fact finding may be adjourned without his approval. Judges fear Judge Williams. He can make their lives unpleasant.

Judge Schwartz, therefore, tries to order her day. The parties in several cases have not appeared, but she is not allowed to adjourn cases for nonappearance until 11:00 A.M. She calls a PINS case to see what it's about. A blowsy, disheveled, overweight woman tells her that her fifteen-year-old daughter "is in great danger. With bad people. She'll be killed in the streets. She needs to be supervised. Please protect her!" This woman shows no inclination to stop talking. "I'm going to rely on your being a lady," Judge Schwartz says, against all available evidence. The problem with PINS cases is that they may in fact be neglects; if a woman complains about her daughter, who is primarily at fault? The daughter says to her mother, "When I go out on the city, it is my judgment. You are not concerned." The mother replies, "I'm your mother. I *am* concerned." The girl's lawyer, in an undertone, says, "This mother dotes on her in a hateful way."

Recessing this case, Schwartz turns to her neglect. A school psychologist gives the principal testimony: the mother, Doreen Alvaros, approached her one day to ask why her daughter Olivia wasn't getting perfect scores on her tests. Olivia is ten, has an IQ of 118, and does average work in school. The mother admitted to the psychologist that she "disciplines" Olivia for not doing perfect work, once banged her head against a wall. Mother, apparently, is suicidal: "She often tried to take her own life. She wanted to jump in the Harlem River. She would take her children with her"—Olivia has a brother, who is eight —"and they would restrain her. She'd tell the kids that she was going to jump out the window and they would restrain her again." Mother has been diagnosed a schizophrenic and has been getting psychotherapy at Roosevelt Hospital, also chlorpromazine and Artane—the former a drug to keep the schizophrenia in check, the latter an antidote for the bad side effects of the former. Without these drugs she can't hold still or communicate clearly. Still, she forgets to take them and then "she flips. She would come to school, unable to focus or concentrate, and shout a lot. She has reviled the other children for picking on her daughter. When she forgets she has children, she will stay out all night."

Doreen Alvaros, a dull, beaten-looking woman of about thirty, interrupts: "*You're* a mother," she says to her accuser. "How can you *do* this to me?" She picks up a pair of sunglasses and puts them on. Judge Schwartz asks her to remove them: "It's part of my responsibility to evaluate individuals."

"I think there is a role reversal here," the psychologist continues. "The daughter must make decisions for the mother. Mrs. Alvaros sees her daughter as more competent than she in many ways. Olivia does the mothering." Olivia at the moment is placed with an agency, St. Christopher's; she has told the psychologist she thinks her mother "needs a rest."

On cross-examination, Marvin Fruchtman, the mother's lawyer, tries a cultural tack: "Are Latins tempestuous?"

The psychologist appears confused, waves her hands.

Fruchtman (as if addressing a half-wit): "Are they *placid,* like Nordic people?"

Psychologist: "I can't answer that."

Fruchtman (shrugging): "I'm upset that you refuse to concede that Latins are more ebullient, tempestuous than other people."

Robert Levy, the law guardian, having objected to this line of argument, asks about Olivia. The answer he gets is that "her behavior is deteriorating. She's imitating her mother's problems, losing sight of reality. I think there is real cause for concern." Throughout her testimony, the psychologist, who has not been in court before, has appeared calm, but (as she confesses later) she was so nervous that she had to fold her hands to control them. As she leaves the stand, she looks ready to collapse.

Judge Schwartz at this point delivers a little lecture. She calls this giving the mother's lawyer "the benefit of my thinking. I think it's fair to them to let them know what they have to confront." She has not made a decision, but she wants to make it clear that a prima facie case has been established. She speaks slowly and softly, reminding all present that an abuse case was filed against Doreen Alvaros two years previously and, it seems, "forgotten. In this country an individual has a basic right to raise her own children, but the state has defined minimum requirements a; to how these children shall be cared for." These requirements, set out in Article 10 of the Family Court Act, have to do with "impairment of emotional health," and "a state of substantially diminished psychological or intellectual functioning in relation to, but not limited to, such factors as failure to thrive, control of aggressive or self-destructive impulses, ability to think and reason," and so on for quite a while. "I am being very strict in regard to testimony. I'm very careful when I think in terms of separating a child from a parent. I draw the conclusion that I am mandated to draw by Article 10, that this mother has not provided minimum care for children as the state requires."

Fruchtman suggests that Judge Schwartz talk to Olivia. She declines: "I never speak to a child during fact-finding stage. I speak to them during disposition. This case will be continued this afternoon."

Fruchtman protests: "Your honor, I can't continue this afternoon. I have other business."

Schwartz: "I will not adjourn this case."

Fruchtman: "I will make no further sacrifices in this case or any other in Family Court. Nobody cares for the private lawyer in this court. I'm not being paid for this case."

Schwartz (irritated): "You must continue this afternoon, or tomorrow. My calendar next week is too crowded."

Fruchtman: "I ask to be relieved of this case."

Schwartz: "Don't do it, Mr. Fruchtman. Don't desert your client now." She is, in fact, furious, ready to hold Fruchtman in contempt, though she refuses to cite even the most outrageous lawyers for contempt during a hearing. "Before I declare a mistrial, I always call a recess," she says during the lunch break. "I may look like I'm frail, but I am not. I am committed to this robe. How does the client feel when he says in open court that he is not being paid?" She has the power to keep Fruchtman on the case, but she won't exercise it, even though she has arranged this hearing to suit his pleas to see his paying clients. "One was supposed to have paid him five thousand dollars yesterday. I'll have to let him go, so the mother can be adequately represented. If I held him, the mother won't get much help from him. He hasn't even read the file. I must not only be fair, but appear to be fair."

During the recess, Fruchtman and the BCW lawyer, Stanley Jacobs, swap opinions on the case.

Jacobs: "Schwartz doesn't know which end is up."

Fruchtman: "Like all women, she's unreasonable. She has no idea what courtroom procedure is. She hasn't heard my motion to dismiss. She talks about the preponderance of evidence, but she hasn't heard any of *my* evidence yet."

Jacobs: "Schwartz is so biased for the defense, she's like another lawyer. I never stood a chance. Judge Dembitz, now, I could file a blank piece of paper in evidence and she'd find for neglect."

Fruchtman: "She lacks a sense of humor. My experience is, the better the judge, the more lenient he is. The worse the judge, the more legalistic."

Jacobs has done only neglect and abuse cases for the past seven years. "I must admit I couldn't do any other kind of law now." Fruchtman, forgetting that his role is to represent his client, says: "Of course, the most important thing is the welfare of the child."

. . .

The afternoon session begins with Judge Schwartz lecturing the attorneys in private. "I have a situation on the record where a respondent hears in open court that her attorney receives no money, can't come back, won't come back. If I were that respondent, I'd say, 'If I had some money, I'd get a good lawyer.' This is reversible. This client can appeal any decision I make on the grounds that she was denied the best representation."

Fruchtman: "Tomorrow I'll be two hundred and fifty miles away from this case in every sense."

Schwartz: "Mr. Fruchtman, that is an insult to this Court."

Fruchtman: "Then I ask the Court to strike my remarks about compensation from the record."

Schwartz: "I'm concerned with this woman's thinking."

Fruchtman: "Has she complained?"

Schwartz: "I never talk to respondents during a hearing. I can't get personally involved with clients who appear before me. This woman will never know what happened in court if we break the case up now. It is important for her to know that justice is done. A case continued for more than a day or two is meaningless to this client."

Fruchtman: "If I may refer to my gray hairs, a client thinks justice is done when she wins a case. You will never persuade her otherwise. I'm sorry to have incurred your displeasure."

Schwartz: "Nothing happens before me that incurs my displeasure. But at times I must vindicate these robes I wear."

Doreen Alvaros is brought into the courtroom, and Fruchtman makes a kind of apology: "Whether or not I was compensated is wholly irrelevant." Judge Schwartz, for the record (because she doesn't believe it), tells the mother: "No matter how much you paid an attorney, you could not get better representation."

The mother, on the stand, proves an unconvincing liar. She denies threatening to kill herself. "Who, *me?* Jumping into the river? Who said that? This is a beautiful life. Why would I do that?" She denies leaving her children unattended. "Just because I'm nervous, they bring me here." Her children, she says, were born with emotional problems; it runs in the family. When Judge Schwartz asks questions, relying on the psychologist's testimony, Doreen Alvaros replies evasively, not looking at the judge. "She just lying, right? Maybe she don't understand my English. Maybe there is a conspiracy against me. This doctor with a high job, is she paid to say these things against me?"

It is not an easy case. This woman clearly wants to help her children and tries, but she just can't cope. Judge Schwartz carries the case over to the following Monday, glad that Fruchtman has calmed down and she won't have to declare a mistrial. "Lawyers sometimes act like that when they want to get off a case," she says at the end of the day. "Or if they think it's continuing too long. They bait the judge." But Monday destroys her optimism: Fruchtman, on the record, accuses her of bias and she is forced to declare a mistrial. Fruchtman asks to have his remark expunged, but it is no good: he will have to do the trial all over again, which may be Judge Schwartz's way of punishing him.

A month later, when the case is recalled, Fruchtman is still complaining. He has an injured foot, he says, and it is very painful for him to be here; besides, as a panel lawyer, he gets only $15 an hour "and I can't cover my overhead with that. So when I'm sitting here in the waiting room for hours the city's losing money and I'm losing money. It makes no sense at all. I know a lot of lawyers, however, who make a living doing it. If you do enough of it. It's been a good thing for them. You know, it shouldn't be for the money. It didn't start that way. It was a way to get out among the people—but you can't take that for very long. This place is a house of horrors. There's no respect for the panel lawyers." He waves his foot in the air. "Getting out of this court is like taking off a pair of tight shoes."

While Fruchtman complains, the law guardian, Robert Levy, talks to Duane Kendall, a social worker at St. Christopher's. Kendall tells him that Olivia is making progress. At first she had to be medicated because she would try to throw herself out of the windows, but now she seems happy, she is able to admit when she lies, she understands why privileges may be withheld. She flirts with the boys, makes pizza, spaghetti, sews her own clothes. Once Olivia introduced Kendall to her friends at a nearby school as her mother: "I wanted the kids to see you weren't crazy." But time is running out. The St. Christopher's psychiatrist doesn't want Olivia or her little brother to remain longer: if they are not going home they must go to a foster home. "We have fifty-five children at St. Christopher's," Kendall says, "and three hundred in foster homes. Foster homes are really the next stage to adoption. We tell foster parents to love, care for and do everything for the kids, but not to get too attached to them. Because we're going to take them away in three months, six months. The Alvaros kids want to go home."

Robert Levy has doubts. "I think they're gonna have terrible problems. When they're teenagers, they'll still have to mother her." He and Kendall agree that Olivia, if she must go home, will fall back into tantrums and beating up children to get her way, instead of explaining what she needs, which she has learned to do at St. Christopher's.

"What would you do," Levy asks Kendall, "if you were the judge?" Kendall admits that the kids will have to go home. In fact, 75 percent of neglected children are returned to their parents, and so, in a few months, will the Alvaros children be returned to their mother. Levy will run into them by accident in a McDonald's on the Upper West Side: "They seemed to be happy enough, but then how many of these stories really have happy endings?"

That, however, is in the future, and now Kendall thinks the children's return should be supervised. "BCW isn't going to do it, you know that," Levy says. "Sometimes it's the parent who needs placement, not the child," Kendall replies.

Marvin Fruchtman interrupts at this point to say that he has been waiting since 9:30 to make an application to be relieved from this case. It is now 12:30. "I'll wait till one, no longer."

"And then," says Levy, "you'll walk away from your case and your client." He says it with a smile, his scorn so cool that it slides right by Fruchtman, who does indeed walk out at one, not to be seen again. Doreen Alvaros, learning this, runs to the ladies' room and swallows a handful of pills. Her case now must be returned to Intake A, where she will be assigned a new lawyer, a new hearing date.

"Seven and a half months I've been in this court!" she cries. "Is that fair? My case was marked 'Emergency'!"

V

The Friends
of Robert Levy

They can't say I'm playing a game. Though of
course I am. That's what litigation is. It's just
knowing how to play it. . . . You're not supposed to
abuse the system. You work within it. If the system
doesn't work well, is injurious to your client, then
you may justify behaving unethically.

A law professor addresses his third-year
students at New York University

In the afternoon of June 14, 1977, two white, upper-middle-class people, each about twenty-five years old, testify before Judge Louis Otten
in Part III, on the fifth floor of Manhattan's Family Court. The man,
Michael Bernier, is an ideal witness—which is to say that his manner
is exceptionally cool and his testimony contains not one superfluous
word. A week ago, he tells the court, "Wendy and I were bicycling
north in Central Park. Wendy was just behind me. We were going
about twenty miles an hour, in tenth gear. I saw two individuals
crouching by the roadway. They ran out behind us. One of them
yelled, 'Give me your mother-fucking bike' to Wendy and struck her
with a tree branch, breaking it on her head. I turned around to come
back as fast as I could. They ran away."

A flurry of court business establishes that it was the older boy, who
has now been dealt with in Criminal Court, who struck Wendy

Turner and that the respondent in court today allegedly acted in concert with him. The respondent, Pedro Almedo, is fourteen, wears a brown afro; though he listens only intermittently to the proceedings, he is very agitated, twirling a white sailor hat in his hands.

When Wendy Turner, as cool and terse as her boyfriend, takes the stand to tell the story again, Pedro's lawyer, Robert M. Levy, turns very technical. When she says, "I closed my eyes when I was hit with the club," Levy objects "to the use of the word 'club,' your honor. I don't know what a club really is," but apparently he is the only one in court who doesn't, so is overruled. He objects to Turner's saying "I must have done": "She should only tell us what she did do." Here he is sustained. When she says, "I believe Pedro was right next to him," Levy objects to what she "believes." Overruled. Sometimes you can reduce a witness to outright mutism with such tactics, and besides, there's the record to think of: inaccurate as it sometimes is to the point of incomprehensibility, a record which shows judicial errors, noted by an alert attorney, is that attorney's best hope for a reversal on appeal.

Sidney Mayer (Corporation Counsel): ". . . these two individuals who came toward you with a tree branch . . ."

Levy: "Objection! There's been no testimony that *two* individuals came after her with a branch."

Judge Otten, an old, gray, quiet man who seems occasionally to smile at what he sees before him, sustains him wearily.

Mayer: "Can you identify the younger of these two boys?"

Turner: "I saw a white hat . . ."

Obligingly, Pedro waves his sailor's hat in the air for all in court to see. Levy this time registers his objection silently, by kicking his client under the table. He doesn't expect actual cooperation from the kids he represents, but visual displays of confession are out of line. "Delinquency cases," he says later, "are nearly always about money or bikes—what these kids don't have."

What Levy is doing here is gambling. He expects to lose. This proceeding might have been a fact finding, an actual trial, but instead it is a preliminary hearing to determine the need to remand Pedro until the fact finding takes place. Levy has decided to risk his client's spending several weeks more in Spofford because he doesn't want to go to trial without seeing the grand jury notes involving Pedro's eighteen-year-old co-assailant. These take time to obtain, but just possibly, Levy can get Pedro off for lack of prima facie evidence. In his summation he argues that the boys did not act in concert: the respondent made no overt act of assault, which the law requires in an in-concert proceeding, but merely tagged along.

Judge Otten disagrees: a prima facie case has been established. He asks for the Probation report to determine the remand question, thereby disqualifying himself from hearing the fact finding; Pedro's case will have to go back to Intake A for reassignment. Probation reports that Pedro has "absconded from several placements." Otten sends him to Spofford for two weeks. Pedro breaks down and weeps. In the antechamber between the courtroom and the waiting room he starts shouting: "You don't know how I mothafuckin' feel!" Sobbing, he is handcuffed and pulled away.

Thirteen days later Rob Levy still hasn't received the grand jury transcript—it isn't even typed and may take another two or three weeks to obtain. Pedro has now spent three weeks in the dreaded Spofford, and rather than prolong his ordeal Levy goes to trial without that evidence. The case comes to Part II, before Margaret Taylor, who thinks she recognizes Wendy Turner—"Haven't we met?"— perhaps because hers is the first well-bred white face she's seen among the parties in this court, but Turner assures her not. She tells her story again, with a coolness approaching boredom, her head supported by her hands.

Levy hopes to get Pedro off on the grounds that he committed no overt action, didn't touch Turner or her bike, that "the act would have been committed without him." To accomplish this he rides herd on the testimony of the policeman who arrested Pedro. The policeman is not allowed to say what Michael Bernier or Wendy Turner said to him—he can only say what he *did,* which makes his actions meaningless. He can't even testify to Bernier's pointing out the boy.

Policeman: "He said, 'That's them.' "

Levy: "Objection."

Sustained. Sidney Mayer, the Corporation Counsel lawyer, is stymied. How to proceed?

Levy moves to dismiss. "A prima facie case has not been established. By Miss Turner's testimony, Pedro did nothing. He was four to six feet away from her. Two boys approached, for what purpose we're not sure until the older boy took out a tree branch."

Judge Taylor: "Took *with* him."

Levy: "Pedro did not act in concert. He said nothing to the complainant. He could have run out with the older boy to see what was happening and when he saw, he ran away. There's been no testimony that he was involved. As for the assault charge, there was no serious injury, as required by law." He reads the assault section, 120.05, of the Criminal Procedures Law. "There was no deadly weapon, no serious injury."

In fact, Wendy Turner had only to show her bruises to Probation to get her case immediately preferred. Until she ran into Robert Levy, everyone was courteous and sympathetic. So far, for trying to do her duty, to be a good citizen, she has lost four days' pay.

Mayer: "120.05 says that if in attempted crime an injury is caused, that constitutes assault. Subdivision 6." He's right.

Levy: "The definition of physical injury is substantial pain. There's been no testimony to that."

Mayer: "She was in hospital, had to wear a sling."

Judge Taylor rules for him. "Is a tree branch a dangerous instrument?" she asks.

Levy: "There's been no evidence what *size* this branch was. Could it have been a twig?"

Throughout all this, the two court officers have been dozing, side by side.

During a recess, Michael Bernier and Wendy Turner talk in the waiting room with the policeman who arrested Pedro. It is 12:34, Tuesday, July 27, and the digital clock on the waiting-room wall reads: 26 October, 8:16. A sign on the wall says "No Smoking," so only the policeman smokes. Across the way, in the door leading to the tiny anteroom to Part I, where this case began, there is a slot with a hinged flap, rather like a slot for mail. Nobody knows why it is there, but at the moment children are waving their fingers through it and giggling. These children are too young to be left unattended in the waiting room, and the judge doesn't want them in the court with their parents, so there they are in the anteroom having a high young time.

The policeman complains about his unhappy lot. "We are told we have to read the kid his rights in the presence of his *mother*. When we get the kid we have to say, 'Shut up, you're not worth talking to.' The mother has to waive the kid's rights, too."

Michael Bernier is unsure what he feels about Pedro. "I have mixed feelings. I don't want to ruin his life, but I don't think I am. I think he's done this before and hasn't been caught. I think he'd do it again. Wendy was lucky she wasn't hit the wrong way. The way she was going, he had to hit her from behind. If he had hit her from in front he might really have hurt her."

Wendy Turner has no regrets, except for her lost pay. "What I want for this kid, and I've thought about it a lot over this time, is that they send him to some detention place where he could be trained. I don't mean stamping license plates, but learn to do something useful. I'm tired of these court appearances, but it is a duty."

When the case resumes, Robert Levy moves for dismissal because prima facie has not been established. "Pedro makes no aggressive action. He just follows his friend. He could have been out there to stop him, or to find out what was happening."

Sidney Mayer is visibly irritated by such implausibilities. He cites cases involving lookouts, blocks away from the crime. "If a person is confronted by two persons instead of one, that constitutes guilt. It *seems* as if two are coming at you. His presence encouraged the act."

Judge Taylor denies Levy's motion for dismissal, but Levy keeps fighting for it: "You have to prove a common design. We're inferring that this respondent had guilty designs on circumstantial evidence. I think there are other interpretations we could make." Probably no other judge would have listened for so long to Levy's argument, but he loses anyway and has to put his client on the stand.

Pedro, who manages to look plausible, says he was alone in the park, got tired, sat down next to "this guy. I didn't know his name. I didn't know what he was gonna do. The guy picks up a stick and I ask him was he gonna leave. He swung at the lady. I ran up to stop him, then I thought I oughta leave. I was just conversatin,' see, and this man got all wild. After, I said, 'Why you do that?' And he said he needed money."

Throughout this, Taylor watches Pedro closely, at one point asking the court reporter to sit back so she can see. Far from puncturing Pedro's testimony, Mayer manages to confuse him by prefacing his questions with "Did there come a time when," the trial lawyer's favorite cliché and a construction Pedro cannot grasp. Judge Taylor tries her hand:

"Where was the tree branch?"

Pedro: "He had a stick next to him."

Taylor: "Did you know *why* he had the stick?"

Pedro: "I didn' bother to ax him what he was gonna do."

Taylor: "What *did* he do?"

Pedro: "He went up to the lady and say, 'Give me your bike.' He use that bad word the lady said."

Taylor: "Why did you follow him?"

Pedro: "I wanted to talk."

Taylor: "Why? You never saw him before."

Pedro: "He seem like a nice guy."

Taylor: "What did you do when he hit the lady?"

Pedro: "I ranned outta de park." Where he ran cannot be established because the terms "East Side" and "West Side" mean nothing to him. He did, however, meet "by accident" the other boy at Park Avenue and 102nd Street, where they were both arrested.

In summing up, Mayer says, "It is reasonable to assume he took part in the event. A prudent person would assume it. Take into account the credibility of the various witnesses. The credibility of the respondent is dubious. There are too many coincidences. It's curious that he should have run into the same person on 102nd Street that he had just fled in the park. This is a contrived and strained story which the Court should take with a large grain of salt."

Rob Levy, however, specializes in uncertainties. "What we are doing here is speculating what his motives were. When we begin to speculate we have to admit that more than one inference can be made. There's not much doubt as to what happened, but what was the intention? Did Pedro add anything to this event? Did his presence reinforce it? The answer is no. His flight: it's reasonable to believe he was scared. If he was innocent—or guilty—he is smart enough to stay away from this person. The issue is whether the Court wishes to speculate, to make a metaphysical inquiry into Pedro's mind. The actions give us no clue as to whether he was involved."

Taylor reserves her decision until five, then calls the parties into court. Scratching her head, she says, "Court has reasonable doubt. Petition dismissed."

As everyone files out, Pedro says to Wendy Turner, "I'm real sorry, miss, about what happened."

Turner says thoughtfully, "I am, too." Later, she says: "Maybe this boy has learned something from his court experience and his time in Spofford. If he hasn't, we've all wasted a lot of time."

And a lawyer from Corporation Counsel says, "That judge is a real menace on the bench. She never convicts. There's no telling how much harm she can do before they take her back to Civil Court."

Robert M. Levy, who sowed so much doubt in a field well prepared to receive it, is twenty-nine, a slender man of rather darkly romantic appearance. Although he was born in Minneapolis, he has, on his several trips through Turkey, been mistaken by the inhabitants for one of their own. He wears a mustache "because the Turks are more hospitable to a man who has one." He is taking classes in Turkish at night and in Rumanian, too; he is already fluent in German, French and Spanish—the only law guardian in Manhattan, for that matter, who can understand some of his clients' parents without using the child as interpreter. In high school, Levy was a debater. At Harvard, which he left for a year to study in Paris at the new counterculture division of the University at Vincennes, he managed after a great row to rearrange the requirements for graduation to suit himself. He then went to New York University, which was reputed to have the best clinics in criminal law. While there, he studied photography with Ansel Adams and Philippe Halsman, and took up the piano: "I didn't go to that many classes after the first year."

By the time he was graduated in 1975, and had passed the bar exam, he knew that corporate law—all those tedious journeys over thick carpets to root among file drawers in search of imperial profits—was not for him. "I wanted to work with poor people. I wanted trials. I had worked as an intern at Harlem Assertion of Rights, a Legal Services office. I worked as a student with the Parole Revocation Unit of Legal Aid and with the ACLU." His first priority, however, was to go to Turkey "to film a group of people on the Black Sea called the Laz, who have a very interesting culture; they're not really Turks." On his return, he was drawn to Legal Aid—not to its Criminal Division, which is chiefly involved in plea bargaining, but to the Juvenile Rights Division, where the trials are. His first assignment was to sit in the Brooklyn office reading the "Manual for Law Guardians" —so he took it home and read it there. Juvenile justice, for those of an independent or fanciful turn of mind, can be an accommodating field in which to work.

And so, on any given morning, Rob Levy may spend the whole morning moving restlessly about the building's fifth and ninth floors, where the courtrooms are, and the sixth floor, where an attendant guards the way to the Designated Felony Part, trying to promote a little action in his cases. He checks to see who has appeared, whose lawyer hasn't shown, which Part is too congested to hear his case. He swaps gossip with the court officers, feeds bits of information to Corporation Counsel and BCW lawyers, tries to persuade them to change their minds. He chats with his clients and their mothers.

On a Monday, at 9:30, a young woman comes into Levy's office. Her son was picked up Saturday night on a burglary charge. She can hardly believe it: the boy is due to be in court tomorrow on another petition, and a third will be heard next week. She doesn't know where the boy is. Levy tells her without having to check: "He's in Spofford. He'll be here at 10:30. You can see him in Intake A, or go to Probation on the fourth floor." The mother sighs. "Somethin's gotta be done. I was goin' to school but now I've drop out—just to look after him. I can't get no job. The welfare, I can't live on that. I love my son, but I gotta do somethin'." Knowing the boy, Levy nods. This boy is fourteen, has two findings against him—one burglary, one looting— and now these three petitions. For five days after the great blackout, he was held with adult prisoners at Rikers Island because the police didn't believe his birth certificate. His mother pulled him out of school because he had fallen in with a tough crowd, but he liked school, and now—smart, hyperactive, needing medication—he is getting into a lot of early trouble.

Levy's memory for past clients is excellent—"for the ones I like" —and he can, after a year, recognize a mother and ask after her daughter by name. Sometimes his clients send him notes: "I Love You," said one. "I hope I can stay with my Mother'n Father, I do not wat to leav them pleas I Lov them." On the wall of the office he shares with another law guardian, he has taped comic strips drawn by his "regular customers"—The Mighty Thor and The Two-Gun Kid—and a poem, written in pencil, called "Don't Go To The Wrong Person":

> *Don't go to your friend*
> *Don't go to your school mate*
> *Go to your lovers*
>
> *Your friend can't help you*
> *Your school mate can't help you*
> *It's your lovers can help for your problems.*

> To Robert Levy my lawyer

"The author is seven," Levy says. "A neglect. When his mother wanted him back, his aunt offered him a hundred dollars to stay with her."

Talking to very young children is, if not an art, a highly specialized craft. "I've never given up on any child yet," Levy says. "I've gotten something out of a three-and-a-half-year-old. You say, 'Who's your daddy? Who's your mommy? Who's your *other* daddy? Are you ever bad? Does mommy hit you?' You find out what resentments they have. I discovered an abuse case that way. You have to be so sensitive with kids that age, their lives are so frail." With older children, a few law guardians use the kids' own street language—"You told your mother a lotta shit, you know; you can only fuck people over so far and get away with it"—but Levy's tone is generally affectionate. To a boy who tells him he plans to run away from a mental hospital, he asks, "What would it take to keep you there another two weeks?" Boy: "Five dollars." Levy, who sometimes doles out carfare to his clients, talks him down to $2 and hands it over. This is witnessed by his supervisor, Steve Hiltz, who says, "You can't take *that* out of petty cash."

After a disposition, a mother tries to press a $10 bill into Levy's hand. Refusing it, Levy says to her son, for whom he has arranged a parole on condition he attend a center, "Listen, you really gotta go. If you don't, you'll be back here and you'll undo everything we've done." The boy, Levy fears, is too weak to comply with the court's conditions. Despite the belief of many in court, particularly in Probation, that the kids are operators, skillful in manipulating their lawyers and the entire system, the law guardians generally believe that their clients often have no idea of what their options are, or even how to present themselves in court. One of Levy's children, a boy whose brain has been weakened by glue-sniffing, comes to court in his jogging costume: running shorts and an undershirt. Another, a fourteen-year-old girl, stands before the judge in a tight T-shirt that bears the legend: "I HAVE SMALL TITS."

Or, on another morning, Rob Levy may start the day with a fight with a judge, Blossom Heller being a likely antagonist. Judge Heller, a former prosecutor, is in her fifties and, as the kids would say, "a tough lady." Once Heller interrupted a hearing, summoned opposing counsel to her robing room and, when the stenographer had been excluded and the door had been carefully shut, addressed them in a voice that could be heard in every warren and cranny on the fifth floor: "I THINK I'LL THROW YOU THROUGH THE GODDAM WINDOW! DON'T YOU DARE SAY THAT. . . . NO, SIR! I WILL NOT READ IT! I AM NOT INTERESTED IN THAT!"

In accents immediately identifiable across the country as pure New York, Heller attempts to keep lawyers in line. "Mr. Levy, *please!*" she says one morning as she discards assorted clauses from Levy's motion for discovery in a Designated Felony case. "Clauses I and J are evidentiary," meaning they cannot properly be advanced until the trial begins. "*Any* statements made during the course of the crime are *evidentiary.* Read Richardson"—the standard book on evidence—"*all* the cases."

Levy: "I thought it would speed up the trial."

Heller (not at all taken in by such disingenuousness): "That may be all very liberal. But that's not the *law.* If you wanted a speedy trial, you would have brought this motion in earlier."

Levy: "Surely I'm entitled to the records . . ."

Heller: "Just because you're a law guardian, you're not entitled to no juvenile records. You've just fouled up my whole day again. Thank you very much. Why did you wait two weeks filing this motion?" Then, in a noisy aside: "That's why I get gray: *lawyers.*"

This kind of banter is easy enough, but occasionally Heller shows her teeth: "Act like a *lawyer,* Mr. Levy!" she suggests one morning in Intake A. Levy's offense is that he has been consulting with his client's sister to see whether she will take the boy on parole. "I've never seen such discourtesy in all my life!" Heller bellows, and then orders Levy into her robing room, where she tells him she will hold him in contempt should he do this kind of thing again—by which she means, presumably, conferring to work out an arrangement for his client. Levy considers this possibility: "I'd be taken down to adult detention. Another law guardian would have to represent me, I suppose. I might be fined. I don't remember such a thing happening."

Most law guardians see the judges, not Corporation Counsel or the bumbling BCW, as their principal adversaries. Some judges are ignorant of the law and must be unobtrusively coached; some are volatile and must be soothed; some are overbearing and must be resisted; some are weakly evasive and must be propped up; a few (it must be admitted) are right and must eventually be accommodated. After all, as Levy knows, 90 percent of his clients are guilty—if not precisely of what they are charged, then of something not far removed. "Only two or three kids have fooled me," he says, and then adds: "But how do you know?" In any event, whatever the cause of a judge's intractability, the attorney's options are limited. Tomorrow, or even later today, he will have to confront that judge again in another case. He has to look out for his credibility. He has to learn how to play the judges, too, to aim his defense at their susceptibilities. "The lawyer who trained me," Levy says, "told me always, when I was before Judge

Schwartz, to stand as tall as possible beside my client. The idea was to make the client look small and childlike. It can be really tough. You have to be really polite to the judges, yet you have to be ready to yell at them, too."

One of his mornings begins in Part I, with a brace of cases before Judge Otten. The first, a disposition, is for Levy a routine matter of extricating a fifteen-year-old boy from a lot of trouble and putting him back on the street, the kind of case which, if the press were allowed in the courtrooms, might cause the public some concern. In the recent past, this boy has survived four other petitions: one for assault, dismissed in Probation; one for robbery, dismissed when the complainant didn't show; another for assault, adjourned in contemplation of dismissal because there was some dispute about who began the fracas; and one—an alleged heroin sale—which will be dismissed this afternoon when it is shown that the white powder the boy carried was not a prohibited drug. This morning's disposition, which follows a finding made fully three and a half months ago, involves the boy's admission to a charge of Burglary 2. Originally he was charged with Robbery 1, Assault 1 and Burglary 1, all of which Levy negotiated away. "He was overcharged. That's why they thought him such a dangerous kid." And so, perhaps, he was, this limpid-eyed boy who says "Yessir" when Judge Otten asks him: "Can you make it on probation? Will you continue the program that the Legal Aid Society has developed for you? Will you meet with your Probation officer?" Levy has got this boy admitted to Manhattan School, a "special education" school on the West Side. Otten's disposition is that he remain there, on probation, for two years.

Levy's second hearing, which follows immediately, involves a pile of guns that have been stacked on the waiting-room floor since early morning, to the fascination of all assembled. Despite a decree from Administrative Judge Joseph B. Williams that no case may be adjourned unheard for more than ninety days without his personal permission, this one has been stalled for more than seven months, and the respondent, Quentin Torres, is now two days short of his sixteenth birthday and about to move to Puerto Rico.

Judge Otten calls Levy and Robert Kalish, the Corporation Counsel lawyer, to the bench. "We have two days' work to do in fifty-eight minutes," he says. Kalish promises a short hearing: "Half an hour, your honor, I guarantee it." Levy agrees to stipulate that the guns are operable (had he not, he could have won another adjournment for testing), "but only because this case has been adjourned so often I'm desperate." Otten says, "Let's start it, but let's finish it," a suggestion which, anywhere but Family Court, would seem unnecessary. Nevertheless, they cannot start it for a while: the interpreter is missing. "It would be nice," Otten observes, "if someone could wait two minutes for the court instead of the other way round."

By now the guns, roped together, have been brought in and placed on a table before the bench. A policeman is telling Kalish: "I observed two rifles on the floor next to the respondent." Levy objects: the one thing he does not want to emerge in this trial is the proximity of these intimidating weapons—two rifles, one with a sniper scope, a sawed-off shotgun, three handguns and a mess of cartridges—to his client. "I don't know where this is." A flurry of talk about addresses follows; whoever drew up the petition got the address wrong and Levy makes a note of that for the record.

The policeman continues. Chasing suspected burglars in an empty building, he entered an abandoned, doorless apartment. With his flashlight beam he picked up "two males flat against the lefthand wall. These were not the men I was pursuing. Two rifles lay at the edge of the wall. The other guns were a little further forward. All were loaded. I arrested the two men."

On cross-examination, Levy establishes that some apartments in the building were occupied, that there was a social club on the ground floor, an unlocked door at street level. "Anyone could walk right in." He moves for dismissal: "There has been no testimony that Quentin held any of these weapons. The case law is clear: if the respondent is not the lessee of the building or touching the weapons, he is not 'in possession.' I can offer four or five cases. Petitioner needs to prove dominion and control."

Otten denies Levy's motion, so Quentin takes the stand. "Just relax," Levy whispers to him. Quentin admits he was present with the weapons. "I don't know what I was doing. I was playing pinball and pool in the social club and the owner asks me to go upstairs. A lady had come in saying there was heat on in this empty apartment. He wanted me to check it out." He took with him another man, who has long ago plea-bargained his way out of this particular mess in Criminal Court. "We heard a noise. We thought men were on the roof"— the policeman, perhaps, who was chasing his burglars—"so we ran into this empty apartment." He never knew what was in the room, had never put anything there. The first time he saw the guns was in the precinct.

Throughout all this testimony, Kalish objects to hearsay, which Otten allows "not for the truth of it, but because I want to know what was said." The air conditioning in Part I is not working today and the court reporter looks ready to faint. When Levy finally yields, Kalish begins his cross-examination, trying to get Quentin to show him on a diagram which room he was in.

Levy: "Objection. It's too unclear. I can't make it out."

Quentin: "It don't look like the apartment to me."

Kalish: "Well then, *you* draw a diagram."

Levy: "Objection."

Otten sustains him. Quentin is proving adept at fending off Kalish's challenges. The social club, he says, has closed down, so he can't find the caretaker who sent him upstairs; he can't find the woman who reported the unseasonable heat.

Levy moves again for dismissal. "The police officer got the address wrong on the petition." May as well throw everything in. "The case has not been proved beyond reasonable doubt. Corporation Counsel has not proved possession or dominion. Just finding two boys in a room with weapons does not mean they brought them there. In an unoccupied building, proximity is not enough to make a finding. In *People* v. *Israel Diaz,* there was a stolen auto being stripped, the defendant standing beside it, but the case was dismissed." Levy continues in this vein for a while: he even has a case of a man standing next to a stash of cocaine in an apartment, but because the lessee was also there the man got off.

Nevertheless, Judge Otten, perhaps working less from the law than common sense, finds against the boy. "This boy beyond reasonable doubt was in possession of the weapons." He uses an interesting phrase, "constructive possession of these weapons," then goes on,

"The respondent's story of how he happened to be in that apartment is entirely incredible. Therefore, I put no credence in it."

Levy then makes a pitch designed to retrieve victory from ad-judicated defeat: "This is Quentin's first petition. He will be sixteen in two days. He is moving to Puerto Rico; his mother wants to get him out of the city." Although he doesn't say so in court, Levy believes the boy not guilty: "The other guy probably said to him, 'Come look at what I've got,' and he did."

He asks for an adjournment in contemplation of dismissal on condi-tion that Quentin move to Puerto Rico. Presumably there, as with the mad Hamlet sent to England, his irregularities may pass unnoticed. Otten rejects the fanciful plea, but grants the ACD anyway on even more fanciful grounds: "On condition he stay out of trouble after he is sixteen." *Sweep the kid out of sight.* That's what conservative voters demand in the hope that it will solve the problem without anyone's actually having to get involved; that's what, in this case, the law guardian wants because it is an attractive alternative to placement in a children's jail; and that's what, on occasion, the court will accede to, when the course seems most efficient. After all, the kid could have fired the guns at someone.

Kalish's guaranteed half-hour hearing took only an hour and a half: really very good time indeed.

Outside the courtroom, Levy asks the policeman, "Was Quentin right next to the guns?" The policeman says he was. "I didn't want to ask you that. I was afraid you'd kill me with it." The policeman nods.

Law guardians are assigned, on a rotation basis, to cover a different Part each day of the week, with one day "in reserve" for preparing a difficult case, interviewing witnesses, or visits to centers and hospi-tals to talk to their clients. On one of these days they cover Intake A, looking out for their regular customers as they are brought in on new petitions and picking up new ones. Because two law guardians cover Intake A each day, they try to sneak looks at the petitions as they arrive and divide the new cases between them according to preference. Robert Levy, for instance, prefers cases that he thinks will actually go to trial. He knows that his partner doesn't care for sex crimes; like many female lawyers, she is not eager to defend the rapists, sodomists and child molesters who come before the court. Theoretically, this rotation means that on any given day most of a lawyer's cases should be appearing in the Part to which he is assigned. What happens is that constant adjournments bounce a case among several Parts, utterly disrupting court policy, which declares that a single judge should follow a case from its first hearing through disposition. The lawyer, however, must follow the case and is often wanted in two Parts at once. No judge understands why a lawyer cannot be present when his case is called; none believes that the law guardian may be held elsewhere by a judge who will not release him. Once a judge told Levy that if he did not appear immediately, never mind what case he was trying, he would have him brought into court in handcuffs.

One of the clients Levy picked up in Intake is Richard Scott. Black, fourteen and virtually inarticulate, Richard manages to communicate primarily by rubbing his hands over his eyes and across his mouth, and by shrugging. For several weeks he has been a resident of Manhattan State, a psychiatric hospital, which is said to be good for children, but depressing. There he is given drugs which, he tells Levy, make him "sleepy all the time." He would like to go home and see his friends; still, matters could be worse: sitting here in the waiting room day after day he sees a lot of his friends. "The whole neighborhood, East 105th and 106th streets, is here," says Levy, "all up on some petty charge."

Richard likes to drive. A small fourteen-year-old, he once stole a city bus and drove it at sixty miles per hour from 116th to 177th streets, considerately flashing his lights and blowing his horn to lessen the chance of someone's being hurt. Richard was heading full tilt for the George Washington Bridge before the police managed to stop him by blocking his way with a sanitation truck. Another time, he stole a Greyhound bus and is now charged with "possession" of a stolen sanitation truck. Levy has doubts about this one: the police picked Richard and a friend up when they found them sitting in the cab of the truck.

Levy interviews Richard and his mother in the waiting room. "Do you have any brothers? Sisters?" "Mmmmm." "How do you like Manhattan State?" Shrug. "What do you want to do?" Another shrug. "You like to drive, don't you?" Impassive response: nothing showing. "Where would you like to go?" After much circling around this question, an answer surfaces: Richard wants to go south to live with his grandmother. "Would you rather go home than to an open setting?" He nods. "Whom do you see?" Levy inquires after several kids by name whom he knows to live in Richard's neighborhood: maybe that way he can get a fix on how the boy is drawn into trouble.

Two benches away, another of Levy's clients rises when a court officer calls his case before Blossom Heller in Intake A. Santos Jimenez is thirteen, claims to be fourteen. When he was picked up for selling cocaine to an undercover officer, he had $201.27 and two diamond rings in his pocket. Richard Rosenberg, the Corporation Counsel lawyer, says this makes Santos a major dealer. "Usually they're caught with five or ten dollars, but this guy must have made at least twenty transactions that day." Santos has been arrested ten times in the past five years, but there have been no findings against him yet. A rape charge in the Bronx was dismissed when the girl involved failed to prosecute. There have been other petitions, "mostly for token-sucking," Rosenberg says. Minor charges like blocking subway turnstiles to recover tokens are usually thrown out at Probation. "He's graduated. Now he's making more money than we are."

Levy makes a pro forma stab at parole for his client. He has no chance: Santos has lived on the street for weeks; his mother says she can't control him.

Judge Heller: "This is a very serious charge."

Levy: "It's not heroin, your honor. It's cocaine."

Heller: "Cocaine's the same as heroin."

Levy: "It's not addictive."

Heller: "Exactly the same. Remand. Remove him."

Santos: "I don' wanna go back to Spofford!"

He starts to hit the wall. A court officer grabs him and he fights back: "*Fuck you!*" Another court officer, and then a third, hold him. Nobody can get his handcuffs out, but Santos is wrestled to the anteroom where, finally, six court officers subdue this thirteen-year-old: one on each of his hands, one on each foot, two at his middle. They force him to the floor, one puts a knee in the boy's back, and another handcuffs him. Amid the "Fuck you's" Santos cries: "Hey, lawyer! Get my mother!" Levy, as soon as the flailing began, ran after his client to the anteroom just in case charges of brutality were in order. He believes his presence at such encounters helps keep the guards restrained. A guard emerges from this particular encounter bleeding from a scratch on his elbow. Judge Heller tells him to file an incident report, which is designed to protect him against just such a brutality charge as Levy may have had in mind.

Later in the day, the case returns before Heller. To get Santos paroled, Levy persuaded him to plead guilty only to possession of cocaine. "Don't say anything to the judge about selling it!" Nevertheless, when the case is recalled, and Santos spots the undercover officer in court, their strategy collapses. The first question Heller asks the boy is: "Did you have any cocaine in your possession?" Santos answers, "Yeah. I sold it to that man there." Levy winces, but what can he do? His clients don't have the formidable wiles endowed them by the press. Having done himself in so efficiently, Santos hears his bid for parole denied. His case will be heard three days from now in the Bronx—at the boy's request, to make it easier for his mother to attend. Levy warns him that his mother doesn't want to take him home.

These events surprise the Corporation Counsel lawyer, too. Richard Rosenberg had thought nothing much would come of the case because the undercover officer was unlikely to appear. "Santos probably doesn't remember him," Rosenberg says only an hour before the recall. "He may have been the eighth sale of the twenty-sale day, and the officer doesn't want Santos to get a good look at him and circulate his description in the streets. If he doesn't show, all we've got is a possession case, and maybe we haven't even got *that:* it sometimes takes more than three days to get the lab report proving that the stuff was actually cocaine."

When the Designated Felonies, with their threat of longer incarceration, were introduced into the Family Court, so, too, was plea bargaining. One early morning finds Robert Levy in a corridor—for some reason, opposing counsel never consult in each other's offices—making a pitch to the Corporation Counsel lawyer. His client, Tommy Gengler, has robbed at knifepoint a boy who had just left a bank, having cashed a check for $51. "Give me your money or I'll cut your throat," Tommy is alleged to have suggested. Levy proposes Robbery 3 as an appropriate charge, which incenses Bob Kalish: "No way! I got him dead. I got the police officer here." Steve Pokart's technique for plea bargaining with Kalish is to say, "What kind of hearing we're going to have depends on how much you want to screw around," but Levy takes a different tack. The thrust of his argument is that Tommy is an unlikely felon. He's not a street kid. He should not be sent to restrictive placement—to Goshen, the children's jail. Kalish replies that the policeman has talked to Tommy's grandmother, who thinks the boy needs supervision and wonders why the court doesn't provide it.

Kalish: "Why worry about it? Plead guilty to Robbery 1 and I won't say anything about restrictive placement."

Levy: "But you know the judge. Doran. He'll put him away."

Kalish: "Not necessarily. You don't understand him at all. You got to learn how to play him."

Levy: "But why take the chance?"

Kalish: "That's what he's paid to do. Make these decisions. It's why he gets forty-five thousand and I get half. Why should I do his work?"

Levy: "But that's the way it works. You know he wants us to settle it here."

Kalish: "I see no reason to let him off the hook."

Levy: "But we can do it. We can agree right here on what happens to this boy. You're a powerful man, you know."

Kalish: "I *am?* Why don't you convince Doran?"

Levy: "You know the judge will ask us what we think. Will you say you're against restrictive punishment?"

Kalish: "I won't say anything. It's not my job."

Levy: "This boy is one day short of sixteen. Why should we be tougher than Criminal Court? They'd throw it out."

Kalish: "You got nothing to worry about in this case."

Levy: "I'm not sure. We have to take some responsibility."

Kalish: "I can prove Robbery 1."

Levy: "But this is not a kid who should be sent away on a Title Three."

Kalish shrugs.

Levy: "Okay. If you want to play games."

Kalish: "I'm not playing games."

Levy: "You're *always* playing games. That's all you ever do."

Kalish: "That's not true. Why should I tie the judge's hands?"

The discussion having reached the sandbox level, Levy tries a final stab: "Will you look at the Probation report? Maybe we can get the CLO to commit himself to nonrestrictive placement." Kalish declines, but even if he hadn't, the court liaison officer, Seymour Gottfried, would have refused. He calls *that* playing games. Sometimes, when asked for his recommendation, Gottfried will talk to the boy and his mother "for two minutes. I ask him if he will accept certain curfews and controls, and report to an ATD—Alternative to Detention—Center on West 23rd Street where they have a nine-to-five program of sports and classes. But I won't play *that* hand until I've heard a probable cause or a trial."

The games motif is resumed about an hour later in Judge Doran's Designated Felony Part. After conferring with Tommy and his mother and grandmother, Rob Levy withdraws Tommy's not-guilty plea, hoping that by an admission and by saving Doran a hearing he might still come up with something less than Goshen for his client. Doran, however, returns tomorrow to his court in the Bronx and wants no part of Levy's scheme. If he accepts it, he is bound to hear the disposition, too—which means he will have to come back from the Bronx for the occasion or have Levy bring it up there. In either event, his Bronx calendar would be upset, so, playing his own game, he refuses to accept the admission on the grounds that Levy is playing games.

As the hearing begins, the police officer testifies that Tommy said to him, "I took the dude's money, I robbed him with my knife." Levy objects, claiming this is hearsay. Doran looks at him amazedly: "An admission on the part of a respondent is *hearsay?*" Matters deteriorate further when Bob Kalish, having announced that he was ready for trial, announces that he is now only ready for a probable cause hearing: he has decided he has another witness he should interview.

Doran orders Kalish into his robing room. "I was threatened," Kalish says later. "I don't like being threatened." Doran tells Kalish in private that this is the second time he has tried this particular game of standing ready for trial and then falling back on a probable cause, and that if he, Doran, were not leaving this benighted borough of Manhattan, he would call in the head of the city's Corporation Counsel for a tongue-lashing. As it is, he settles for calling in the Manhattan chief, Larry Schwartzstein, and, as Kalish eavesdrops with his ear pressed against the robing-room door, bawls *him* out. Minutes later, as Doran sits impassively on the bench, Schwartzstein can be heard bawling out Levy in a corridor: "No more of your games! Maybe we both play games, but from now on you're gonna see something different!"

For all its decibel level, this exchange has been a minor frustration for Larry Schwartzstein, for whom major frustration is a chronic condition. Like Arthur Trufelli in the Bronx, he needs more attorneys; an investigator or two; above all, more cooperation from the police. "The police are merely concerned with the collar; I have difficulty getting them to come in. They are either not working afternoon shifts or they can't be relieved to come into court. We have difficulty getting them to come down prior to the day of the hearing to discuss the case, so we often have to go in cold the day of the trial." This can be embarrassing, because Corporation Counsel is not supposed to present a case in court unless it believes the case can be won. Because its lawyers are often unable to assess a case until the last minute, they are sometimes obliged to withdraw it after the hearing has begun—which is humiliating for them and a waste of time for all who have been summoned. Such debacles do not occur in other courts. To make matters worse, the court warrant squad, once a corps of half a dozen police officers whose job it was to bring in recalcitrant respondents, is virtually defunct. If a judge now issues a warrant for a boy who has failed to show for his hearing, it may take a year or even two for that warrant to be executed.

Morale is a problem, too. Schwartzstein's lawyers are bright and experienced, with three or four years of this work behind them, but their loyalty may possibly be due to lack of other opportunity. "It's very hard out there for lawyers," says Marilyn Schulder, one of his attorneys. "That's why these fellows are here. They're not here for love of the work, I'll tell you that. They're here because it's hard out there and they don't know enough people to get a good job. There are too many lawyers in New York City." Schulder herself would like to go into bankruptcy law—someday.

Salaries at Corporation Counsel have been frozen for three years. "There's really no increments or bonuses for those who do work," Schwartzstein says. "There's no incentive to keep a young attorney in this office. Nothing to motivate him to stay. On the contrary, the motivation is for them to leave as quickly as possible. There's nothing more for them to gain here, no place to go, nothing to strive for. In my opinion, that's wrong." Schwartzstein, who tends to speak of himself as if he will be doing something else next week, sees himself as "more or less the protector of the community when it comes into Manhattan Family Court." Schulder disagrees: "No. Absolutely not. We know we're doing nothing. Most people in the office feel that it's futile. We're there, period. If we weren't there it wouldn't make any difference, frankly."

For some, the frustrations yield before a personal satisfaction in prosecution. "I do care," says Judith Levy, whom the law guardians think the toughest, and one of the ablest, of Corporation Counsel's attorneys. "It's a career. It's not just a job. I enjoy it." In court, Judy Levy fairly seethes with indignation, rolling her eyes to heaven at unfavorable rulings, or turning her back to the bench in search of consolation from the wall. "I take work home with me. Every precinct in the city that we're involved with has my home number. They sometimes call at two in the morning. I think the complainants in this court are entitled to superior representation. Aside from that, it's an ego thing. I don't like to do a half-assed job." "Judy Levy," says Judge Stanley Gartenstein, "has a lot of balls."

Like Schwartzstein, she respects the law guardians and thinks of them as adversaries. "They're hand-picked for dedication. It's difficult to have the same kind of dedication when you don't have the clients. We have a raw petition. We don't meet the people till the day, or the day prior to, the trial. You have to have instead a social idea"— Corporation Counsel is pretty sure the law guardians do not—"and a pride in your own performance. Especially that. That's where it's at, with any good professional. But then one of the easy parts of this job is that you usually know you're right. If I become extremely agitated in the courtroom and start to scream and ventilate a bit, if I try to intimidate a little, I feel as if I have right on my side. I mean, if you go to trial with a case, more often than not you win it." *If* you go to trial: Levy admits that between half and three-quarters of her cases collapse because someone hasn't shown up.

The Corporation Counsel attorneys believe that many of these dismissals for nonappearance are due to the law guardians' under-handed machinations. "I've always resented their dilatory tactics," Judy Levy says. "They discourage a complainant from coming in. They demand adjournments when they haven't got a form. It's an effective tool, one I see all too frequently. Judge Deutsch became infuriated last week in just such a situation. It was a case of bicycle theft. The cop arrested the guy before he got half a block away. The complainant was in court. So was the officer. He had made out both the complaint report and the arrest report, but in court we had only the complaint report. The other was on file. The cop told Judge Deutsch they were both exactly the same. So the law guardian says he has to have the arrest report, he can't go to trial without it. Deutsch got a little crazy. He said, 'That's a dilatory tactic and I resent it,' but he gave him his adjournment. God knows if we'll get the complainant and the officer in court together again, and if we do, maybe the kid won't show. Or the kid's mother.

"Lots of these judges are appeal-shy. I've had four rape cases the past six months. I was ready on two. I got two convictions: one on trial, one on a plea. The other two were paroled out of Intake. Unbe-lievable. A woman is raped. She's been to the hospital. Two or three doctors give her internal examinations. She's had her underpants confiscated. It's a dehumanizing experience. She comes to court and she sees the rapist standing there. Probation says, because of the gravity of the offense, we recommend remand, plus the fact the kid has two or three other petitions. And the Intake judge paroles him."

"Legal Aid's been having it both ways," Larry Schwartzstein says. "They talk about the best interests of the child, but they only care about getting him back on the street. They have nothing to lose by going to trial because the sentencing power is so weak anyway. We may have a complainant who is fearful of her life to cooperate, and yet Legal Aid will not admit to any crime. Prove your case, they say, and maybe we can't, yet it might be in the best interest of the child to start worrying about a structured placement instead of paroling him. Legal Aid doesn't care. I get frustrated when you have a serious crime and you do a lot of preparation and you get a finding beyond a reasonable doubt and nothing happens to the juvenile. You feel kind of frustrated. It's very difficult to explain to the layperson that this is the only kind of sentencing power the Family Court has. They can't understand why a juvenile who commits murder or rape can't get what a sixteen- or seventeen-year-old would get in Criminal Court. Why are they treated so leniently when they commit an 'adult crime'? That's the frustration we have. The problem is that the law that governs Family Court, that is given to us by the governor and the legislature, is weak. Our hands are tied."

Schwartzstein believes that children, "over the past ten years, have been getting too many constitutional rights. They have more, in my estimation, than an adult has. You show me where in Criminal Court a respondent charged with homicide would have to be tried in less than one month. No way. It might be six months to a year. Yet in Family Court the case is tried right away. Plus, the sentencing power is much less in the commission of a very serious crime than an adult would get. A juvenile who rapes a woman at gunpoint is being condoned, in a sense, by the kind of sentence he gets in Family Court. That's what's disturbing, alarming, and at times frustrating for us."

Judy Levy agrees. "Juveniles are being afforded special and lenient treatment for the acts they commit. I had a fourteen-year-old kid whose family have been involved in the court for years. Not just minor matters. A couple of homicides. Four brothers involved. Two are serving life terms. One brother is now eighteen and is convicted of homicide in Family Court, but he's out, of course. Now this kid's arrested for the third time. Possession of a weapon. Loaded. He was standing out on a street corner and the testimony was he was passing a joint. Cops come out of a car and one of them bumps up against him and felt something hard in his pocket and gave him a toss and found the gun. OK. Agreed. Even if half the cop's testimony is hallucinations, he has a fourteen-year-old kid who was on the street with a gun. So the law guardian moves to suppress the gun and I went through a hearing. A very good judge. Whom I respect. He suppressed the gun. I think that decision was an injustice to everyone. Not only to the community, but to the kid himself. Because the kid left the courtroom laughing. He's out on the street, a hero. The judge went crazy, though from the legal standpoint the facts supported him."

Judge Doran says: "What this court needs is less law and more common sense." Which is to say that the experiment launched by Charles Schinitsky is a mistake. Judy Levy agrees with him. "Family Court, as far as I'm concerned, is the most important personal court in the whole city system. You're not dealing with money. You're not dealing with a damaged fender. Or with lost merchandise. You're dealing with the souls of people."

Marilyn Schulder, who before she discovered the prosecutor's calling was for six months a law guardian, takes a darker view. "I have a lot of feeling about this court. But I don't know how to express it. It's a very depressing, horrible place. It's completely not in the real world. The criminal cases, they're a waste of time, a waste of money. You might as well not ever bring them into court. The Catholic Church says, 'Give me a child until he's five and he's mine forever,' so how does this court think it's going to rehabilitate a fifteen-year-old who's lived in an entirely different society?

"And to say it's society's fault is ridiculous. You know, we should stop worshiping poverty. It's about time. The Family Court was made for the little newsboy who broke somebody's window with a stone. That's when the laws were made. Not for the fifteen-year-old who's into drugs and killing. We're still on those laws.

"It's just a horrible place with horrible people. Unfortunately, it's the place that has taught me prejudice. I've become very racially bigoted, and if I lie to you and say I'm not, it's not true. If I say to you I wasn't before, *that's* true. I was not before I came to this job. Being in this place, I mean, it's horrible. I mean, who do you see who comes into this court? How can anybody keep an open mind after seeing what they see? It hasn't done much very positive for me.

"The law guardians, they're very dedicated. I can't believe it, that someone could be dedicated to a cause. I can't explain it. That's ridiculous. I mean, if you have a kid who's on dope and he's walking the streets, don't you want to help him? We have a problem even with the black judges. They go too far one way or the other. Either they get so mad at their black brothers, so to speak, that they can't see farther than their nose, or they completely commiserate by saying, 'We were in slavery, too.'

"I feel guilty, the way I'm speaking about this problem. But I can only feel about what I see, and I know what I see. Obviously, I'm Jewish, and the Jews were one of the biggest factors in this black civil rights movement. I mean, they supported them tremendously. They still are. What they're getting for it is a kick in the ass: lousy Jewish landlords, lousy Jewish lawyers. They're so ignorant. They still think the Jews have horns.

"Every time I see a Jewish kid here on a petition, I say: 'Get out. I'll give you the name of a local rabbi. Get out of here. Out, out, stay out! I don't want to prosecute this case. I don't think the best interest of your child is in this court.' I say, 'You will get nowhere. Where do you think you're going to get? You want the kid out of the house, but if you don't know where you want him, and you don't know where he's going, I say, get out. Just get the hell out.' Not only Jewish families, but white middle-class families as well. I say: 'What do you want us to do? You've been abused. Your kid hits you. Is that what's happening? Fine. Get in touch with the Jewish Social Services, with the Protestant Big Sisters, try to find a clinic or a psychiatrist.' I say: 'You're not going to get it through here. Get out of *here.*' Of course, I can't say it to the other ones, because there's no one they can get ahold of. In Spofford, they're going to get killed, man. Killed."

Marilyn Schulder takes the court elevator up to the ninth floor. At the fifth floor, the doors open. A black woman asks: "Going down?" "Up," says Schulder. And then, as the doors close: "You see? They can't even tell up from down. I'm sorry, but it's true."

Not a day passes in this court without someone's attempting to bend the law in an attempt to accommodate what he assumes to be the best interests of a child. Rob Levy, like most law guardians, believes his clients' interests are often best served by freeing them from the court's benevolence—by returning them to the street, as Corporation Counsel says—but he denies behaving unethically to accomplish this end. He

will try to get a case adjourned if Corporation Counsel hasn't prepared it properly—the missing form, that kind of thing—because the
burden of preparation lies with the prosecution, but he won't lie or
discourage his clients from appearing. "You shouldn't do anything to
lower the ethical tone of the place even further." One afternoon he
found himself fighting not only his usual adversaries, Corporation
Counsel and Probation, but a new judge determined to substitute his
own policy for the law and a panel lawyer representing his client's
co-respondent.

Legal Aid policy forbids its attorneys to represent more than one
client in cases involving two or more respondents; because the children's interests may differ, private counsel, usually panel lawyers,
must be assigned to the others. Panel lawyers, however, are notorious
for arguing against their clients' wishes and in so doing weaken whatever it is Legal Aid is trying to accomplish.

This case, before Judge Joseph A. Esquirol, Jr., in Part III, involves
two boys charged with attempted burglary. Neither boy's mother is
present—Levy knows, but will not say, that his client's mother wants
nothing to do with him—nor is the complainant or the arresting
officer. Because the case cannot be heard today, or for at least six days
to come, the question is what to do with the boys. Levy's client, Victor
Gilman, has already been held at Spofford for six days—longer than
the law allows—and Levy wants him paroled.

Esquirol: "Well, I think in view of what I've got before me, they're
both going to be remanded with privilege of parole to their parents.
I don't have any adult to take them home."

Levy: "Your honor, the statute does not speak of an adult. The
statute speaks of a maximum of three days—"

Esquirol: "I'm not paroling anyone to the streets, counselor. There
is no adult to take him home."

Levy: "We have escorts that can take Victor to his home. There's
no problem with that at all."

David Entes (the panel lawyer): "The respondent Willie Morales
has been in already seven days. You're putting him in another week.
It's true his parent is not here. I have before the Court Miss Leslie
Reynolds, a case worker from Covenant House, who knows the boy
well. If you just heard her speak, I think you'd be thoroughly im-

pressed. Maybe the parent doesn't want to show up, that's true, but I would say this, judge: she knows him for the last three months, and he comes religiously every week."

Esquirol: "And on June 23 a petition is taken out on him for this. So what's she been doing for him?"

Entes: "It's not her job—"

Esquirol: "Don't tell me what she's going to do or not do."

Entes: "I just feel that—it's a problem, though, if you were to parole him: where would he go to sleep? That is a problem, I agree with you." Entes's musings, his desire to cooperate with the judge, have now led him to work against freeing his client.

Esquirol: "That's right."

Levy: "Judge, there's been absolutely no statement that Victor Gilman cannot go home. We can make sure that he gets home. And I call the Court's attention to section 739 of the Family Court Act which states that 'No remand to a detention facility may last longer than three days without a hearing.' And I believe this will last longer than three days."

Esquirol: "Only if his parents don't go to pick him up. I am granting him the privilege of parole. I point out, counselor, that on this case a warrant is outstanding for the mother right now—on your client."

Levy: "Your honor, we have had no warrant officer's report on his mother. We have no indication that she's ever been notified."

Esquirol: "She could have called to find out, after this much time, where her son is."

Levy (all innocence): "Where would she call?"

Esquirol: "I don't know, but I think if I were a parent I would be somewhat concerned if I hadn't seen a child in seventy-two hours, at this age." Victor is nearly fifteen. Esquirol's argument makes perfect white-middle-class sense, but it has nothing to do with the law, and the law is what Levy is pursuing now.

Levy: "She may be concerned. But regardless of that, the statute doesn't require that a parent appear to take a child."

Esquirol: "But I don't parole anyone to the street."

Levy: "Your honor, the statute states—"

Esquirol: "I'm familiar with the statute. I'm remanding him because I have no other alternative. I have no adult supervision to release these boys to. Am I just going to let them out on the streets? They have no place to sleep, no money, no—"

Levy: "Victor has a home to go to."

Esquirol: "That's open to question, as I say. His mother hasn't even taken the trouble to inquire of his whereabouts at this point. It's a very substantial question in my mind that he does have any place to go this afternoon."

Levy: "Your honor, he has a home. Probation has a record that there is a mother. Under the reasoning of the Court at this point, if a mother never appears in court a person could ultimately be remanded for an indefinite period of time—for two months, three months, four months."

Esquirol: "With privilege of parole to a responsible adult."

Levy: "Well, that would make the statute utterly meaningless."

Esquirol (delivering a low blow): "Counselor, I'll parole him to you. Do *you* want to take him home tonight?"

Levy (parrying): "Legal Aid will take him tonight."

Esquirol: "No, no; you take him to *your* home. If you want to be responsible, I'm perfectly willing to do it. But I want to know he has a place to sleep, that he's going to get his food, and he won't be wandering the streets, with no place to go."

Entes now further muddies the process: "Judge, let me step in a moment. Rob, please. I just want to follow the rationale here. I see the problem with the Court. Let's be practical. You do have a problem here. You have compassion for the kids. I don't envy the Court's position. But consider the problem; you've got to be realistic. I have to say this: lots of kids live in the street."

Esquirol: "That doesn't make it right. If that's your argument, forget it."

Entes: "You're not appreciating the spirit I'm thinking in. I'm not saying that's good. I'm saying it's like kids don't go to school."

Esquirol: "I'm here to stop this."

Entes: "I don't say no."

Esquirol: "What do you suggest we do to him? Give him a gold star and send him over to 100 Centre Street and wait till he's sixteen?"

Entes: "Judge, I don't think that. No one in the world's capable of solving all these problems. You do the best you can, which is great.

I don't say it's not great. I want to know one thing: Has Probation determined whether my respondent has been in trouble before? That's the first thing I think you should know." It is, in law, the *last* thing Judge Esquirol should know just now; the wonder is that Entes should suggest it.

Esquirol: "Not if I'm going to a fact finding; I don't want to know a thing from Probation."

Entes stumbles a bit further: "The action before the Court is that the respondents allegedly jostled somebody. At best, it's a nebulous type of case here. I feel as a lawyer I've got a responsibility for the kids. I'm not trying to win this case. I'm trying to help this kid."

Esquirol: "Fine. Have you been in touch with his parents?"

Entes: "No."

Esquirol: "Well, then, you've done as much as the rest of us. Counselor, I'll let *your* client go home with *you.* "

Entes: "Yeah; that's not a fair question."

After a debate about trial dates, Rob Levy throws in another idea: "I ask the Court to remand my client to shelter care. It's a surrogate parent. If the Court can't trust the respondent's parents, then the city, I believe, should assume responsibility as a parent."

Entes: "I'll do the same thing—right?"

Levy: "If my client were fourteen months older, he'd be out on bail at this point. That's one of the unfortunate problems of the juvenile system, where a person cannot be released on bail and, if his parent does not appear, he can be detained indefinitely. I think there are constitutional problems with that. And I think the statute was addressing itself to that very problem."

Esquirol: "I don't think the Family Court Act, which was drafted in 1962, contemplated what we're dealing with in the 1970s. I really don't. It may be that the Family Court Act is long overdue for an overhaul. It's being done piecemeal."

Levy: "But the point is, it hasn't been overhauled."

Esquirol doubts his authority to send the boys to shelter care and is backed up by the court liaison officer, who announces that BCW must approve such an action. "I can tell you right now that BCW is not going to give approval in this situation, particularly in *your* case, Mr. Levy." This infuriates Levy: Probation has as good as told Judge

Esquirol that Levy's client, Victor, has other problems with the court.

Levy: "There has been no evidence of any findings"—he checks himself—"of any . . . reasons why this person who has the presumption of innocence should be remanded. He is being held beyond the statutory limit of three days, merely because his parent is not here."

Court liaison officer: "I'd like to note that the Court has a warrant against Victor Gilman's mother, which was ordered by this Court, and she has not shown; nor has she made any contacts with this Court to indicate or to express a desire for care for this youngster. I should also like to note, there's a finding against respondent. I'd like also to indicate that the respondent's mother did not appear here on the Intake case, and that, when the warrant officer went to visit the home —well, there's been no response."

Esquirol: "No response?"

Court liaison officer: "At all."

Levy: "So the reason for the failure of Probation to explore remand to shelter care is that the mother has not cooperated, and the sins of the mother are being visited on the child. It's not an appropriate reason."

But he has lost. His client, presumed innocent of the offense of which he is charged, proved guilty only of being abandoned by his parents, will spend sixteen days in jail before he goes to trial.

The pressures of the day, however, have finally eased. Because Judge Esquirol, who has been sitting for two months, claims to forget by the day's end the cases he has just heard, "unless I've had to reserve a decision," he concludes his afternoon by exchanging banter with his court officer, Al Deal. Deal is a long, reedy black man with a lot of court experience; he guides the new judge through his calendar, reminds him tactfully whether a case should go to this Part or that. Former respondents stop Deal on the street to ask whether he remembers them. "I've got my own fan club. I've never had to hit anybody, though I've arrested lots. I believe you don't have to hustle people here. You just treat them with dignity."

Esquirol: "What kind of calendar do we have tomorrow?"

Deal: "A good one. All delinquencies. No adults."

Esquirol: "I think I'll bring my mother-in-law. If she saw what happened today, she'd wonder why we are paid so much. And she'd be right."

Deal: "These are good ones. I recognize some of the names."

Esquirol: "All pillars of our society?"

Deal (grinning): "Some are misunderstood."

Once, over lunch during that summer of 1977, Rob Levy and Steve Pokart discuss ethics.

Pokart: "If one of the women judges let you know she'd go easy on your client if you went to bed with her, would you do it?"

Levy: "No. Would you?"

Pokart: "Yes. If I knew it would help my client. I'd do just about anything to help a client."

Levy: "Well, I think it has something to do with self-respect."

Pokart: "My self-respect has to do with getting my clients off. I don't have any idealism. I see what I'm doing here as getting people off. I'm a technician. I help these people by getting them their freedom. Sometimes they use that freedom badly. I've gotten one client off four or five times and he goes out and knifes people. But I have no compunctions about that at all. I feel very sorry for these kids because most of them have been fucked over in every possible way all their lives. I don't have time, I don't have space in my head, to feel compassion for the victims."

Levy: "I do, because the victims are from the same element of society."

Pokart: "A lot are not. Don't forget many are policemen."

In the talk that follows, both admit to having doubts as to whether they, as a respondent's attorney, have the right to prohibit a client from perjuring himself if that's the defense he wants.

Pokart: "I never put a client on the stand who's going to lie, but for purely pragmatic reasons: they're lousy liars on the stand."

Levy: "It's awkward, perhaps wrong, for defending lawyers to be officers of the court. You have to remember the code of ethics was drawn up early in this century by one kind of lawyer, lawyers very different from us. Lawyers representing the Bar Association, which has brought us a lot of other things we don't like. To a certain extent we have to devise our own ethics."

Neither Levy nor Pokart has any interest in corporate law work, however much more money it might provide, and because it is difficult to become a successful independent attorney, each is satisfied with what he is doing now. Pokart thinks he'd like someday to switch to Legal Aid's Criminal Division (and within two years he will do just that) "to learn some more law," but Levy is dubious: "It's all just plea bargaining over there."

"I've gotten so I hate everybody here," Pokart says. "BCW, panel lawyers, judges, case workers, Probation. We're the only ones who are doing the job well. But we have to do everybody else's work, too. If we didn't have to, we could act more like lawyers. There's no end to what you can do in any case, so if my case load were cut in half I'd be working just as hard."

—

Rob Levy left Legal Aid in 1978 and works today for the New York Civil Liberties Union Mental Patients Rights Project, an experimental area of law which argues that mental patients who do not behave in antisocial ways have a right not to be incarcerated. He hopes someday to write something about the psychology of some of the children he has defended, to combine a career in law with a career in photography. He has never photographed his clients for fear of exploiting them, but he has, in Turkey, taken thousands of photographs of people at work. Of one of these pictures, he says: "It's a group of metal workers. They do everything by hand. They cast metal in little molds that they make out of mud or dirt. They pour the molds by hand, heating them in sulfur. They stand there for hours just stoking the fires, sweating immensely, and working in absolute darkness."

VI

Caring,
Kind Environments

The first and most essential thing to do is to make
it plain to the boy who is boss, who is in charge,
and that they are not going to be able to do
anything without being punished for it.

The Director of Clinical Services
at Goshen Center for Boys, quoted in testimony
in *Pena* v. *New York State
Division for Youth* (1974)

On special occasions in Family Court, all the elements for a particularly terrible trial appear to converge—the kind of ordeal by justice
in which prejudice and ill will take precedence over law from the
moment the first motions are made. It is in the nature of such proceedings that those most concerned with the outcome—the children—
understand nothing, or little, of what goes on about them; their role
is to witness a struggle conducted among educated white folk whose
use of an arcane verbal shorthand will result in a conclusion that only
the children must endure. Susan Larabee, a Legal Aid attorney, has
just such a case on her calendar for July 22, 1977: a particularly grim
offense; an unusually shady respondent; a complainant who may not
be what he seems; accentuated problems with her co-counsel for the
defense; an acrimonious rivalry with the lawyer from Corporation
Counsel; one judge who seems mischievously determined to humiliate

her; another judge who makes his bigotry plain. To make matters worse, the situation is exceptionally poignant, revealing as it does that the institutions set up by our society to protect and rehabilitate children in trouble are in fact little better than instruments of their degradation and abuse.

The case, a Designated Felony which will be heard in Part IV, involves an allegation of homosexual rape at Covenant House. Covenant House, a Catholic-sponsored agency in Greenwich Village, is not a secure place of detention but a group home for boys convicted of less than the more serious offenses; like all such agencies, it draws upon federal, state and city funds. Few of these agencies are inspiring places, but Covenant House is said to have recently deteriorated. Susan Larabee's client, Xavier Morales, had been confined there for a minor offense, much to the chagrin of his mother, who, having taken on a new lover, wants nothing to do with her fifteen-year-old son and had hoped to see him stashed away in a prison far from New York City. Xavier, who has a first-grade reading level and can't write at all, has a finely molded face, with delicate, sensitive features; his hair rises from his head like a mushroom cap or a nuclear cloud. An innocent observer might reasonably doubt that such a boy could possibly be involved in a violent sex crime, yet according to one of the court officers, "All these kids know how to do is rape and rob."

Xavier's co-respondent in this case, Youngman Green, is an even more ambiguous figure. Youngman, who says he is also fifteen, has never seen his father and thinks his mother "lives somewhere in New York City." He last saw her two years ago and remembers having lived "somewhere on 72nd Street." At the time of his alleged participation in the rape of the complainant, he had been at Covenant House for one day, sent there by the police. Before that, he tells the court, he had run away from home and hitchhiked to New Mexico, where he "stayed with a friend" for two years before being picked up by the police there and sent back to New York on a plane. Youngman's attorney is a panel lawyer, Oswald Dimond, an elderly, spreading man who is hard of hearing and has to keep asking his client and other witnesses to repeat their testimony. Because Dimond is of that breed of defense counsel that scorns the "bright lawyers"—he means the Legal Aid attorneys—"who get kids they know to be guilty off, not considering their best interests," he joins Judge Joseph Doran in a rigorous cross-examination of his own client.

Doran: "Do you have any idea, counselor, why the New Mexico authorities had sent him back? Was it to take him off the back of their taxpayers down there, or what?"

Dimond: "That is the impression that I got from him when I first saw him this morning."

Doran: "Yes."

Larabee: "Your honor, I feel this line of inquiry is prejudicial to both the respondents at this time."

Doran: "If you have an objection, make it and I will rule on it."

Larabee: "I am objecting."

Doran: "Overruled."

Dimond: "I guess they returned him as a runaway. They were glad to get rid of him. No question about it. They were happy to get rid of him."

Incredible as such a comment is from defending counsel, the court reporter records it as being said by Judge Doran. Minutes of proceedings in this court often vary from what is actually said. The reporters do their best and are reasonably skilled; it takes them between six months and two years to learn to use their machines properly. They must then pass a test, recording at least 180 words a minute, but people talk faster than that and often trample over each other's offerings; when the going gets complicated the reporters are instructed to follow the words of the judge. Nevertheless, this reporter, who thinks "this court is a farce," and who says he doesn't "pay attention to what's going on; if I did, I couldn't write it down," has just mangled the record in such a way that if the case were ever brought before an appeals court it might well be overturned.

Dimond continues his cross-examination of his client, adducing further damaging evidence against him: "What were they holding you for?"

Youngman: "Holding me for being a runaway. I told them I had run away from here. They said, you know, that they would put me in a D home."

Dimond: "What is a D home like?"

Youngman: "Like a lockup place."

Dimond: "Like a detention?"

Youngman: "Yes. A detention home."

Not satisfied with this, Dimond tries to trick his client: "What is the date of your birth: the month, date and year?"

Youngman (not fooled): "Nine twenty-six sixty-one."

Dimond: "When his honor asked you your age, you said...?"

Youngman: "I said, fifteen."

Dimond: "You were going to say sixteen?"

Youngman: "Yes. Because I am going to turn sixteen."

Dimond (last stab): "When?"

Youngman: "September 26."

Dimond: "All right. That is all."

Throughout these proceedings, Probation's court liaison officer, Dorothy Bass, remains impassive but skeptical. "He looks older," she says during a recess. "He's probably living somewhere under another name. Everybody's got *some* family. There *was* one kid, though, who was placed, hospitalized and died—and no one ever knew who she was."

With the identifications, such as they are, out of the way, the hearing should now be set to proceed, but Susan Larabee is not. Larabee is a tall, lean, attractive woman of twenty-nine; in the courtroom she behaves more aggressively than the other women law guardians and occasionally lets the edge of her temper show. Within two years she will be named attorney-in-charge of the Manhattan office, which will somewhat reduce her courtroom work, but at the moment she is erecting the law guardians' first line of defense: missing records that Corporation Counsel should have supplied.

Her opponent, Robert Kalish, will have none of this. "Your honor, may I say something? Legal Aid knows very well that all they have to do is to fill out a subpoena duces tecum and to have it signed by the Court and to serve it on Police Plaza and the reports will be obtained." Nevertheless, as Larabee reminds him, the judge at Intake A ordered Corporation Counsel to furnish these documents. Kalish calls this unfair. "I think it is unfair that they are now going to ask for an adjournment because we did not furnish the reports. The statute provides a hearing in three days, judge. We are ready for a hearing in three days."

Doran: "So noted."

Kalish: "They are asking for an adjournment because we have not given them reports which they very well know can't be obtained in three days."

Doran: "You may be right."

The usual bickering follows over whether the respondents should be remanded until a trial date in early August. Youngman Green is remanded without protest from his counsel, who asks Probation to get in touch with the New Mexico authorities "to find out what they have on him, okay?" Larabee suggests shelter care for Xavier Morales, to which Dorothy Bass replies, "To send this youngster to a shelter is like paroling him out into the streets."

Larabee: "Well, your honor, it is my feeling that there is insufficient evidence before the Court to justify a remand for detention care."

Doran: "I see."

Larabee: "Xavier will assure you that he won't get into any more trouble and that he will return on the adjourned date."

Doran: "Do you guarantee his word?"

Larabee: "Your honor can speak to Xavier."

Doran: "I am asking *you.*"

Larabee: "I can't guarantee another person's word. You know I can't do it."

Doran: "Why do you expect me to take his word, if you won't?"

Against such sophistry Larabee has no defense. Rather than let her client stew for another twelve days in Spofford, she moves for an immediate probable cause hearing, hoping she can show that Kalish's witnesses have misidentified Xavier, who claims not to have been present at the rape scene. Kalish, still irritated, fights back: he is ready for a full hearing, he says, but *not* for an abbreviated probable cause hearing. None of the law guardians has ever heard a prosecutor claim to be ready for the full-dress affair but not for the rehearsal, yet Judge Doran immediately agrees to a three-day postponement—perhaps because, as the law guardians later agree, he doesn't like to hear trials, or perhaps because he wants to punish Larabee for capping her successful appeal for an adjournment with yet another motion; he knows Larabee will feel guilty about Xavier's time in Spofford.

Larabee asks what the "special circumstances" are that justify postponing a probable cause hearing.

Doran: "Surprise, counselor." He means Larabee has surprised

Kalish by her request for probable cause. "I don't buy ploys. If that is the way you want to play the game, you can spend a weekend in Special II"—an appeals court—"and get him out on a writ if you want to."

Afterward, Larabee is thoroughly angry—at both Kalish, "who shall hereafter be known as 'Snake-in-the-Grass,' " and Doran, whose spiteful invitation to her to file a writ she is at first inclined to accept. "We have to let them know we'll hit them with a writ every time." She is concerned about how she will appear on the record, however —"Did I speak in complete sentences?"—and when she sees the minutes decides to let the judge's invitation slide.

On July 26, probable cause day, Bob Kalish is the first to arrive in Part IV. A man who likes his work and would prefer a larger audience than a locked courtroom can afford, he seems edgy, eager for the scrap to come. Of Susan Larabee he says: "She's a maniac. Yelling. She should learn to keep quiet sometimes." As Larabee enters on the heels of these words, he adds: "I'm showing no mercy this time."

"As opposed to last time," Larabee sniffs and then proceeds elaborately to ignore him.

Probation's confidence that it could come up with some background on Youngman Green has proved vain; he remains as amorphous as before. Xavier Morales's remarkable hair today is coiled in ten short braids secured by rubber bands; his red plaid trousers, on loan from Spofford, are more than a foot too long and rolled several times at the ankles.

Kalish begins by calling the complainant. Zachary Raines is sixteen: very dark, handsome, with delicate features and an effeminate bearing. Now that the court's attention is for the first time focused on this boy who claims to have been raped, there is a flurry of whispers at the defense table. Oswald Dimond asks Youngman: "Did he have a reputation for being a homosexual?" Both Youngman and Xavier agree that he did.

Speaking so softly that Dimond must many times call for a repetition of his testimony, Zachary works his way through his dismal narrative. On the night of July 18 to 19, his first night at Covenant

House, he was attacked by several boys on a stairway, beaten, and forced to commit oral sex with "them two right there." The encounter, which roamed from a common room to a stairway to a tiny bathroom crowded with perhaps ten boys, lasted for thirty or forty minutes before the appearance of a counselor brought it to a hurried close. Throughout this time, Zachary says, he was screaming and crying.

At first, Kalish has difficulty phrasing his questions properly—he asks leading questions and elicits testimony that fails to distinguish between the two respondents—but as Larabee takes over the cross-examination he recovers, peppering the record with his own objections: "Beyond the scope of this hearing!" "Miss Larabee is attempting to obtain the names of all the witnesses and we are concerned only with these two respondents!"

Larabee: "What were they wearing?"

Kalish: "Objection!"

Doran: "Sustained."

Larabee: "I really need to know!" And she does, if she's going to suggest that Zachary has improperly identified his tormentors, but Doran won't yield her an inch.

Larabee: "What was the counselor's name?"

Kalish: "Objection! Probable cause is not for discovery."

Doran: "Sustained."

Nor is she supported by her co-counsel for the defense: "Your honor, I object to this inquiry going beyond probable cause."

Kalish (grinning): "I join in Mr. Dimond's objection."

"Maybe," suggests one of Larabee's colleagues later, "that's the way old lawyers behave." "None of *us,*" Larabee snaps back, "is *ever* going to be as old as Oswald Dimond."

After a lot of this sparring, Larabee moves for dismissal. "The complainant didn't kick or fight back when this allegedly happened," she says, thus hinting to Doran that what he has before him is a homosexual in a mood for revenge after a consensual act. "There has been no corroborative testimony offered, although nine or ten boys were there. There has been no medical testimony to support the third-degree assault charge in the petition. There has been no showing that he knew Xavier. Part of the time he was in the dark. Part of the

time he was face down. Most of the time he was crying and upset."
Dimond, seemingly disinclined to muster an argument, simply says
that no probable cause has been established against his client.

Nevertheless, Doran finds against them both and sets a trial date
for August 3. By that time he will have kicked the dust of Manhattan
from his heels, and the case will be heard in Part IV by Judge Stanley
Gartenstein.

Testy as Doran has been in this case, his replacement by Gartenstein
does not move Larabee to joy. The law guardians think Gartenstein
arrogant, obnoxious, and intelligent. If Doran's contempt for the
lawyers who prance before him is wintry, Gartenstein's ranges unpre-
dictably from tart criticism to angry bullying; he is fond of citing
codes and acts which he urges hapless attorneys to read. "You can't
follow his switches in moods," Rob Levy says. "Yesterday he cited
a section of the Family Court Act that doesn't exist. He taunts new
lawyers, trying to work them into untenable positions, and then ridi-
cules them." Gartenstein is a former rabbi; he has written a novel, as
yet unpublished; he can, when he wishes, exude considerable charm.
He likes to tell a story of how, as a young man, he worked in a Domino
Sugar warehouse, swinging 240-pound bags on a hook. "You had to
learn very quickly to get the hook out of the bag before it took you
along with it. If you got the rhythm just right—get the hook in, swing,
get the hook out—you didn't need any muscle at all." In this way, he
runs his courtroom: no waste motion allowed, particularly from attorneys who are sometimes too slow or too uninformed to make objections. Gartenstein makes them before the lawyers have even tensed
their leg muscles to rise: "Objection sustained." *What* objection? If
asked, Gartenstein will explain. Hook in, swing, hook out, and the
case has been disposed of, somehow.

On the morning of August 3, proceedings begin with Gartenstein's
noting that Judge Doran has assigned the court clerk as Youngman
Green's guardian *ad litem,* which prompts Oswald Dimond to a spate
of further prejudicial remarks about his client. "I sense somewhere
there's got to be a parent. The boy is reluctant to reveal addresses."
Susan Larabee smiles wanly. Youngman whispers something to
Xavier Morales.

Gartenstein: "Will defense counsel remind their clients that they are in a courtroom. I don't insist on formality, I don't insist on respondents standing. But will you please give them a short lecture on courtroom discipline."

The tone being thus established, Bob Kalish draws once again from Zachary Raines the story of his humiliation that he told Judge Doran. At 12:30 A.M. on July 19, he says, he was asleep in his third-floor bedroom in Covenant House when "one of the twins" woke him to say there would be "a meeting" downstairs in fifteen minutes. "I got up and went downstairs. I was jumped."

Larabee: "Objection."

Gartenstein: "Sustained."

Zachary: "One of the twins grabbed me by the neck."

Some tedious back-and-forth follows: Where did you go? What floor are you talking about? Zachary refers only to nameless boys— a lot of "theys" and "thems."

Gartenstein: "Mr. Kalish, if you think you are scoring points by vague identifications, I certainly hope you're going to get to the core and identify one of these respondents sooner or later. You're in a criminal trial, Mr. Kalish, and I expect you to move expeditiously."

Kalish: "Zachary, do you see any of the persons who were in the lounge area on the night of July 19?"

Gartenstein: "I don't see conspiracy alleged in this petition. Do you want to get to specific acts that these respondents are alleged to have committed?"

Kalish: "I can't lead the witness. . . ."

Gartenstein: "I'm going to give you some leeway, counselor, but obviously it's not going to be very much."

Kalish: "Specifically, Zachary, what was done to you in the lounge area?"

Zachary: "I was beaten and stomped, grabbed by the hair."

Kalish: "What, if anything, did you do while you were beaten?"

Zachary: "I was, er, crying."

Kalish: "What, if anything, happened after that?"

Zachary: "I was drug to the stairway."

Dimond: "I don't understand. Is that a misuse of 'dragged'? Or does he mean he was drugged?"

Zachary: "I was drug by the hair."

Larabee: "Your Honor, I object to the use of the word 'stomped.' I don't know what it means."

Gartenstein: "I know what 'stomped' means, counselor. How long have you been in Family Court?"

Larabee: "Obviously not as long as you."

Kalish: "Zachary, while you were being stomped and kicked, what, if anything, did you do?"

Zachary: "I was screaming: 'Stop it!' "

Kalish: "What, if anything, then happened?"

Zachary: "Youngman said to me, 'The mothafucka bit my hand, now I'm gonna kick his ass.' He hit me in the face and my glasses popped off. Youngman step on my glasses. Then they all started hitting me. Stomping me. Then Xavier took over and started hitting my head and saying, 'You're gonna suck my dick now.' "

Kalish: "Where were you located in the stairway at this time?"

Zachary: "On the landing."

Kalish: "What, if anything, did Xavier do?"

Zachary: "He made me suck his penis. He pulled it out and kept putting it in my face. He kept pushing my face until I opened my mouth."

Kalish: "Did he put his penis in your mouth?"

Zachary: "Yes."

Larabee: "Objection. Counsel is leading."

Gartenstein: "Overruled."

Kalish: "Now, Zachary, how long did that last?"

Zachary: "About five minutes."

Kalish: "Now, while Xavier had his penis in your mouth, was anyone else there?"

Zachary: "Yes. Him," pointing to Youngman Green. "The twins. And J.C. One of the twins suggested to take me upstairs. Youngman pulled me by the hair. The other dudes were standin' around and started hittin' me. They said, 'Let's take him in the bathroom.' They still hittin' me there. He, Xavier, said, 'Open your mouth,' and then he took out his penis. I was sittin' on the toilet. I sucked his penis. One of the twins suggested I suck their penises in turn and that someone stick his penis in my rear. Youngman said he would stick his penis in. They tole me to get up and take off my pants. One had ripped my pants. One of the twins stuck his penis in my mouth, Xavier push him away and say, 'You'll get your turn.' J.C. stuck a clothes hanger up my rear. Xavier say, 'Don't do that, just stick him.' Youngman say, 'I'll do that.' Xavier, he had his penis in my mouth. I felt something come out."

Dimond: "Your honor, I can't hear. . . ."

Zachary: "He urined in my mouth. He say, 'Don' worry, I didn't come. I just peed.' "

Kalish: "And what happened after that?"

Zachary: "Then the counselor come upstairs."

As Susan Larabee rises for her cross-examination, so does Judge Gartenstein; he walks to a corner of the bench, folds his arms across his chest and glares at Zachary. Larabee runs through a sequence of routine questions: his age, height, weight, how much time did he spend on the stairwell, where were the doors. "Isn't it true that some of the boys on the stairwell weren't doing anything?"

Zachary: "Um, yes."

Larabee: "How many boys were on the stairwell?"

Gartenstein: "Miss Larabee, a point of instruction, from one lawyer to another. When you've brought out a discrepancy in testimony, it's probably the worst tactic a lawyer can use to ask for an explanation. Leave that to your adversary. No, you've asked it already." To Zachary: "Go ahead."

Zachary: "Five or six, not counting me."

Larabee: "Now, Zachary, you didn't hit or kick anyone, did you?"

Gartenstein: "Counselor, don't you think you ought to ask what he thought he was doing going to a meeting on the first floor at 12:45 in the morning?"

Larabee, who is no novice, could do without all this instruction and advice, but court decorum provides her no means to decline it. Besides, she doesn't want to ask Gartenstein's question because she doesn't want to hear the answer. Judge Gartenstein's priorities are not hers.

Larabee: "I'm not finished. How many boys were in the bathroom?"

Zachary: "Seven."

Larabee: "Isn't it true that you testified last week there were ten boys in the stairwell?"

Zachary: "Yes."

Larabee: "Today you say five or six. And didn't you testify there were ten in the bathroom?"

Zachary: "Yes."

Larabee: "Now you say six or seven. Well, which? Were you mistaken before?"

Zachary succumbs to confusion, and Larabee sits down. Oswald Dimond, true to form, says, "I have no questions, your honor." Gartenstein, however, does. During a break, he had said to the assembled counsel that Zachary "is as queer as a three-dollar bill"; the question now is to discover how his aberration came about. "How did you get into Covenant House?"

Zachary: "I come from Detroit, I was upset at things there, to live with my sister. Her apartment was too small."

Gartenstein: "In other words, you didn't get along with your sister?"

Zachary: "Yes. I couldn't stay there and see her do things to herself." He went to a place called The Door for counseling. The Door sent him to an agency called Under 21—"a kind of hangout, you look at TV"—and after three days he was sent to Covenant House.

Gartenstein: "Have you ever before gone to a meeting at one in the morning?"

Zachary: "No."

The next of Kalish's witnesses, Avery Willets, is fifteen and nearly monosyllabic; he testifies by grunting. "Some kid" had said to him, "Let's jump this dude," but he, Avery, had nothing to do with what followed. "This kid had cut the light. I was in the room when they beat up on Zachary. He couldn't help himself. He just stood there and let them hit. They were provoking the dude because he bit this guy's finger. I tried to get into the bathroom but they wouldn't let me in. I kicked in the door. I saw Xavier had Zachary sucking his penis. I left."

Larabee: "Did you hit Zachary at all? Did you touch him in any way?"

Avery: "No."

Larabee: "You didn't see anyone get bitten?"

Avery: "No. I heard the scream of a guy gettin' bit: 'I got bit!' "

Dimond: "Did you know why Zachary was awakened?"

Avery: "Yes."

Larabee: "Objection!"

Gartenstein: "You can't object. If Mr. Dimond brings forth information prejudicial to his client, it's his right to do so."

During the lunch break, Judge Gartenstein speaks to counsel about Zachary's long fingernails. "What *is* this horseshit?" he asks Bob Kalish. Oswald Dimond says privately to Susan Larabee: "The complaining witness has a problem. This court won't solve it. The behavior of these kids isn't going to be changed. What are we doing here?" His client's arms, he says, are scarred. "Youngman says they come from fighting with a knife. Some choice over drugs!" When the parties assemble for the afternoon session, the look that Youngman gives Dimond as he enters cannot be one of trust. Zachary, oblivious to everyone else, has been reading a paperback novel: Irwin Shaw's *Rich Man, Poor Man.*

The next witness, Benjamin Arroyo, was Zachary's roommate in Covenant House. His story is roughly similar to those preceding, with an important exception: he testifies that Zachary did not leave his room prior to going down for the 1:00 A.M. "meeting"; Zachary had said that he did. Larabee thinks Zachary's version may suggest to the judge that he had left to set up an after-lights homosexual encounter. She is furious when Dimond, on cross-examination, tries to get Benjamin to reconsider this point.

Gartenstein (to Dimond): "Counselor, you're doing the same thing that I admonished your co-counsel for. When you have a discrepancy on the record, leave it to your adversary to straighten it out. If you want to go on, go on. You've opened the door. Answer the question, please."

It is doubtful that Dimond understands what all this has been about. The question is never answered because Dimond changes course, immediately further jeopardizing his client by his determination to reinforce Zachary's claim that he was tricked from his room.

Dimond: "You heard him say there was going to be a meeting?"

Larabee: "Objection, your honor!"

Throughout Dimond's cross-examination, Gartenstein has rolled

his eyes and clutched at his head. "I can't stop your adversary"—
Gartenstein uses the word advisedly to Larabee—"from going along
this line. It may be damaging to you. It may be damaging to his client.
However, it *is* admissible and I can't stop him." Still, as Gartenstein
has reminded them, "I'm not a jury. My passions are not inflamed by
what a witness says."

Larabee doesn't doubt that by now Gartenstein has sorted the
incident out to suit himself—"You'll win on homophobia," a colleague tells her. After inconclusive testimony from the counselor, who
claims he never heard the forty minutes of shouting, screaming and
bottle-breaking but intervened in the course of a routine check, and
after Oswald Dimond tries to persuade his client to take the stand
(Larabee signals Youngman with her eyes: No! No!), she moves for
dismissal.

"Your honor, at this time I would move, as to the respondent
Xavier Morales, to dismiss all three charges on the petition for the
petitioner's failure to put forth a prima facie case. As to the charge
of third-degree assault, which is section 120.00 of the Penal Law, that
section states that the petitioner"—she reads from the text—" 'must
put forth prima facie evidence that a person is guilty of assault in the
third degree when with intent to cause physical injury to another
person he causes such injury to that person or to a third person.'
Referring back to the definition section of the Penal Law, Article 10,
I find that physical injury means 'impairment of physical condition
or substantial pain.' There is absolutely no evidence in the record that
this petitioner sustained any physical injury and in fact he has not
testified himself that he has suffered substantial pain. More than just
a mere scratch. There were no hospital or medical records of any kind
introduced to substantiate that charge.

"Now as to the charge of sexual abuse in the first degree, also
sodomy in the first degree, both sections of Penal Law require forceful
compulsion, and I would argue that the petitioner has failed to put
forth a prima facie case as far as forcible compulsion, as defined in
Article 130, section 8. It means 'physical force that overcomes earnest
resistance or a threat, expressed or implied, that places a person in fear
of immediate death or of serious physical injury to himself or another
person, or in fear that he or another person will immediately be

kidnapped.' In forceful compulsion, earnest resistance is required to be shown. It's got to be something more than passive. It's got to be active. Both the petitioner and the witnesses have testified that he did not so resist."

Gartenstein: "What do you do with the testimony about his tears?"

Larabee: "That's open to interpretation. People cry for many different reasons. As to whether the testimony offered by the petitioner and witnesses is credible, I would suggest to the court that they are not. Their testimony was filled with inconsistencies. One thing I think is extremely important is that Zachary never mentioned anyone putting an unbent hanger in his anus. One of the other witnesses mentioned it. Your honor is certainly aware of the complaining witness's attention to detail, and it strains the imagination—"

Gartenstein: "Counselor, let me stop you right there. There is testimony from the petitioner."

Checked, Larabee presses on: Zachary claimed to have gone downstairs after he claimed to have gone to sleep. "I suggest that this is incredible. The counselor testified that he came upon the incident not as a result of forty minutes of screaming, but merely through a routine check. Yet his office is on the first floor, where much of the action, if I may phrase it that way, occurred."

Oswald Dimond says simply: "The testimony is so woefully weak, especially in regard to my client."

For the next ten minutes, Gartenstein silently writes his "endorsement"—his decision—in a bold hand on the files of both Xavier and Youngman. The endorsements are the same:

> After hearing on the merits the court finds that the charges of sexual abuse and sodomy, both contingent upon forcible compulsion, have not been sustained either as charged or the lesser degree. The court finds that the CW [Complaining Witness] embarked on a course of action at the very first point of the incident alleged from which it could and reasonably is inferred that his participation in deviate acts was consensual or could reasonably be foreseen under the circumstances. His agreement to accompany an alleged uncharged co-perpetrator to a purported meeting at almost 1:00 A.M. cannot be viewed in any other

way other than to impart knowledge to him that events of this type would follow. The court holds that a course of conduct by which it may be inferred that voluntary sexual participation took place cannot be abandoned by one of the participants when matters get out of hand and that compulsion cannot follow on these facts. Further, the testimony of CW was replete with inconsistencies wherein it is possible to & the court does in fact discount his testimony as to the sexual acts. This does not obscure the fact that testimony as to the assault was clear, lucid and with sufficient specificity not to be shaken on cross-examination. Accordingly, the charge of Assault 3, PL 120.00 is sustained beyond a reasonable doubt and a finding made accordingly.

Inasmuch as a designated felony has not been established, the Clerk is directed to strike out all reference to a designated felony and to have the case re-assigned to an all-purpose part.

I&R ordered.

RC [Recall] 8/12/77 Part 5

Stanley Gartenstein.

Larabee now makes the law guardian's traditional plea for remand to some place other than Spofford while awaiting disposition. Xavier has been at Spofford since June 21; she suggests shelter care. She reads letters from Xavier's teachers at Spofford attesting to his progress.

Gartenstein: "This shows the laudatory effects of remand."

Larabee: "No. It doesn't."

But she loses: Xavier has too many petitions against him; Youngman has no family. "You're all piss and vinegar," Gartenstein tells her after the court reporter has packed up his machine.

Larabee thinks the verdict crazy. "Somewhere along the line things got out of hand. But can you call that rape? The case I gave him involved a woman who took off her clothes and got in bed naked with a man, then started kissing him. Later, he initiated sexual intercourse. Can you call that a rape? But I don't see how he could have found Assault 3. Assault 3 requires substantial pain or serious physical injury. There was nothing on the hospital reports." She thinks, too, that the Covenant House counselor lied: "What does he *mean,* 'routine investigation,' when the kids have been throwing things at his door all evening? He testified he saw Xavier zipping up his pants when Xavier had been wearing shorts without a zipper."

Bob Kalish, going to the elevator, is equally indignant. "He wouldn't agree with me on anything today. That decision had no foundation in law! Their inconsistencies is what made them credible! I was about to dismiss the Assault Three charge."

Youngman Green's disposition occurs first, on August 12. The judge and Oswald Dimond discuss whether there is a way to get Youngman fingerprinted for identification. There isn't; it's illegal, and Youngman, who has no wish to be identified, is resisting. Still, judge and defending attorney debate the ways and means. Carol Sherman, the assistant attorney-in-charge of Legal Aid lawyers in Manhattan, is covering the Part today and is appalled at what she hears. She makes an objection, but there's nothing she can do because Legal Aid is not involved in Youngman's case. Briefly, she wonders whether Legal Aid cannot in some way take the case over—but it is too late.

Twelve days later, by some maneuver, Youngman is fingerprinted. He comes out clean; no identification can be made. He is put into a group home and, on his first night there, disappears.

Xavier Morales's disposition, called the same day in a different Part, must be postponed because his mother continues to refuse to appear. She has told the court she won't come, and hasn't attended Probation meetings either. Meanwhile, Xavier has received a certificate at Spofford for excellence in math, which he gave to his mother. Mrs. Morales has told Susan Larabee that she wants her son sent to jail for good this time; she even has a specific jail in mind—"a deteriorating pile," says Larabee.

The court liaison officer observes that "a good report from Spofford is no reason to remove him from Spofford." Two agencies have rejected this boy, she says; the Division for Youth hasn't had his file long enough to place him.

Judge Aileen Schwartz, reluctant to send anybody away for a long term without a parent present, decides to try the mother one more time. A great sound of handcuffs rattling can be heard as a court officer prepares to lead Xavier away. "I thought they were coming after him with a ball and chain," says the court liaison officer.

On the morning of August 23, Mrs. Morales still has not appeared, but toward noon she is reached by telephone and promises to come in that afternoon. Judge Schwartz is pleased. Because the mother is opposing the proposed placement of her son in a group home, which is what Probation recommends, the court's action would be reversible, even though the mother wants something stiffer, more unpleasant, for her boy.

The disposition proceeds quickly. Probation recommends "Placement in Title II, DFY." Susan Larabee is tied up with another hearing, so Carol Sherman stands in for her and agrees: "We feel this is appropriate. MHS"—Mental Health Services—"recommended long-term placement. This facility offers psychotherapy on a daily basis and will keep him as long as necessary."

Judge Schwartz: "Mrs. Morales, I'm going to ask your opinion on this matter. I have visited these places. They are good; they are pleasant. This one has special services for psychotherapy. It's a place where he won't be transferred about. There's a special program for Spanish-speaking youngsters. There's a reading program. I'm also impressed that this is the place your son wants to go to. He will have to be there a long period of time."

Mrs. Morales consents.

Judge Schwartz: "I never do anything I don't think is right. If you or your son have a problem, please get in touch with the Legal Aid Society."

Unedifying as the course of the Morales-Green case may be, it is significant to the extent that it suggests the terrifying consequences of confinement in an institution established with public funds for the protection and rehabilitation of the young. These cases, and worse, are so common that the Legal Aid Society finds itself constantly suing the city or the state to have laws concerning the confinement of children

changed or institutions closed down. Most of this expensive and exhausting work is conducted by the Juvenile Rights Division's Special
Litigation Unit.

In the fall of 1977, Michael J. Dale, head of the unit, reflected on
his critics. "Some people look at Special Litigation as academic law
practice, a steppingstone to somewhere. Other people look at it as an
ivory-tower situation where you have no idea what's going on in the
real world, the pits, the blood-and-guts aspect of representing kids.

"It's not necessarily so. Take *Daratsakis* v. *Smith*—that's J. Henry
Smith, head of the city's Welfare Department. It was a very important
suit, the quickest, most successful suit we've had. It involved a place
called Children's Center, the last remaining temporary shelter, a place
for kids who haven't committed offenses. It's a beautiful old building
at Fifth and 103rd Street that had been donated by some wealthy
family. This facility has a long and sordid history. A year ago January
I started getting reports about kids getting beaten up, about rapes,
about homosexual attacks, liquor and drugs being used extensively in
the facility, about beatings by staff. We also found the authorities
there bringing kids from that facility into Family Court and charging
them with delinquency. So the person charged with the care of these
kids said, 'Kid A beat up Kid B.' Our response was, 'Well, why didn't
you stop it? That's your job. This is supposed to be a caring, kind
environment for these kids.'

"Well, the horror stories went on and on. It really was bad. In
January there were approximately 150 kids there and I was visiting
almost daily. I filed a lawsuit alleging that conditions in this place
constituted cruel and unusual treatment. It was ghastly. The girl, Joan
Daratsakis, on whose behalf I filed the suit, had attempted to commit
suicide on a couple of occasions there. Another girl had attempted to
rape her. They had taken a broom handle and a girl was attempting
to put it into her. There were allegations that staff members knew this
and didn't do anything to correct it. This kid was being thoroughly
destroyed. She could have been killed. During the period I was investigating, she was taken to Bellevue Hospital on two separate occasions:
she had reacted psychotically to what was happening to her. She was
fifteen. She was from the city, had been in foster care for a long time,
had been taken away from her foster parents because she didn't get

on with them, and was placed here, *temporarily.* She'd been there, when I met her, two months. In fact, she was still there when I brought the lawsuit: seven months.

"So we filed the suit in late June, early July, 1976. There were over a hundred kids involved. By the time the case came on to be heard for a preliminary injunction to close it, seven days later, seventy-five kids had been removed. The judge heard testimony and we entered into a settlement. Because of the horrors, the case made the papers. We would close the place in one year. And during that time, they would allow no more than fifty kids in the facility. There was room for three hundred and fifty. Where there was more than one child in any location, there would have to be a staff member there. After all, there were three hundred and fifty *staff* for fifty children. It cost two hundred dollars a day to keep a child there. The judge was appalled. He couldn't believe what was being said to him. His comment was, 'You can house them at the Waldorf for that amount.' We also got them to make cosmetic changes in the facilities: small things, like shower curtains for the girls. There was no privacy for them and, because they were in adolescence, it created sexual tension.

"This place had been open for over twenty years, and it had never worked. There were always problems. You had a staff that was not responsive to these children's needs. We felt there was no way you could correct conditions there. Our view was to set up some small facilities—ten, fifteen, twenty—around the city. In a similar case the judge had made the same point. He said there's too much history, too much tradition in the bricks of this building, to allow it to continue as a place to house children.

"They closed it this past March. We're very pleased about the outcome. The question now is, what are the *other* facilities like? Sometimes you feel you're spending your life chasing after bad agencies, and to an extent that's true, but somebody's got to protect the kids from the conditions in those places.

"As for that unresponsive staff who were not fit to take care of kids, they're still around. They found jobs for them—in other agencies, I presume."

· · ·

The brutalization of children in these institutions achieves an exquisite refinement when the city's Department of Social Services refuses to help a child and is supported in its dereliction by the Family Court. DSS is charged by law with the responsibility "for the welfare of children who are in need of public assistance and care, support and protection," but the agencies to which it has the power to send such children are not obliged to take them. To run through the Bureau of Child Welfare's list of authorized residences is to stumble in a thicket of restrictions: most seem to want Catholic children with a minimum IQ of 70 and cite numerous disqualifying factors. St. Dominic's Home in Blauvelt, New York, is typical in its definitions of those it will not accept: "Children who are autistic, psychotic, chronic fire setters, absconders, those with severe pathology such as extreme promiscuity"—this in a home that takes children only up to the age of thirteen —"or drug addiction, and physically handicapped (e.g., blindness, grave cardiac or orthopedic children [sic] who cannot climb stairs) are not considered." Such prohibitions make sense if one cares primarily for order and decorum, but they exclude many of the city's children who most desperately need help.

In 1974, Michael Dale became involved with such a child—a boy whose problems, although by no means unique, are about as severe as Legal Aid has had to deal with. When he was eleven, José Gomez either fell or was pushed from the sixth-floor roof of his home. "He had sustained very serious brain damage, had been operated on," Dale recollects. "The result was aphasia: he walked with a limp, face partially paralyzed, a speech impediment, visual problems, lost certain motor skills and part of his ability to think." His IQ tested at 47. When he was thirteen, his parents abandoned him. A neglect petition was filed and José was sent "temporarily" to the Jennings Hall School for Boys in Brooklyn. "So now he was in this facility. Legal Aid had represented him in the neglect charge against his parents, so one day his lawyer came to me and said, 'Look, this kid has been in this temporary shelter for over a year and I can't get BCW to find a residential facility to care for him.'

"I represented this kid for two and a half years. Only at the end of this time was I able to force the city to find a place for him. I appeared in court on his behalf on approximately thirty-six occasions before eighteen different judges—all the way to the highest court, the Court of Appeals."

What had happened in the interim was that Dale had written to Elizabeth Beine, director of BCW, pointing out that the boy was long overdue for placement in an appropriate facility. He received no reply. He filed suit in New York State's Supreme Court against her and the commissioner for social services, James R. Dumpson. Life was not proceeding as it should for José Gomez, Dale charged: at Jennings Hall the boy had been subjected to ridicule for his impediments, to beatings, to cigarette burns, lacerations and homosexual attacks. This was not the kind of treatment the state had in mind when it wrote the law, and besides, José had been illegally detained at a "temporary" home. José must now be either properly placed or returned home: "Upon information and belief, when José entered the school covered with snow, he told the school staff, 'God, I want to die . . . God, God, God help me . . . I don't want to be here anymore.' "

Helene Holmes, representing the commissioner for social services, insisted that her client "has not been sleeping away his responsibilities," but actively trying to place the child with agencies that would have none of him. Dale pointed out that the agencies named by Holmes would never have taken him: they catered only to younger children, or children with higher IQs.

"The Family Court judge who heard it felt that they were doing the best they could to find a place for the kid. He was concerned, but he was running for the state Supreme Court and he didn't want to stick his neck out. I had innumerable run-ins with BCW, who accused me of all sorts of things: trying to make a name for myself with this case and so on. The Appellate Division had no time for the case. Their attitude was that it ought to stay in Family Court.

"The Family Court judge sat on the case for six months. I finally called up and threatened his law clerk. I said I was going to sue the judge. Right after that, I got a decision, and of course it was against us. Unbelievable. Then it went before the Court of Appeals. They all sat there, asked one question and denied my appeal. We had to go back to Family Court, which wasn't doing anything. In time, Judge Breitel, the chief judge in the state, wanted to know why we hadn't found a facility. I had given them a list of thirty-five facilities; BCW had called up two of them. Then Breitel ordered the commissioner to find a place for this kid forthwith, or else the court would hold him in contempt of court. They would not rule on the other issue, which was what court do you go to to try to get a resolution of this problem.

"That was in November. It was not till February that they found a place for this kid, in Florida. Out-of-state placement of kids is now the subject of a lawsuit brought by the NYCLU. It's adequate, not great. We've visited him there. He's now seventeen.

"Up to that point no other judge had shown *indignation*. We've convinced the Family Court judges to hear these things, but only by doing them over and over again before them.

"The question that's always raised is that we spend a hell of a lot of time litigating this stuff, and spending a good deal of money, and is the result acceptable in the light of time and energy? My feeling is that it's one of the tools that lawyers representing kids have to use. Just as you represent the kid today in court, there's got to be somebody in your organization that's filing the lawsuits that say: 'Hey! Stop this practice! Stop this policy!' This is just one of the tools that's used to protect kids. Up until recently, nobody's been doing it."

Those familiar with Family Court are well aware that a child who appears on one kind of petition will presently be brought in on another. The line between a neglected child and a PINS is so tenuous that a child alleged to be a PINS by his parent may in fact be a neglect in disguise: the easiest way to dump a child you can't or won't care for is to insist that he's ungovernable. The line between a PINS and a delinquent is equally vague and was once defined as the difference between a child brought into court by a parent and one brought in by the police. What is certain is that one kind of appearance tends to lead to another and that the removal of a child from his family is (except in cases where his survival is concerned) detrimental to his welfare.

Any law guardian can pull from his file a sheet like the one that follows, which shows an inexorable progress from neglect to delinquency:

CHRISTOPHER DEVLIN

AGE (APPROXIMATE)   CURRICULUM VITAE

Before birth   Father deserts mother after "casual affair"—father was pusher and addict.

3 months   Mother gives child to grandmother.

3 years   Neglect case in Brooklyn; Christopher given to mother on trial basis.

4 years   Mother turns herself into Bellevue. Feels guilty about severe beatings she is giving to Christopher and is afraid of what she may do—mother has been jailed previously for prostitution. Christopher returns to grandmother.

6 years   Grandmother stabbed to death by uncle. Christopher watches from next room. Christopher sits with body all day. Uncle returns, pretends to find body, calls cops. Christopher says nothing. Great-grandmother comes. Christopher tells her—cops arrest and jail uncle. Christopher goes to great-grandmother.

1 month later   Great-grandmother dies of stroke. Christopher goes to aunt and uncle.

7 years   Child runs away, winds up in Children's Center. Says aunt and uncle beat him badly. (Later, aunt abandons all of her own children and uncle drinks himself to death.) Christopher termed "depressed."

9 years   After several spells in Children's Center, Christopher goes to foster home.

12 years   Back to Children's Center. Foster parents "deny his problems."

13 years   To Geller House.

1 month later   To Bellevue, not psychotic. Doctors feel he could be worked with. Has "depressive neurosis."

Later   To Mount Loretto, back to Bellevue

14 years   Phoenix House. Stays a year or so and leaves.

15 years   Juvenile Detention Center (Spofford).

A couple of
months later   To St. Agnes. Inappropriate. Back to Juvenile Center.

16 years   After 8 months of Juvenile Center, to Holy Cross. After 1½ months, sent back to Juvenile Center.

RECORD

1973 PINS   Children's Center PINS—absconding and truancy. Dismissed. (Note: case brought by center, not parent.)

1973 Delinquency   Petty larceny. Dismissed.

1973 Delinquency   Some sort of robbery. Adjusted.

1974 Delinquency   Taking penis out in subway station. Dismissed. (Christopher says he was urinating.)

1975 Delinquency   Stealing wallet. Dismissed.

1975 Delinquency   Stealing watch at knifepoint. Finding: Robbery 3.

I.Q.

Has been as high as 107 Full Scale and 110 Verbal with higher range possible.

Latest testing was 95 performing, 97 verbal, and 90 Full Scale. But, qualified by stating that considering lack of motivation and background, this is a very good achievement and indicates a *much better* potential.

Bright enough to go beyond high school if he receives proper academic tutoring.

It is unlikely that he will, highly salvageable child that he may be. Probably Christopher sees himself already on a kind of invisible track, as did one of the plaintiffs in an important case, *McRedmond* v.

Wilson, in which the Legal Aid Society compelled the state to stop warehousing PINS children, who had committed no crimes, in state training schools with delinquents, who had.

Willie Bosket, eleven years old, had been living with his mother and her other children in Manhattan; his father had been serving a prison sentence in Wisconsin for murder and armed robbery since some time prior to his birth. In 1973, he was adjudicated a PINS, his mother complaining that Willie stayed out late at night and had not been attending school. Willie was sent to the Wiltwyck School for Boys in Yorktown, where he was given psychological tests which described him as "precocious, warm and empathetic." However, said his examiners, "in order to reach his above-average intellectual and creative potential," Willie needed "support from the adults in his life." Willie's stay at Wiltwyck ended in 1974, when Family Court Judge Louis A. Pagnucco ordered him placed in a Title III facility—in other words, a children's jail.

At Brookwood Center, a maximum security institution 115 miles north of his home, Willie was never visited by his family. Whenever he got angry he was confined to his room or to the infirmary. "Plaintiff Bosket does not like Brookwood," Michael Dale wrote in his brief. "He believes he is being introduced to older, more institutionally experienced youths. If he does not do as he is told he believes he will continue to be transferred from institution to institution. On the other hand he is afraid that if he does as he is told he will only learn to live in the institution and will never be capable of returning to and remaining in a family and community setting. He thus views his future as institutional and believes that he will soon graduate to Goshen Annex (a Title III facility for juvenile delinquents) and then enter the adult prison system."

In testimony given before the Temporary State Commission on Child Welfare in September 1976, Charles Schinitsky cited two similar cases. Then he said: "What is perhaps most disturbing about these cases is that they are not unique. Instead, they point out the way the child-care system functions in New York City and State. The lack of a strong public body to oversee and, more especially, to enforce the provision of appropriate care and treatment is a cruel deficiency. This situation is extremely detrimental to the thousands of children who enter the child-care system through their early childhood and adolescent years. It is equally detrimental to the community at large—for it is not only ineffective, but extremely expensive as well. The failure to plan for the care of a child who has entered the system, the failure to provide adequate aftercare services to the home, and the failure of the state and city to require that the public and publicly funded child-care and mental health agencies be both responsible and accountable for these children all lead to the inappropriate and excessive use of the courts. Agencies that are unwilling to deal with the behavioral problems that arise out of their own failure to care for and treat these children turn to the court as a dumping ground. Unfortunately, the court is essentially powerless to compel public and private agencies to provide the necessary care to any and every child coming within its jurisdiction. Consequently, one child waits six months before being placed in a facility; another waits twenty-seven months. In either case, the situation is inexcusable."

Ever since its construction in 1958, the Juvenile Detention Center at Spofford Avenue and Tiffany Street in the south Bronx has been under attack. The eight-story white-brick building sits on a hill surveying four acres remote from any transportation to the rest of the city. Access is controlled by an electrically operated gate and door. Spofford, formerly called Youth House, was originally operated by a private agency; since then proprietorship has fallen successively to Probation, the Department of Social Services and, in 1979, the newly formed Department of Juvenile Justice. It was intended to be a stopping-off place for children in transit to various stations of the juvenile justice cross: children remanded pending hearings, children awaiting acceptance in permanent facilities. In fact, children are incarcerated in Spofford for a variety of reasons: they are picked up at night, or over a weekend when court is not in session; they are held there when no parent will claim them. In 1977, the median length of stay for a child at Spofford was twenty-four days—at a cost to the city of $136 a day. Many had no business being there, having been assigned to nonsecure facilities, or having been, as it sometimes seemed, forgotten by the Division for Youth.

Throughout the years, Spofford has been investigated by various committees and commissions—eleven reports had been filed as early as 1967—many of which have recommended that the institution be closed and replaced by smaller facilities dispersed throughout the city. The most celebrated uproar occurred in 1971 when the Legal Aid Society filed a suit, *Martarella* v. *Kelley,* which exposed in detail the conditions prevailing at Spofford at that time and the catastrophic effects of confining PINS children, accused of no crimes, with confirmed juvenile delinquents.

"Spofford," in the words of the complaint, "has become a jail for children. Incarceration in this maximum security institution is a frightening and dehumanizing experience that creates a serious risk to the plaintiffs' physical, psychological and emotional well-being. . . . The conditions . . . are so shockingly oppressive and degrading that they are an affront to basic human decency; moreover, they are so inimical to their health, safety and welfare that they violate the fundamental constitutional rights of the plaintiffs. . . ."

The complaint cited conditions at Spofford and two other secure centers, now closed: "large water bugs" in the rooms and food supplies; cockroaches; mice; overcrowding; poor ventilation; windows that don't open; sinking buildings; improper insulation so that the buildings were hot in summer, cold in winter; falling plaster; peeling paint; cracked walls and ceilings; leaks in the roof; showers in disrepair; inadequate clothing; bad hygiene—an epidemic of "crabs" in the girls' center, Manida, had forced the closing of a dormitory; lack of psychological, psychiatric and social-worker services; insufficient medical care; the physical abuse and humiliation of children by the counselors, who also sold them drugs; lack of recreation and a library; prohibition of phone calls unless "the favor of a social worker is gained"; homosexuality, both consensual and forced; failure to attend to the children's most urgent needs—in two and a half years, fourteen hundred children with hepatitis were left untreated, and one died of it after lying unattended for seven days; and suicide attempts—"a recurring and serious problem."*

The history of one of the co-plaintiffs in this case (for it was a class-action suit) is typical of what was happening at Spofford. Joe Tyson, fourteen years old, was charged by his mother with truancy in the Brooklyn Family Court. (In New York City, on any given day, sixty thousand children are truant from school.) Found to be a PINS, Joe was remanded to Spofford, where, on his third day, he was ordered by his dorm counselor to do two hundred pushups for talking in the lunch line. After completing twenty, Joe stopped, informing the counselor that a knee injury prevented him from doing more. As he began to stand up, the counselor struck him on the head; he was knocked unconscious when his head hit the floor. He was taken to the infirmary with blood dripping from his ear; there he was found to have a tympanic rupture of the right ear. After twenty days' hospitalization, he was returned to Spofford.

Bad as the brutality at Spofford was, a major thrust of the argument on behalf of the plaintiffs emphasized a more insidious brutalization:

Q: "As far as you saw, Robert [Martarella, age fifteen], were the kids up there for like running away and not going to school treated any differently than kids like you said, who were up there for killing people or shooting up drugs?"

A: "No."

Q: "Were they all pretty much in the same dormitory?"

A: "Yes."

Q: "For instance, did you know anybody up there who was actually there for killing somebody?"

A: "Yes."

Q: "Did you have any conversations with him, or other kids who were up there for committing crimes, about the things that these kids actually did for getting up there?"

A: "Yes. But me and him are good friends."

---

*Suicide attempts are still endemic at Spofford—there were forty-six such between April and September of 1980—but it was not until November 1980 that one succeeded: a 15-year-old boy from the Bronx hanged himself with a sheet which he attached to an air vent in a room in the infirmary, to which he had been assigned because beds were unavailable elsewhere.

Q: "Did these kids actually tell you how they did whatever they did?"

A: "Yes."

Q: "For instance, did you learn anything up there that you didn't know before you went there about crime?"

A: "Yes."

Q: "What type of things was that?"

A: "They tried to teach me how to rob a pocketbook. They tried to teach me how to rob a car."

Q: "Had you ever done any of that stuff before you went up there?"

A: "No."

Q: "For instance, what did they tell you about robbing a pocket-book?"

A: "Swing the lady around, knock her down, just run the other way."

Robert Martarella testified that he was "so mad for getting re-manded" that he would "punch the walls." His counselor wouldn't speak to him about his problems, but his social worker sent him to Spofford's psychiatrist.

Q: "How often did you speak to a psychiatrist when you were there?"

A: "Spoke to him once. He put me on Thorazine."

Q: "Do you know why he put you on Thorazine?"

A: "Yes. He said I was going crazy. He said I was hyperactive."

Q: "Anybody ever tell you you were hyperactive before?"

A: "No."

By way of rebuttal, the defense marched a phalanx of psychiatrists through the witness box, all attesting to the salutary effects of secure detention on the young. From hundreds of pages of testimony, three principal points emerge:

(1) *The children want it.* "This is what the children need, is struc-ture," said one psychiatrist, who went on to suggest that the symbol-ism of substituting a secure jail for an insecure home was not lost upon the kids. "It's as if they finally got at one level what they really wanted. . . . Somebody has finally taken a hand." In this, he was supported by a colleague: "In many instances the security is a relief for the child and, indeed, a protective situation in terms of what I was

saying before, in protecting him from emotional stimulation." A third, on cross-examination, offered a short answer to a long question:

Q: "Would you agree that a child who finds himself in a closed setting where all the doors are locked, doors to each room into which he is told to go were locked, where he has to wear a uniform of blue jeans and a shirt with the name of the institution stamped across it, where he must move through the institution in silent lines, march in silent lines, and where many of his fellow inmates there are there for the commission of crimes, wouldn't you say that that child would consider himself imprisoned and being punished?"

A: "Again, you are implying that all kids react the same way to wearing an insignia or wearing a T-shirt or wearing jeans. You see, many schools ask kids to wear uniforms."

(2) *We psychiatrists need it.* The doctors were all agreed on this point. One said that part of the reason for secure detention "relates to having the children available in a relatively secure situation where one has the opportunity to assess and evaluate the child. . . . The secure situation gives you the opportunity, if you will, to titrate—that is to say, in measured ways allow varying degrees of freedom, or lack of freedom, understand and measure to some extent the child's response to that situation. . . . Without the secure facility we really are hamstrung in terms of being able to make a proper determination about that child." Even the child's anger at his imprisonment benefits the doctors: "It is all grist through the mill, in my opinion, for working with the children."

(3) *Prison is really a good place for kids to be.* "Secure detention per se is not traumatic in itself," said one of the psychiatrists. "I definitely feel that for some of the children secure detention is therapeutic." What it is for the rest of the imprisoned children, no doctor would volunteer. Another declared secure detention to be "a milieu which is healthier than letting them roam the streets finding the people they want or being caught up by people who are looking for them"—which indeed it might be, were not all those people already in Spofford, waiting for the new guy. A third belittled the problem of keeping order: "The kids will, you know, begin to control each other in a particular way to make for a harmonious environment for themselves."

Judge Morris E. Lasker of the Southern District of New York remained unimpressed by so much learned speciousness. A year after hearing the testimony he delivered himself of a seventy-seven-page decision in which he cited "the rapid urbanization of the United States in this century and the heavy influx of the poor to the cities" which have "produced a numerous class of children whose conduct, although not criminal in character or legal designation, results in their incarceration." After reviewing the facts that had been set before him, he based his decision on a narrow legal principle: "When the State, as *parens patriae,* imposes such detention, it can meet the Constitution's requirement of due process and prohibition of cruel and unusual punishment if, and only if, it furnishes adequate treatment." Although the plaintiffs had sued for the removal of PINS from secure detention centers, he would not go so far. The key to the problem was "adequate treatment," which other courts had ruled was the right of those held in long-term noncriminal custody—and adequate treatment was not being offered to PINS. Five months later still, Lasker issued an order defining treatment standards: the qualifications necessary for counselors and social workers at Spofford were upgraded; the children's access to recreation and psychiatrists, and the ratio of social workers to inmates, were spelled out. Lasker's most original stroke, however, was to impose an ombudsman at Spofford, a presence he described in other than human terms: "a continuing mechanism, outside the normal chain of responsibility . . . a capacity for rational persuasiveness."

The embodiment of that abstraction, in September 1977, was Maurice L. Nixon, for two and a half years Spofford's ombudsman and as of that month its executive director. Within a year, after a seventeen-year-old boy and two friends *invaded* Spofford, drew guns on the unarmed counselors and escaped with the boy's fourteen-year-old brother, Nixon would resign, citing the city's frustrating unresponsiveness to the crisis in its juvenile justice system. But that September Nixon was in charge of the peeling palace of Spofford Hill, a place that some people called "the sieve" because 130 kids were escaping from it every year, even though, simply to eat breakfast, the boys were marched through ten or twelve locked doors. Through the suspiciously clean window of the staff dining room one could see on the asphalt outside the shards of last week's window, broken during a successful escape. On a ground-floor wall of this building there is a mural, so crude that it may have been painted by a child, depicting an anguished brown face over which is written, in dramatic lettering, "PRINCIPLES: GUIDANCE, DISCIPLINE, DIRECTION, DIGNITY." Far at the bottom, in small letters, someone has written "Peace."

Maurice Nixon is black, a policeman for seventeen years before he went to Spofford. "My role in the Police Department was an advocate for youngsters. Throughout my years, the youngsters have always been the most vulnerable I know. They have no say in anything that affects them. As they grow older, sixteen or seventeen, they still have no say in the running of the city, or the making of the laws that affect them so vitally. We should be taking a hard look at that. They're very vulnerable people. I've stood in front of other policemen when they were going to hit youngsters, and got flak for that.

"This system, you know, it's a system that feeds on itself. It's a recycling system, and that's all it is. A kid who's a PINS, staying out late, the next time he comes into court, he's a delinquent. Because once he comes into the system and he's put in Spofford or a group home and then he's released to go back home, he's not going to listen to his mother or father. He's told, now you go home and not stay out late anymore, he's not going to pay any attention. That's bullcrap. He goes out and he says, well, you put me away and everything, and he goes out and becomes a delinquent. Then he comes to Spofford and he's in with other kids, you know. When he goes back home, you cannot control him. He's been to jail and he's a big man. So the mother goes to court and gets a warrant on a PINS. It's a vicious circle.

"There used to be pride in having come to Spofford. It used to be a kid would come back to the community, and where you been? Oh, I was in Youth House, it was called then, and I met so-and-so up there. I used to rap with these kids when I was a policeman. They'd say all the things they did in jail. And I'd say, OK, fine, now tell the kids how many times the counselor kicked your ass, how many times you got put in the cold shower. You only tell the good parts, that's not real. Let's do it real. Is Youth House the answer? Is Youth House great? It was a status symbol, now it's not. I think symbols change with the times. Before, years ago, a kid was not so violent, not doing the crimes they do now. So anyone who was put into Spofford was a big person: they played hooky or they stole something from the fruit stand, you know. Now I think the status of crime, the offenses, I hate to say it but it's looked on secondary. Hey, so he killed somebody, he mugged somebody. It's not so bad. I think it's graduated where now Rikers or Elmira is the status symbol. Spofford, you're in Little League. We have kids fourteen, fifteen, who claim they're sixteen just so they can go to Rikers, say, 'Hey! I been to Rikers.' To stop that you got to get into prevention."

During his brief tenure at Spofford, Nixon was much admired by the law guardians. True, Judge Lasker's order had changed little. Spofford's residents, when they weren't punching holes through the screens affixed to the bedroom windows, holes through which they would lower blankets for escape, tried to steal the wads of keys that the counselors had to carry to move from one room to the next. The counselors carried these keys on lanyards, the better to use them as a kind of ball and chain to break open the children's heads. Steve Pokart arranged a counselor's dismissal for this kind of violence and encouraged his client to sue the city. The girls at Spofford remained, in the words of Wilbur Wiley, Nixon's deputy, "harder to deal with than the boys. They are less rational, very much into lesbianism. A male presence they see as a threat. I can have a fight with a boy one day, he will be my friend the next, but the girls are much more moody." Still, under Nixon, there was a sense of an attempt at humane restructuring of a hopeless environment. That he and the three men who succeeded him between September 1978 and July 1979 were finally unable to accomplish very much is due to the failure of the agencies associated with Spofford—Department of Social Services, Division for Youth and the Family Court itself—to provide the necessary managerial support. In the absence of that support the staff ran Spofford to suit itself.

On July 1, 1979, the responsibility for Spofford passed to the city's newly created Department of Juvenile Justice. By the summer of 1980, the department's commissioner, Paul A. Strasburg, had decided that

"Spofford is unsalvageable. If its objective is to do something constructive for a kid who's arrested, then it will never succeed. It's too big ever to be good. The layout is like a jail rather than a child-care center and the security is minimal. The kids are treated as if they're in a cold institution. Since we've taken over, there have been no escapes, but the place still has nothing to do with child care. The public expects something constructive to happen. It never will happen. People have done a lot of soul-searching in the last ten years and every study group has recommended small institutions."

Everyone agrees that to place around the city four or five detention centers, each with a capacity of twenty or thirty children, is preferable to maintaining Spofford, but the problems such a plan poses may prove insuperable. The first is economic: small facilities are very expensive to maintain and will necessarily lack the recreational and educational facilities Spofford affords. The second is political: no one wants such a facility in *his* neighborhood. Why should he? In the summer of 1980, an elderly woman in Westchester, who had gone out of her way to employ the delinquent boys of nearby Lincoln Hall, was beaten, raped and murdered for her trouble. The third problem is bureaucratic: once a city owns a crumbling pile like Spofford, with its large gym and swimming pool, there's not much to be done with it except to use it.

Moreover, Spofford is *needed.* Its population rises. In November 1980, the number of children held there peaked at 244, exceeding not only its capacity of 212, but the capabilities of its staff, who were prepared to deal with 180. PINS are no longer held at Spofford, but in April 1980, 100 children who, under the Juvenile Offender Law of 1978, were being tried in the slower adult courts, had been held there six months and more. Forty-two youngsters already adjudicated and placed with the Division for Youth had been held there for up to four months, simply because DFY's facilities are overcrowded.

To make matters worse, Paul Strasburg's problems have been compounded by allegations of abuse, sexual and otherwise, of the children by staff members. In April 1980, four counselors methodically beat four boys, one after another. The Citizens' Committee for Children of New York, founded by Eleanor Roosevelt thirty-five years before, issued an "urgent appeal": "The situation is grave and it is dangerous." They did not mention that Strasburg had had the men arrested and relieved of their duties.

> This facility serves children who, by virtue of racial, ethnic and economic background, already have carried on their young shoulders the heaviest burdens of living in our world. They are now in the care of the City. It is a measure of the humaneness, of the civilization of New York that this moment at Spofford be seized to begin a process of social justice. It is not too late. We must believe it is never too late. Not with children, not with youth.

Vintage liberal rhetoric for sure; no one could disagree. With words like these the first children's court was delivered into Illinois in 1899. And yet to men like Paul Strasburg, who didn't disagree, there might have been in this mural-like image of brown-skinned youngsters shouldering life's burdens something missing—perhaps the trace of the beast that lurks in all men and is often most explicitly evident in the behavior of moist-eyed children. In Spofford, where the counselors are young, an outsider finds it sometimes difficult to distinguish between the keepers and the kept.

Strasburg shrugged. The Citizens' Committee for Children was giving it to him from one end and his staff from the other: his employees, thinking he had gone too far, staged a walkout. Strasburg could not condone the incident, but he could understand it. "In the absence of training or professional background, many of these counselors are thrown back on their own devices. They control kids by intimidation. Sometimes it's subtle intimidation. The kids know they can get hurt. It's one of the few things that keep them in line."

Intimidation and abuse work as well to keep children in line in the city's foster homes as they do in Spofford. That they are so used is perhaps the least understood of the tragedies attending the juvenile justice system. Understandably, no one wants to think about the matter. The irony of the city's assuming custody of an infant, removing him from parental incompetence or abuse, only to expose him to more of the same, or worse, cannot be easily considered. To prevent such consideration, the city—through the Bureau of Child Welfare and its parent agency, the Department of Social Services—has erected elaborate baffles. If BCW learns that a child is being abused by his parents, it investigates; it takes the case to Family Court; if the case is bad enough it may even be publicized in the press. But if BCW suspects abuse in a foster home, the matter is handled differently. The case will not go to court. In fact, unless a particularly alert law guardian is involved, no one will ever hear of it. The foster parent involved was chosen by an agency—the Catholic Home Bureau for Dependent Children, for instance—which in turn was chosen by DSS for custody of the child. The agency, which relies for 90 percent of its income on DSS placements, doesn't want to hear about abuse on the part of foster parents whom they have selected. Because abuse reflects adversely on the agency, some intentionally cover it up, or refuse to investigate. DSS, through a special unit set up for these contingencies, attempts to negotiate with the offenders it does hear about. If negotiations fail, the child is placed elsewhere.

In August of 1965, a two-year-old girl who would become known to the courts as Evelyn Roe was voluntarily placed by her parents in foster care. So were her three sisters. Her mother had been hospitalized, and her father, a laborer, was unable to care for the girls alone. Antonio Roe and his wife are Hispanics with little grasp of English. They were, they said later, promised by the Catholic Home Bureau that their children would be returned to them, which is standard procedure in foster care.

Foster care is not intended to be a permanent condition—the children it embraces are meant to be returned to their families in time or placed for permanent adoption—but there are so many financial incentives for the agencies to keep their wards that the condition does, in fact, often become permanent. In New York State today there are 43,000 children in foster care—24,000 from New York City. Three-quarters of these, like Evelyn and her sisters, have been voluntarily placed; the rest are there by court order. Both the foster parents and their sponsoring agency are paid for the care of these children: about $375 million a year. Half the money comes from the federal government, a quarter from the state, another quarter from the city. In 1977, the average payment was $29 per child per day.

For whatever reason, the Catholic Home Bureau refused to return the Roe children to their parents, on the ground that the girls had been surrendered for adoption. They produced papers, in English, which the Roes had signed but later claimed they could not understand. One girl was adopted, another sent to a Bronx foster home, where she was beaten. Evelyn and her remaining sister were sent to Staten Island, to the home of Nick Sligurney, a former policeman, and his wife, Arlene. Evelyn today remembers Nick Sligurney as "big, tall, heavy. He had muscles. He was ugly." Arlene, the foster mother, "was nice: brown hair; she keeps dyeing her hair." The Sligurney home was "a simple house, middle-class." The Sligurneys' own four children shared two bedrooms on the second floor; Evelyn, her sister and two other foster girls slept in a large attic room.

In 1968, when Evelyn was five years old, her foster father began to beat her in a regular way and to humiliate her by insulting and ridiculing her before other members of the family. Once he cut her with a knife. Before long, he was subjecting Evelyn to sexual abuse —forced fellatio was his usual preference—and by the time she was ten he had begun to rape her. For good measure, he did the same to her sister. After beating and sexually assaulting the girls, he would send them to their attic room for long periods of time. In the words of the complaint that Evelyn's lawyer finally filed with the Southern District of New York, "At all times when Nicholas Sligurney was abusing, battering, unlawfully imprisoning, and/or neglecting plaintiff, he was acting as an agent of defendants Catholic Home Bureau and DSS."

Evelyn spent twelve years in the Sligurney home. Repeatedly she asked to see her parents, but the Catholic Home Bureau, which had terminated her parents' rights in 1975, refused her permission. Nor would the agency tell her where her parents were, though Evelyn knew very well that the agency had their address. For a while, Evelyn hoped she might be adopted, yet her incarceration with the Sligurneys continued. Her sister gave her no support: "She was a tattletale—she would always tell on me." The girls would not talk among themselves about their foster father's behavior: "There was no reason to tell about it. Even the next-door neighbors could hear when we were getting beaten. Mrs. Sligurney had seen it." From time to time, social workers would come to check on her, but seldom did the same worker come twice and no trusting relationship was ever established. "If they wanted to talk to us," Evelyn says, "the Sligurneys were in the other room listening. Mr. Sligurney would say, 'You tell these people that everything's all right.' He threatened that we would be sent away."

Evelyn was so scared by her foster father that she didn't dare tell anyone, not even her friends at the Catholic school, what was going on. "One time when I was being punished I was in my room. I ran away and went to the church. I spoke to some of the people there and they suggested that I talk to the priest. I told Brother Michael about it. He said he would have to talk to my father. Then he said I'd better get home before it got too late. Mr. Sligurney got really steamed up. He was swinging at me, hitting me, pulling my hair. I got two black eyes. He sent me to my room and said, 'Now you can stay up there and rot.' He got around to seeing Brother Michael and convinced him that I was making up stories."

In fact, Nick Sligurney, who could be a charmer when he wished, convinced agency workers that both Evelyn and her sister were promiscuous. "He was supposed to go for psychiatric tests, but he refused. He didn't want the doctors to know nothing. He told the agency I was having intercourse with a lot of boys. I was scared of him, so I made up silly stories. He accused me of going with this man, so I'd say, 'Yeah, I was with so-and-so.' I'd make up a name, just so he'd leave me alone. Every time I'd say no, it was a crack across the face. I spent most of my time in the attic. I think Mr. Sligurney was putting me and my sister in the criminal's place. He used to lock us up as if we were animals. He doesn't like to hear no. He called me a liar, a deceit. He ran me down low in front of the family. He succeeded. He succeeded all the way. They would never talk back to him."

One day, Sligurney announced that he was getting a divorce. "He had all his things on the table. He said, 'Now how would you girls feel if we were divorced?' I said, 'I can't say nothing. It's between the both of you.' Then he took off. He had his girlfriend Kathy"—who was seventeen—"waiting in the car. I had seen her before. Then he left. He told me to be a good girl."

Shortly after, Evelyn "took off." She and her sister bounced around among foster homes they didn't much like. For a while, Evelyn was confined in the St. Cabrini Home, where, according to her complaint in federal court, she "was attacked and beaten by other girls residing at St. Cabrini, and sustained numerous injuries. Despite defendant St. Cabrini's knowledge of these injuries no medical treatment was provided." Meanwhile, the jilted Arlene Sligurney, who had finally discovered her husband in one of his sexual assaults on Evelyn, filed a complaint, but when trial time came she refused to testify. "She was afraid of him," Evelyn says. Because the Catholic Home Bureau continued to refuse to identify her natural parents, Evelyn, age fourteen, struck out on her own. "I just put my foot down. I found two names in the phone book that could have been my father's. I called. My father came down. He was really happy to see me."

What makes Evelyn's case, and her sister's, different from most of the countless unreported cases of foster-home abuse is that they filed suits against everybody in sight: DSS, the Catholic Home Bureau and St. Cabrini, but not Nick Sligurney, who couldn't be found. Community Action for Legal Services undertook the cases, protesting the "huge profits" that accrue to the agencies. "They usually keep at least half of the ten thousand dollars or so in government funds allotted each child," says Carolyn Kubitschek, the lawyer who tried the case. "Their bookkeeping calls this 'administrative expense'—although some agencies haven't been audited for years. A study by New York City Comptroller Harrison Goldin revealed that at least one-third of foster children were held years longer than necessary. The agencies obviously wanted their cut."

Presenting first the case of Evelyn's sister, CALS asked for $2,-500,000 in damages. In Missouri and Pennsylvania, cases were pending that challenged the whole concept of foster care, but CALS decided to go for the money. "This case," said its attorney, Louise Gruner Gans, "strikes at the failure of many agencies, and the resulting damage to children in public care. The agency was irresponsible in its selection of foster parents. It never examined the foster father, although the case record describes him as 'weird.' It never made regular examinations of the foster homes, nor spoke to the children alone. The law forbids corporal punishment of youngsters, yet many agencies tolerate it. These forced adoptions—no judge has the right to review an agency adoption when the parents sign—destroy the constitutional rights of parents."

This argument got her nowhere at all. Tried as a civil rights suit in federal court in June of 1980, the case against the city and St. Cabrini was settled for insignificant amounts and the case against Catholic Home Bureau, from which $750,000 had been sought, was lost. Carolyn Kubitschek objected to Judge Milton Pollack's "prejudicial remarks. In private he implied that she wouldn't have been raped if she didn't want to be, and he told the jury to look at the sexual behavior of the girl."

Frederick Magovern, attorney for the Catholic Home Bureau, pleads pity for "poor Catholic Home Bureau, over a hundred years of placing children with a minuscule budget, and they have to fight a publicly funded legal battery with a limitless budget." The children, he insists, received "exemplary care—if anything the foster father was overbearing and injected himself too much into the child-raising. If the wife didn't know about it, how could Catholic Home Bureau know about it? If the wife is there twenty-four hours a day, how is a social worker who makes weekly or biweekly visits supposed to see what is going on? Do you make them guarantors of every child that is placed in foster care? The way it's presented, it's as if the agency is hiring someone to rape people."

Well, yes. Evelyn's case against the city and St. Cabrini has now been settled for similar sums, but her case against Catholic Home Bureau was set to be heard in the fall of 1980. Although the trial was postponed to the following year, her lawyers are optimistic: it will come up in a state court, and much evidence that was denied her sister should obtain.

Meanwhile, Evelyn, now seventeen and with a child of her own, lives with her natural father in Manhattan. A tall, heavy girl with dark skin and black hair, she holds herself in such a way—her head inclined slightly forward and a hesitant look in her eyes—that her past seems only barely contained. She says she has no friends, knows nobody. "I just stay at home with the baby. I still feel scared. I don't know where he is, but I feel he is around here somewhere."

VII

The Key
to the Quality of Life

Yours is not to finish the task; neither are you free
to desist from it.

The Talmud

Few who are familiar with New York City's juvenile justice system
look confidently to the future. Even the most unreconstructed optimist, having heard the sirens sing of tax reduction, senses that the
years immediately ahead will not bring more of the same, but rather
something worse. Family Court does not breed Panglosses; saving a
dedicated minority, it breeds people who want to get out of Family
Court. Reflecting on the daily abuse she must absorb from judges and
other court personnel, and the "absolute grimness" of the families
with which she has to work, one law guardian concludes: "Anyone
with any sensibilities at all can't stay here more than two or three
years without burning out. I'm coming up on my second year now."
And yet Legal Aid work, or some kind of public-sector work, is why
this young woman, who took time out for marriage and motherhood,
went back to law school. She wants someday to go into appeals—
where the work is less visceral, more intellectual, and confined to
papers presented to a better class of judge in higher, more respected
courts.

Yet if there is little progress in the system, there is unmistakably change. Let an innovation appear to work effectively and the legislature, with unaccustomed swiftness, moves to disable it. Such was the case with the legislature's Juvenile Justice Reform Act of 1976, which created the idea of a "Designated Felony"—that is, a case involving a fourteen- or fifteen-year-old in murder, homicide, arson, rape, sodomy and robbery in the first degree—and decreed for the first time that "the court shall consider the needs and best interests of the respondent *as well as the need for protection of the community*" (emphasis added). It was, to an extent, a political act—the legislators responded to the voters' cry of protest against increasingly violent juvenile crime by offering slightly tougher sentences—and the law guardians responded at first with trepidation: the emphasis seemed to have shifted from rehabilitating kids to punishing them. The following year, in another political move, the legislature announced that the district attorneys would replace Corporation Counsel in the Designated Felony Parts. Larry Schwartzstein ground his teeth. Every voter knew the DAs were the big-time adult prosecutors, but to be practical for a moment, what did they *know*, what could they really *do?* "It's a slap in our face," he said at the time. "The DA can come in and try a murder, but he's not going to get any more of a sentence than Corporation Counsel can. To me, it's like the wool was pulled over the public's eyes. DAs coming in, like now we're going to get tougher sentences. Not true. No way."

Schwartzstein was right: bringing the DAs in on their white horses *was* a slap at Corporation Counsel. "It's a practical matter," says John O'Donnell, an articulate assistant DA who until recently was in charge of the operation. "Our lawyers have been trained in criminal law, and DAs are more experienced in conducting criminal investigations. We have a better idea of what to tell the cops to do." In any event, the innovation seemed to work. Eighty-five percent of the cases tried in a Designated Felony Part resulted in convictions, approximately 60 percent of the children found guilty were placed away from home on a long-term basis, and—a nicety peculiar to Family Court —more than half of those accused of violent crimes were detained while awaiting trial. In June 1978, the state's Division of Criminal Justice Services concluded that: "For the first time, violent juvenile crime is efficiently and successfully prosecuted. The Family Court is able to cope with serious crime and the youthful violent offender faces a real possibility of incurring a severe sanction."

But the public and the government in Albany were not convinced. By the spring of 1978, children appeared to be involved in more extravagantly violent crimes than ever before. One boy raped and tried to electrocute an elderly woman. Two others, in what the press called the "laughing boy murder," shot a young seminary student they didn't know because they thought he had laughed at them. Still another, who while he was imprisoned at Brookwood had explained on network television that he had seen the light, was released to commit two murders and an armed robbery. Again the cry went up: we've got to get tough with these kids. Governor Hugh Carey summoned the legislature to an extraordinary session in July. There, without consulting the people involved in the juvenile justice system, and with what the Legal Aid Society called a "hysterical dash towards massive change without adequate analysis," the legislators converted New York State from its accustomed role of an enlightened leader in juvenile matters to one of the most repressive states in the Union. It was an election year and their response was appropriately political.

Passed in August 1978 and put into effect almost instantly, on September 1, the Juvenile Offender Law for the first time exposed children aged thirteen to fifteen, who had been accused of specified violent crimes, to the adult criminal system. For the first time, the legislators appeared to conclude that the rehabilitation of children, which was the Family Court's principal concern, was not working and so, instead of seeking to make rehabilitation effective, they jettisoned it altogether. No one remotely aware of the workings of Criminal Court could have thought it particularly efficacious in dealing with adult offenders, yet to send the "worst" of the children there gave the impression—if one did not scrutinize the matter closely—that something vigorous, something tough, was at last being done. A thirteen-year-old convicted of Murder 2, no matter whether it was his first offense, faced a mandatory sentence of at least five years to life. Other Class A offenses would earn boys of fourteen and fifteen between four and fifteen years. The accused child would be photographed, fingerprinted and made the subject of a computerized "rap sheet." He would be denied the opportunity to present in court information concerning his background, his criminal history (or lack of it), or social and family difficulties that might be germane to his case. If found guilty, he would be swept into a prison system unequipped to secure his safety or to offer rehabilitative services. "In short," said Craig Kaplan, president of the Association of Legal Aid Attorneys, "this piece of legislation panders irresponsibly to the false and racist stereotype of a new subspecies of child that has emerged in our cities; a child of the underclass who, at the age of thirteen, is beyond all hope or healing. A society that consciously writes off its youth in this fashion disgraces itself in writing off its future."

What made this legislation so reactionary—aside from its appeal to the majority of New Yorkers who don't want to think about troublesome juveniles, who are just as glad to have them swept out of sight —was that it set New York in opposition to forty-eight states and the District of Columbia, which place original jurisdiction of such cases in the juvenile court. True, loopholes exist along the way. A district attorney could "decline to prosecute" and the "d.p.'d" case would be removed to Family Court. Judges and grand juries had the privilege of removing juvenile cases to Family Court "in the interests of justice." A great deal of this went on in the first two years of the new law. By the end of August 1980, 2,489 cases involving children subject to prosecution in adult courts had been processed in Criminal Court. The DAs had "d.p.'d" 14 percent of these; another 37 percent had been removed to Family Court; another 12 percent had been dismissed. Clearly, something was wrong with the new law: 74 percent of the children arrested under it were not being held for trial in an adult court. Some, like the first fourteen-year-old tried for murder (he had been thirteen at the time of the slaying), were tried and found guilty of a lesser charge, which obliged them to be returned to Family Court for sentencing.

In time, other flaws in the law appeared as well. John O'Donnell would say, "I tell people, 'Show me where we've botched things up. Show me the horrible things.' They can't come up with anything." Nevertheless, some people *could*. The Citizens' Committee for Children of New York, for instance, observed that violent children appearing in Criminal Court were allowed the privilege of bail; unlike their colleagues in Family Court, where a tradition of preventive detention prevails, they were returned to the streets pending their hearings, and some were rearrested. If the intention of the legislators had been to protect society from this kind of child, they had in fact made matters worse. Then it seemed there was some discrimination at play in the bail proceedings: to no one's surprise, 96 percent of those arrested under the new law were blacks and Hispanics, but these children were far more likely to be held without bail than were white children. Girls, who accounted for only 10 percent of the arrests, were more likely to be released than boys; children attending school were returned home more often than those who were not. Moreover, the decision to prosecute a child under the new law varied widely from borough to borough. For a while, depending on his case load or his personal whim, the DA in Manhattan "d.p.'d" four times as many juvenile offenders as did the DA in Queens. Because it made a great difference to the child whether a charge of Robbery 1 was heard in Criminal Court or in the more benign and confidential Family Court, some observers professed concern that the idea of equal justice under the law might be taking a battering from the new statute.

There was, too, the problem of the law's delay. Because the adult court system moves much more slowly than Family Court, children awaiting trial were being held up to seven months on Rikers Island with virtually nothing to do. Nor were children wrongly accused offered Family Court's protections. The Citizens' Committee for Children cited a case involving the son of a hospital administrator: "He was arrested, charged, sent to Rikers Island with full media coverage. He was subjected to detention and exposure to the criminal justice system, in spite of no previous history of violence or trouble with the law. His case was eventually dismissed by the judge on the facts, but the experience was a searing, destructive and frightening one, and should have been avoided."

To make matters worse, the Division for Youth, which is charged with imprisoning juvenile offenders, has long been unable to care properly even for the children sent to it by Family Court. It needs more money to build more secure facilities and to try to isolate children who belong in mental health units from those who require less extreme rehabilitation. Yet at the time he was promoting the Juvenile Offender Law, Governor Carey was actually cutting DFY's budget in such a way as to *reduce* the secure facilities available.

Popular as the new law may have been with voters and vote seekers, it was widely regarded by those familiar with the philosophy and practicalities of juvenile justice as unworkable. In August 1979, it was amended to allow juvenile offenders, under certain circumstances, Youthful Offender status—which is to say that judges were allowed to impose sentences of either five years' probation or prison terms of less than four years. Young people between sixteen and twenty-one had been eligible for Youthful Offender status long before the new law was passed; it seemed only just that it should be extended to younger children as well. At the same time, the law was amended to allow juvenile offenders to be arraigned directly in the state Supreme Court, thus speeding up the process a bit, because the Supreme Court's calendar is not as crowded as those of the Criminal Court and Family Court. John O'Donnell is delighted by the move: "Supreme Court talks to the kid like an adult. It impresses him that this is no longer kiddie court. It responds with less concern for his wellbeing than for the victim's. It gives kids some incentive. The law is applied in a manner where absurdities don't occur. Supreme Court offers more creative disposition than Family Court. It will order DFY to do things that a Family Court judge won't do."

Still, these were cosmetic changes. The Legal Aid Society urged a return of jurisdiction of all children to Family Court, from which some, if it seemed advisable, could be sent to the adult courts. The Citizens' Committee for Children pressed for repeal of the Juvenile Offender Law, which it rightly saw as a further humiliation of a Family Court that was already held in contempt by the legal community and in urgent need of reinforcement.

Someone is always proposing to reform Family Court. In 1969, a lawyer in the state Appellate Division submitted a report advocating widespread changes. "I've had the experience of proposing a thorough reform of the Family Court, seeing it enacted and then dismantled," says Merril Sobie, who now works for the state Division of Criminal Justice Services. From 1971 to 1975 he served as executive officer of the city's Family Court under the then administrative judge, Florence Kelly, and the present incumbent, Joseph B. Williams. Sobie was in charge of all nonjudicial operations: calendaring, procedures, hiring personnel—"everything to the point of the case appearing before a judge. My appointment was an attempt to bring strong administration to a court that was in dreadful shape. I was granted an unusual amount of authority in that court."

Consistency without specialization was Sobie's philosophy. He converted the specialized Parts of each court into all-purpose Parts: Parts that had hitherto heard only support cases or paternity cases were now exposed to every kind of case that came before the court. The invigorating effect of variety, however, he thought inappropriate to cases involving children, and so he ruled that one judge must follow a juvenile case through its hearings and disposition. "That's been violated on a wholesale basis," he says. "Charley Schinitsky is furious, and rightly so." The advantage of one judge to a case, Sobie said in his 1969 report, would be judges who could become familiar with a case and the parties concerned. Moreover, it would minimize the likelihood of conflict in ordering tests: "Judge A, for example, might not feel that psychological evaluation is important for deciding a given case; however, when the case next appears on the calendar, Judge B, who places great emphasis on psychological evaluations, will probably adjourn the case and order the tests, thus lengthening the entire proceedings. But under the present structure, by adjourning the case, Judge B has probably removed himself from it and the case will be heard next by Judge C, who may have entirely different views concerning evaluation techniques."

Sobie introduced a Rapid Intervention Program into the court. The theory was that a child often comes into court with serious mental problems that can't wait for reports and disposition; an immediate application of the court's Mental Health Services might save the family. He began the program with about $900,000 a year in federal funds. "It was a large program. We recruited a staff of psychiatrists, psychologists, social workers. A judge or a Probation officer could send someone to RIP immediately he entered court. You could get a preliminary evaluation in an hour or two. It helped make preliminary decisions easier. Judge Williams cut it off rather precipitately. On the eve of third-year funding, he wiped out the program, wiped out nine hundred thousand dollars a year in federal funds. He cut back Mental Health Services drastically. What we have now is about twenty-five to thirty percent of the MHS that were available in 1974. What hurts even more is that in such a retrenchment, under the Civil Service System, the people who lose their jobs are the younger, more aggressive people.

"There are no federal funds in Family Court now. This is Judge Williams's decision. I tend to believe he doesn't want people looking over his shoulder. He doesn't want anyone in the court he doesn't have complete control over. It may lead to reports that are very critical of the court. He doesn't want to be subject to outside order, monitoring, evaluation. You should have a Family Court administration that attempts to obtain the resources needed instead of attempting to push the problems under the rug. The court doesn't have enough judges, nonjudicial personnel at almost every level. Probation has been gutted even more than the Mental Health Clinic." Sobie would have brought in federal funds to support the Designated Felony Parts. "There's no reason why federal funds shouldn't be used to establish new Parts devoted to Designated Felony cases—with all the subsidiary services they require: Mental Health, Probation, Legal Aid. It's a new program based on new legislation.

"I have a very low opinion of Judge Williams and his policies. I think he very intentionally produced a system where no one can really tell what is going on. And then he commissions reports to vindicate his policies. For instance, he wants to control the statistics about how many cases the court handles—to manipulate them and to manipulate the court and the type of image that he wants to represent, regardless of its relation to reality. If someone sits around the court long enough he may find that a certain case has been pending for ten months without a resolution—but that won't show up in the court's statistics. When I was in the court the statistics I was receiving from the clerk of court were at wide variance with those I received from the Department of Social Services. So I asked the clerk to explain to me the difference. He said, 'Oh, we have boxes full of cases that haven't been docketed. We haven't been docketing them until we're ready to proceed.' You cannot have a case until it's docketed: *that's* their position. I maintain you have a case as soon as someone walks through the door with a petition. It's sheer rhetoric to claim that a case isn't pending until you docket it. It's called 'abolishing the backlog.' Yet that's how the court operates. There are other ways of juggling your backlog. Old, inactive cases are periodically dismissed. I don't disagree with that, but they should be accounted for separately. The critical issue is increasing or decreasing the *active* cases. Also, instead of drafting a petition, a court can calendar a case before a judge to determine whether a petition *should* be drafted and what method of service should be used for that petition. No petition, no case. And the individual, who used to be able to get a petition immediately, goes to court to get placed on a calendar for some future date. Eight or ten weeks away.

"There's one statistic that should be easy to generate with a very high degree of accuracy. That is the number of petitions filed. At least with those you can count docket numbers. *If* they've been docketed. *If* they've been numbered consecutively. But they don't even do a good job with that. It is not known how many cases are processed by Family Court. The court used to present its own statistics—which were inaccurate, but at least ballpark figures. They abolished that in 1974. No one knows what the situation is now. And it's intentional."

At the end of November 1976, Sobie wrote a "Dear Dick" letter to Richard Coyne of New York City's Economic Development Council documenting the incredible mess that statistics relating to Family Court had become. He had known Coyne well for years, but he never received a reply.

A symptom, at once blatant and mysterious, of the disorder within the Family Court can be found in its system of rotating judges from one Part to another, and from one county to the next. Before Sobie came into the Family Court, judges were moved about every month. As Sobie reminded Coyne: "The judge who conducted the fact-finding hearing and was accordingly conversant with the legal and factual issues (and hopefully attuned to the family's needs) would not preside at the dispositional hearing. A family would appear before a multitude of judges who might issue inconsistent preliminary orders. Embarrassing facts would be presented again and again before different judges. One judge would issue a warrant—when it was executed the 'new' judge would have little knowledge of the reasons for issuance or the respondent's danger to his family or the community." At its worst, this kind of bureaucratically enforced ignorance led to tragedy. In 1969, a child named Roxanne Felumero was murdered by her stepfather *after* they had appeared before several Family Court judges. A committee investigating the case concluded that the rotation system contributed to Roxanne's death.

The rotation continues today, loathed by judges and law guardians alike. A judge with a toothache in Brooklyn wants to know whether he can go to his own dentist or must find another, next month, in the Bronx. Law guardians, nursing their cases from one hearing to the next, dislike surprises. Judges often are assigned to a Part for as long as two months, sometimes three, but they are equally likely to find themselves removed from a Part after a week or two. Because the official schedules of judicial assignments do not necessarily tally with reality, the law guardians make for their own use maps of the judges' peregrinations. In February 1977, for instance, eight judges were assigned to cover three of the Parts in Brooklyn. That July, ten judges presided over six Parts in Manhattan.

Some rotation *is* desirable, to keep the judges awake and refreshed by the city's variety. Charles Schinitsky thinks nine months in one Part, followed by two in Intake and a month's vacation, might be ideal. But no one understands why Judge Williams plays with his court as if its judges were so many counters on a backgammon board. "What possible excuse can there be for not letting a judge know where he'll be next month?" Sobie asks. "Some judges do better at Intake than others. You need some experience. The judge at Intake controls the calendar of all the other Parts. It's necessary for him to know the strengths and weaknesses of all the other judges: how many cases and what kinds of case to assign to him." In fact, the court clerks make those decisions for the Intake judge to approve. "But I haven't detected any pattern on Judge Williams's part for putting the best judges in Intake. I've seen him put virtually brand-new judges there. And now judges in Intake have no idea what judge will be in what Part next month when the case comes up.

"There are other motivations in rotating judges the way Williams does. It's a system that insures a very high degree of control by the administrative judge. He can reward or discipline judges at a mo-

ment's notice. A judge who lives in Queens can find himself assigned
to Staten Island—as a punishment. More importantly, Judge Williams wants to continually shuffle the deck to avoid the kind of
working relationship that he thinks is harmful, that he views as a
threat to himself. Judges becoming entrenched in particular com-
munities, working together continually, becoming familiar with nonjudicial personnel—that isolates things. It means there are certain
centers of power outside the administrative judge. They also may be
able to solve problems. They have working relationships; they can
speak with some knowledge of the people involved. If in Queens
Probation reports are not coming in on time, a judge can say: 'Come
now, what are we going to do?' He can even go to the assistant
administrative judge in Queens. But if he's continually rotated, what's
he going to do? If he attempts to negotiate with Probation, they're
liable to take a bureaucratic approach: 'We don't know the judge; he
doesn't know us.' So they have to take it to headquarters. To Judge
Williams."

Getting to Judge Williams, however, is not a simple matter. He is not
much seen about the court, but his presence is felt through a constant
flow of memoranda and directives that come literally from on high.
The administrative judge's offices in the Manhattan Family Court
building are on the eleventh floor—a floor that most of the court
familiars are vaguely aware exists but that few have seen. The girl at
the information desk on the ground floor is not certain that anyone
can actually *go* to the eleventh floor; certainly you can't just take the
elevator up. Judge Williams will not necessarily respond to phone
calls or letters or requests to visit his court.

By acting thus as a master puppeteer, Judge Williams has spread
a certain amount of fear and resentment about the court. This may
not, say those who must deal with him, be unintentional. Fear saves
time. No need to debate a procedure; we know what the judge wants:
he wants cases *moved.* If we don't know what he wants, no need to
place a call he won't answer: we can think like him. Thinking like him
means we're not going to take the handcuffs off your client, counselor;
no need to waste time arguing. The law guardians worry that he is

trying to diminish their role by ruling that they may not confer with their old clients until arraignment at Intake, and by offering respondents the alternative of defense by an "Appellate lawyer," who is actually a panel lawyer, though the term sounds grand. Judges worry that Williams will criticize them for not moving cases fast enough, that he is indifferent to the care—and time—these cases require. A few people, like Charles Schinitsky, who have their own bases of power in the Court, are contemptuous of Williams; others, like Larry Schwartzstein, insist that their relations with the judge are a model of courtesy and efficiency. Some attorneys find it difficult to *understand* Judge Williams. His speech, they say, is unencumbered by any recognizable syntax. He can talk for five minutes without making any sense at all. This, too, may be deliberate. One of them observes: "When he says, 'What we're going to need here is more substance and less form,' it's *unclear,* perhaps even ominous. Maybe he means more jail and less law."

"I am an optimist," says the source of all this awe and mistrust. "I couldn't be here if I weren't. I think we can do something about all this, but before we can clean up the mess out there"—he gestures broadly out his office window, toward the Criminal Court, the Supreme Court, the federal courts, the entire city—"we have to clean it up in here." Outside his office, in a waiting room decorated in mustard-colored furniture of the Motel Modern persuasion, an air-conditioning vent in the ceiling leaks a milky-colored substance to the tile floor below. As he strides from his elevator, however, and through a glass door hurriedly opened for him by a court officer, Joseph B. Williams looks neither right nor left. A short, brown, intense man of fifty-six, his appearance and manner suggest that he might easily be the leader (not necessarily elected) of a small, unstable country.

In the 1960s, Williams was respected as one of the better judges sitting in Family Court. In 1970, he left to work for Mayor John Lindsay's Model Cities program. In 1974, he returned to the court as administrative judge. When, in 1977, he was appointed and then elected to the state Supreme Court in Brooklyn, his critics hoped his new duties might prove so engrossing that he would relinquish his hold upon the Family Court; they were to be disappointed. Now in August 1977, as he reflects in his office on new disciplines to be imposed, he speaks voluminously, letting his voice trail off to leave sentences and trains of thought unfinished, then accelerating, thrusting his words out in loud clumps. Sometimes he appears to seize a difficult question, eager to answer it, only to drift away to another subject. Sometimes he engages himself in debate, speaking in different voices, switching imperceptibly among them: Williams versus the incompetent judge; Williams versus his critics.

"The Family Court's problems," he says, "I've approached in three ways. First I tried to stabilize them, then standardize them, then refine the process. We are now moving to a point where we will try to concentrate on productivity. We must give some attention to the reasons we're keeping matters here before this court the length of time that we do. Our biggest problem seems to be inefficiency due to inattention, or maybe carelessness, which means we are repeating ourselves a number of times, going over work that we had here before. That, combined with indecision on the part of the judges and nonjudicial personnel in moving stuff through here, almost doubles the burden. Plus the fact of the image of how the court is viewed by the public suffers.

"It's difficult because we have very fixed, very set patterns. What I'm dealing with today is patterns. So far the objection is that I'm working people too hard. Opening new Parts, making the court more flexible, to put people where the problems are, where the balloons are, rather than just fix a mistake. I'm in the process now of taking out all cases that were filed before this year. I'm monitoring them every day. You want an adjournment, you got to call me. These cases *must* be heard that day. There are cases fourteen, fifteen months old with no fact finding, no jurisdiction. It's unthinkable. We should have them all out by the end of next month. But it takes hard work. That's what they're worrying about. I'm putting in what resources I have. I'll put a judge in, I'll put a stenographer in, I'll put a court officer in. Let's go to work. We don't need three people, two sitting and one looking at the others. *That*'s the problem they're talking about. I'm not going to buy the argument. Because that's his job. That's what he's supposed to do."

Rotation of judges is an integral element in Williams's traffic-moving program. "This is a citywide court and you're appointed not to a county but to a citywide bench. Some counties have varying needs. They fluctuate. I may very well have to move a judge from one county into another. Most of our cases should be finished in one day. Most. We're a mass court. We're a speed court. OK? And so we try to do some quality things and say we're doing quality things, but to the extent that we do that we then deny serving the public. To put a case over, a family that needs some support, to come in here and calendar it for three months from now: kids would starve to death in the meantime. We take summary action. That's the reason we're set up this way without all the formality of pleading and the rest of it.

"Now part of the problem is judges who want certain specific assignments. It's normal. I know the argument. So you come around with a county-based judge. What's wrong with that? It gets a little clubby. You can get certain judges doing all the heavy lifting. All the cases is not equally distributed. You can get certain judges who will be shielded from certain kinds of cases. It's a work-distribution system. You don't want to get stuff in your system that don't go out. You get a new and fresh point of view. I've had situations change merely by moving judges around and being told, 'Joe, do you know what's happening here?' It has its advantages. Now if I were to do what people say I should do, the bulk of my judges are New York County judges. They'd all have to stay in New York County. Bronx has two judges and I have six Parts in the Bronx. They want it for convenience. But the point is, they *do* know where they going. The appointments are made on a three-month basis. They're trying to wriggle, is what they're trying to do. What's coming is accountability."

Cases, Judge Williams says, should be assigned randomly from Intake to the various Parts, without concern for where the law guardians will be on any given day. Why should the problems of Legal Aid affect the judges' business? Of course, such random distribution presumes that all judges are equally competent. Williams grins. "Well, you *must* assume that. Nobody's admitted that they're not, right? OK? And none of the judges will say that they're not. OK. I must move with that. I can say to a judge, 'You got ninety days to get a fact finding. Why are you duckin' that? Why you moving that over?'

Sure, it's done. I had a judge who was doin' all the neglects. That's
too heavy. He asked me, 'Joe, assign me to another court; if I have
to do another neglect, I'll just go up. Everybody's leavin' them for me!'
I know there are five or six judges—ten, I guess, twelve—heavy lifters.
I know where the lifters are, and I know who used to leave stuff for
me. They'd leave it for vacation and somebody'd come in and he'd see
a calendar that's in shambles! It's so dangerous for you to pick up and
move it. That's one of the problems.

"I can tell you who's producing, where they are producing. My
producers will produce in New York, Bronx, Brooklyn, they'll produce anywhere you put 'em. The nonproducers won't produce and I
don't care if you got rotation, if you keep 'em. I can demonstrate it.
I'm sending this to the judges." Williams has had prepared a record
of adjournments broken down by category. "Most of these are
dummy, questionable, totally unacceptable. It means a judge who
doesn't want to move. I have it by judge, by county. In the month of
April we had approximately two thousand cases were granted adjournments and I only received one thousand, four hundred and
twenty-three forms or reasons. Now I just sent them a note: account
for them. Account for each one. Go over your calendars. Now we
gotta get back to work. That will tighten them up.

"This record I'm gonna send them, I've keyed it. I've got the key.
I've put Judge X, Y, but I have the key as to who they are. When I
have a meeting this month, I'm gonna tell 'em, you just one month
removed from the *names*. The names are gonna appear in the next
group. I'm gonna give them the names, as to who's doing and who's
not doing. And I know they're gonna tear me limb from limb. And
I find out that those who complain most and talk so much about how
hard they're working are my light lifters. They aren't doin' anythin'
and they're tryin' to cover their lack of activity by talkin'.

"This place has never had any systematic approach to really analyz-
ing the work and the activity here. We've been activity-oriented rather
than results-oriented. Hell, we're *busier* 'n hell. We can show you
activity. And you can go all day and not make a daggone determination. 'I finished my calendar!' That's his *activity:* he finished his *calendar.* That's not it! The end result here, and the performance measure-
ment, is how many people did we help and what did we do today?

Nobody want to go at this one; it looks like spying on them. As soon as I come out with it, 'Joe, you *can't* use that!' I'm not after qualitative things. He shouldn't waste the court's time."

Discussing the judicial vacancies which Mayor Beame insisted, that summer, on maintaining in Family Court, Williams says: "I think it probably has something to do with the work and the people who appear in this court. Which to me is silly, because what happens to this court, what problems we see, is the key to the quality of life in the city of New York. Unless we are able to deal with and cope with the problems that surface here in a systematic way, the city's in for some tough times. The whole social fabric might very easily deteriorate and impact very seriously on the economic life of the city. Things are going to be chaotic. Nothing's happening. We're churning. I can demonstrate: we're churning. I've taken out thirty thousand warrants. We are within a thousand cases of having fact findings on everything in this system that appeared before 1977. When I took over, we had '71s, we had '63s—just layin' there! Then we said, what is the size of the court's backlog, what does it look like, nobody could tell you. If I had all my judges, I could get current in about eight to nine months, if I did a personal monitoring thing on it myself. That's what I believe. A lot of people would be unhappy with me, as they are now.

"I can look at a calendar. I can tell you what's heavy. I can look at the allegations and tell you what's heavy. You see, I *know* how long a case should take. I guess I've tried about everything in here. I know when they're draggin' their feet. I know *who's* draggin' their feet. I know who's fluffin' and puttin' down nothin' endorsements. The ironical thing is, counsel know and nonjudicial personnel know. It impacts negatively on the individual judge and he thinks the robe is goin' to shield his ignorance, his indolence and his inactivity. But it won't. I'm tryin' to instill it with 'em: You can't fool people! You've got to make *decisions!* That's what you're paid to do! You can't slough it off and say: 'Law guardian, Probation clerk—you are the last resort.' The *judge* is. That's his job"—Williams bangs the table, WHAM! WHAM! —"to decide the case."

Williams touches upon other institutions that add to his traffic jam. One is the statute that requires the same judge to preside at both fact finding and disposition. "Unless you go to a punishment question,

what difference does it really make? A homicide, a serious robbery,
a sodomy or arson where a death was involved, you do it. But what
does the average situation require? The bulk of 'em are goin' on
probation. In any event. What difference, and what does it matter, and
what's going to happen when he goes out on probation? Do you know
what supervision he's gonna get? None. Only time Probation Department know anything about him is when he gets involved again. He
come in and they'll violate him on the basis of the new charges against
him. '*I* don't know anything about him.' The number who are actually placed with DFY: very small."

Another is Legal Aid. "In Foster Care and PINS they relate too
much to the youngster. Some of these law guardians grew up in the
so-called permissive age. Any interference that was anti-establish-
ment. Well, some of the results were absolutely ludicrous. You know,
you got a runaway, 'The law says you can't do this; we want a parole.'
Where the hell is the child gonna go? The law says it! The law says
you can't fingerprint him. OK, so I've violated the law, but I've found
out that his dad was in the State of Washington looking for this child
who's fifteen years old and is up at Broadway and some damn pimps.
It's *that* kind of thing that we get into the problem with and I would
say that maybe I might be technically in violation, but I don't say that
it is the kind of thing that happens all the time. But if you move, they
admit nothing. They have a policy. Rarely you get an admission. The
kid say, 'Look, I did so-and-so: Not guilty!' No defense. Just grind you
out of this and *always* resist a placement. Always. That's what gets
the judges. And rightly so. Judges want to short-cut sometimes.

"To the extent that the law guardians have a legitimate point to
urge, I would *compel* them to urge it, *demand* that they urge it, and
would criticize them if they *didn't* urge it. I frankly would. *But* to the
extent that they're just arguing and urging to be arguing it bothers me
because if there's one thing that characterizes the families that come
here, it's lack of structure. We can't show a lack of structure here. We
can't show that this is a game. By the same token, we judges must be
very, very careful that we give the impression of concern, commitment
and fairness. Acting within the law.

"The law guardians are not only better than their adversaries, but
they got all the money. And all the support. The City of New York

supplies the Corporation Counsel, and they have Corporation Counsel that are just as skillful, but they don't have any investigators, got no appeals bureau, got no support staff. Most cases, Corporation Counsel is ready to go to trial. The person who wants the adjournment is the law guardian. He's doing some of the things that the old practitioners used to do. 'Shut your mouth.' " Williams slaps his desk. " 'Make 'em pay.' " Slap! " 'Make 'em not come.' " Slap! "Soon as you don't come"—slap!—" 'Move to dismiss!' " Slap! " 'Failure to prosecute!' " Slap! " 'Respondent? I don't know where he is, judge, I object to a warrant for him.' It's that kind of thing, and rightly so. Make it!

"But you got that kind of situation in because judges were not judging all the time. Judges abdicate their roles, let them go out and make adjustment situations and the judges accept them. Adjournment in contemplation of dismissal? Why? Either the public has a right for me to take jurisdiction of this child or the child has the right to walk out on the street. Unless you give me a good reason. What's the reason? 'I can't prove it, judge, there's some weaknesses in my case, the child has gone to school and he's going into certain things and there's nothing before and we don't want this on any kind of record. We don't think he needs supervision, it's a kind of one-time shot, it's more of a technical violation than anything else. In the interest of justice, the mother does not want to go forward with it.' Something."

His parody of the law guardians' pleas comes easily to Judge Williams. In a moment he will do the same for the Bureau of Child Welfare. "You've got to move *something!* And there's got to be recognition on the part of the youngster of some wrong. That's the point, but we aren't doing that. I'm in a big struggle now with that because one day the public is going to say and hold us accountable for why did we turn all these people out, use all this police time, all this Probation time, to draw up a petition in the court and then let him walk away in the street? We're doin' it."

As for the charge that he has blocked federal funds from coming into the court, Williams shrugs. The Rapid Intervention Program, he says, would have had to be funded by the city after its third year, and "the city was not prepared to pick up that nut. In fact, they not only did not pick that up, they reduced their commitment to the court by about thirty-five percent in mental health areas. I took a lot of flak

on that, but *I* wasn't reducing it. It just couldn't go any further; it had
to make do." As for other federal funds, "I don't make the applications now. The programs and planning come from the Office of Court
Administration." In this he may be less than candid: OCA is the
agency to which Judge Williams reports, but he is also a member of
it; he could easily guide his colleagues in the search for taxpayers'
dollars.

In any event, moving money is not Judge Williams's priority; moving cases is. And if that means moving people, that's what he's there
for. "That's management's prerogative. Management *must* have the
right to bring the resources to where the greatest need is. That's what
we're doing. To some, that's unheard of; to others, it's heresy. I'm
prepared to take that, too. But that's the only way progress is going
to be made in this thing. Now talk about sittin' on these cases. Look
at these, in Brooklyn: '76, '76, '76: almost a year on some of these. It's
appalling. Here's a '75. Now this is almost two years old: no fact
finding. The judge that's got this case, he's got a letter on top of it
saying only I can adjourn it. There's *nothing* he can do to delay it.
I'm told I've been working people too hard. I'm not concerned about
it. I'm going to do it until I see some results and we get it done or
somebody takes me out of here. I'm all right. I'm perfectly happy.
They aren't working any harder than I'm workin'. A guy told me the
other day, 'Judge, I'm sorry I lose my temper, but you had your foot
on me.' Yes, I *do*. I have my foot on everybody; I have my foot on
myself. I'm not goin' to listen to any foolishness of somebody who tell
me I'm technically violatin' some kind of contract and he has a
woman outside who needs some services.

"Maybe that's radical. I don't know. But it seems to me what a
manager ought to be doing. It not only shakes up the troops, it helps
the work load. It's working. We're not there yet. It hasn't been without conflict, not everybody agrees where it's going, but at least it's
going. It's moving forward every day."

Not everybody agrees where juvenile crime is going, either, but it does
seem to be moving forward. In the summer of 1980, Judith Levy—now
Judith Levy Sheindlin and chief of Manhattan's Corporation Counsel

—remarked on the changing fashions in teenage crime. What with the Juvenile Offender Law and the DAs taking over Designated Felonies, her office is less concerned with the heavy stuff than once it was, but she claims to be just as busy. "Current cases involve more preparation. We used to have simple, nonviolent crimes five, eight years ago. Now most of those cases are adjusted in Probation. Eight years ago, graffiti was a big crime in Family Court. You don't see it anymore." They don't see as much drug use among teenagers, either, though there are still a lot of cases involving the sale or possession of drugs. Sheindlin thinks kids sixteen and older, who can get a life sentence for drug dealing, use the younger children for this work because "the worst that can happen is the kid comes in and is placed on probation." Another kiddy crime, unauthorized use of a motor vehicle, has also declined, to be replaced by teacher-assault cases, which are accelerating rapidly. There is less gang crime than there once was: the Chinese youth gangs seem to have disappeared. The trend today, says Sheindlin, is to "Robbery 2 acting in concert; Robbery 3; grand larceny; possession of stolen property." Particularly fashionable that spring were chain-snatching crimes: as the price of gold soared, children were increasingly brought in for ripping gold chains from the necks of women on subways.

"The Family Court system is not working as well as when it was first envisioned," Sheindlin says. "The original idea behind Family Court was that children do not commit bad acts. But today's fifteen-year-old is involved in crime on a repeated basis. The majority of the kids are not here for the first time. There are prior arrests. And that means the system is not working." The system does not work, she says, because it lacks appropriate correctional facilities and because the right to a speedy trial is not observed. "Cases are still put off for months, even with the standards and goals that have been adopted. As a parent, I know that if a child does something wrong and is not told right away, the effect of any putative treatment is lost. Now I'm talking about a recidivist. If that juvenile is not treated *swiftly,* if he is not told that his conduct is unacceptable, he comes to feel that the system is not serious. That's why many kids are involved in drugs as sellers. Nothing happens to them.

"Change will only happen when the system has had it up to here.

You get a kid who keeps coming back, you place him away from home, in the least restrictive placement. He absconds and commits another act. Kids like that know the system does not deal seriously with them at first. If, with the first serious transgression, a kid is treated seriously, I would venture that he would think twice before committing another crime."

In 1979, at the suggestion of Charles Schinitsky, the New York legislature created a Temporary Commission to Recodify the Family Court Act. The commission's mandate, says its executive director, David Gilman, is to pull together all laws regarding children and families, to make substantive revisions in the laws relating to neglects and abuses, PINS, delinquency and other areas, and to make recommendations for improving the court system. The commission hopes to have a new act, the first complete revision of the Family Court Act of 1962, ready by 1983, but no one can guess how long after that it will be before the legislature brings the act to a vote. In the meantime, the nine commissioners are supposed to be digesting twenty of the twenty-three volumes of *Standards of Juvenile Justice.* This project, sponsored by the American Bar Association and the Institute for Judicial Administration, has to date consumed ten years, $2.5 million and the efforts of hundreds of people in an attempt to bring to juvenile justice a set of national standards. To the surprise of no one familiar with the politics of the subject, the enterprise ran into difficulty at the ABA's midwinter meeting early in 1980. The ABA's House of Delegates voted to withdraw permanently a volume relating to schools and education and to return for redrafting a volume involving abuse and neglect. The principal controversy erupted over the recommendations concerning status offenders, or PINS; this volume, by a vote of 145–142, has been indefinitely deferred. "I don't even know if we will bring it back," David Gilman says.

The problems confronting reform of PINS legislation are both philosophical and political. There are those within the juvenile justice system who are still debating—as they have done for more than a century—how the relation between courts and children must be defined. Some see the courts as a "treatment agency" which has the responsibility to identify children who are approaching trouble with the law, and which has the ultimate authority to enforce parental rights. The PINS are just such children. Others maintain that status offenses are difficult to define. PINS behavior has been satirically defined as "behavior that is disturbing to someone." "What is 'habitually disobedient'?" Gilman asks. "What is 'incorrigible?' It's hard to define. How much lip or mouth can a kid get away with?" In practice, PINS proceedings have been openly discriminatory. Until 1972, when the law in New York was changed as a result of a suit by Legal Aid, girls were subject to PINS proceedings up to the age of eighteen—two years longer than boys. Seventy percent of girls who are incarcerated are "status offenders," and of these 50 percent are first offenders. Most of these girls are charged with sexual promiscuity, which many people feel is not a valid reason for imprisonment. "You never hear of young men being incarcerated for being sexually promiscuous," Gilman says. "Whatever that means. Probably it means being sexually active. Men can sow their oats, but we have to keep our young women virgins."

Critics of present PINS legislation argue that all the studies and statistics have demonstrated that exposure to a court does a child more harm than good, that a disproportionate number of the cases coming before juvenile courts involve "status offenses," that the more contact children have with the courts the more trouble they get into. Therefore, the courts should narrow their jurisdictions. "We should not have courts intervening willy-nilly in the lives of kids," Gilman says. "Judges can apply all the law they want, but family conflict is not amenable to judicial solutions."

Indeed it is not, which is why most people who are knowledgeable about juvenile justice favor the removal of PINS cases from the courts. And yet there is an opposing argument: in PINS cases, petitioners and respondents alike are desperate people without recourse to the normal structures of family and community; they need help and cannot get it except through the courts. The National Association of Family Court Judges, which is opposed to removing PINS from the courts and which is responsible for the indefinite deferment of the PINS volume from the *Standards of Juvenile Justice* project, asks: If we take these children out of the court, then who's going to help them?

We're just throwing away these kids. We have to help them—through the legal procedure—and that's what we're going to do. Furthermore, the judges undoubtedly feel—though they will not say so—that to remove the PINS cases, as the juvenile offenders were removed, is further to denigrate the Family Court and therefore what little prestige the judges have. Why not strengthen the court instead?

The influence of the judges was sufficient to sway the decision to defer at the ABA convention. Most lawyers in this country are reluctant to think long or precisely about juvenile matters, and it is probable that those assembled at the convention were glad to see the unseemly dispute brushed aside. Nevertheless, the issue persists, if only because the federal government has recently decided not to reimburse the states for prison costs if status offenders are locked up. There are no PINS at Spofford now, nor at any secure detention center in New York. Only rarely does a PINS in New York City go into placement today unless he agrees to do so. If, in an interview with an open facility or private agency, the child says, "I don't want to go and I'll run away if you put me there," the agency won't accept him. "So," says David Gilman, "there's a real push to de-institutionalize. The court won't have much teeth." He sees a certain irony in that "reform is happening in spite of itself. Even though the states may not remove the old rules, it will happen because of reimbursement. The program follows the dollars."

Inevitably, Charles Schinitsky was picked to be one of the commissioners to recodify the Family Court Act. Once more into the breach. At first he doubted that he was up to the assignment; then he decided that with good staff work the task should not prove arduous. He will be sixty-five in February 1981, an event he has anticipated with some ambivalence since 1977, when he discovered that retirement at that age was compulsory. "I looked into the pension. It's not so great, but it's better than it was. I don't know. Sometimes I think I should go. Give someone else a chance and write something, maybe. But I don't really want to. It's true I don't move quite as fast as I used to. It may be I'm more selective in what I do now." Looking back on his career, he thinks of the Juvenile Rights Division as a family. "We've had deaths, births. Former members send cards." Some of his best lawyers leave—Robert Levy to the New York Civil Liberties Union, Stephen Pokart and Morris Kaplan to Legal Aid's Criminal Division—but, the Juvenile Rights Division being what it is, they are readily replaced. Every day brings Schinitsky "three or four good applications. We have a waiting list."

By the summer of 1980, retirement seemed less of an imposition. "I want to do something in art—a gallery, maybe. I don't think I have to do anything important, but something with structure." For several years he had been concerned with the problem of succession. The Juvenile Rights Division was his creation; to whom would he leave it? The heir apparent for several years, an exceedingly able woman, had recently been appointed to the Family Court bench. Schinitsky was determined that he would not leave until he had groomed the successor of his choice, though in fact it is Legal Aid's board of trustees that must make the final decision. He wanted to retire knowing that the division remained strong, unified and committed to the programs he had developed.

To this end, he chose Carol Sherman, a bright, pleasant, petite woman of thirty-four who since her graduation from Harvard Law in 1971 had worked only for Charles Schinitsky. Sherman had served as a staff attorney both in the Manhattan office and in the Special Litigation Unit, where she had worked on some of the most complex class-action cases that Legal Aid had ever developed; she had been the assistant office head in Manhattan, and then briefly the attorney-in-charge; since February 1980, she has been Schinitsky's deputy in the Brooklyn headquarters. Like the great majority of lawyers who have worked for Schinitsky, Sherman is both admiring and loyal; if she entertains any heretical thoughts about what the division has done in the past or what it should do in the future, she may not yet be aware of them herself.

She has, however, a set of entirely orthodox ideas about what the division should strive for in the immediate future. She would like to see the Juvenile Offender Law changed to return original jurisdiction to the Family Court. She wants to resist what she perceives to be a trend toward making Family Court more of a criminal court: "We believe due process and individual treatment are not mutually exclusive." She wants to resist pressures from both the Division for Youth and the Department of Social Services to have exclusive discretion in placing children; the judges must retain responsibility. She wants to see the PINS removed from the court, to reduce the court's increasing tendency to fingerprint children and file information about them in computers: "More and more people will want to use the computer and they will eventually be allowed to." Awkward though it is for the law guardians to say so, she would like to see an improvement in the selection and training of panel lawyers. Like Schinitsky, she wants to press for a better concept of treatment in the facilities to which children are sent. "In Neglect and Abuse areas, we would like to see even more emphasis on preventive services, and continued pressure toward preservation of the family, or expeditious return of the child to the family. Or if that's not possible, then a movement toward adoption and an end to long periods spent in foster care. We'd like to see the agencies really *work* with families—you rarely see that." If she could raise the funds, she would want to have law guardians representing foster children when their cases came up for review: "The purpose is to have the agency come in with a plan for the child, or terminate parental rights and put the child up for adoption. We don't want children staying in foster care for year after year and nobody caring, or knowing about it." She wants, of course, more lawyers, more social workers, more impact on other areas outside the courts—the educational system, for example. She would like to have renewed a grant that Legal Aid obtained from the Law Enforcement Assistance Association which provides a special task force to monitor what is happening to the division's clients in twenty agencies.

"And," she says, "we'd like to continue to be a model of advocacy in representing children. And in showing the need for a specialized agency to do that kind of representation."

In the summer of 1980, Schinitsky could point to two encouraging trends—one with a chance to pass the legislature; the other, perhaps not. The first is a proposed merger of all the New York courts. Should this come about, the Cinderella of the family would benefit from a much-needed boost to her dignity and morale. Just now, however, the

Supreme Court justices, possibly fearing contamination, oppose any such move that would include the Family Court. The other trend is toward the merit system in the selection of judges. A few years ago, Schinitsky thought it made no difference whether judges were elected or appointed—equally dismal judges emerged from either method—but he has changed his mind. Recently, the governor has been appointing judges not on a political basis but from a list of candidates recommended to him by a committee. Mayor Edward Koch has followed a similar procedure: the quality of his appointments is markedly better than that of his predecessor, Abe Beame. Schinitsky, however, is pessimistic about the legislature ever passing a bill requiring merit selection: "It would have too much impact on the political system as it now exists."

Other trends—particularly the Juvenile Offender Law, and the failure of the state to continue his Neglect and Abuse Bureau, thereby reducing his complement of social workers from fifteen to six—leave Schinitsky depressed. "We're really castrating Family Court, the whole concept, without it ever really getting off the ground. If it continues and these youngsters stay in Criminal Court, we'll be back to where we were a long time ago: the 1890s, say. I suppose our present thinking is to be expected." There was, after all, no Family Court until 1962. The experiment has been under way for only eighteen years, and the pressures have been immense—so why *should* all the problems have been resolved? What disturbs Schinitsky is that the experiment seems not to have produced the research, the effort, that he thought was required. What authority should be given the court to compel the development of programs? No one has really asked. How can you take large numbers of children and deal with them effectively at a cost the state will not find prohibitive? Again, no one has asked.

"I can understand how someone feels when he's mugged, why the Juvenile Offender Law is a popular program. One would expect changes, modifications, deletions of the Family Court Act, but not such a traumatic change. If it spreads across the country, it will affect one, one-and-a-half million children. We've said there's a Family Court, now let's make it work. It hasn't been given a chance."

Schinitsky regrets that the social upheavals of the 1960s and 1970s, with their complex challenges to authority, have passed relatively unexamined by those who should have been thinking about how the institutions of authority, the courts in particular, must respond. Nor has anyone seriously looked at the problems that the courts themselves have created.

"I'm pessimistic," he says. "I don't see any leadership. It's not the courts' function to resolve the problems. The judiciary, the legislature, the governor should all be doing better. The problems just continue and grow."

What does not change—and it is in this point of stability that Schinitsky finds hope—is the concept of due process. Once children were locked away and forgotten. Due process, now that it is being applied to children, makes such forgetting difficult: it forces those in authority to take a look, from time to time, at the children who have been placed in institutions. Due process suggests that if a child must be punished, that punishment must be combined with some degree of concern that the child not go on being punished for a lifetime.

"The bottom line is basic fairness. What lawyers, the public, newspapers fail to understand is that it isn't the individual case that's thrust upon us—the kid who commits a sensational crime—but a process that has to exist. It's part of our judicial system. It's part of America. It's a process that's growing, that's being defined."

The problem is not to attract people's attention, but to maintain public interest in maintaining the basic fairness of our society when the country's mood seems to shift, when one administration succeeds another. So much that took so many years to establish and refine can so easily be swept away—simply because people get tired of thinking about one problem and turn their attention to another.

"The only constants we have are in science and mathematics," Schinitsky says, "where discoveries are written up for those who come after. We don't have anything like that in human or social relations. Every time a child is born, he starts from scratch. What he feels has been felt for thousands of years, but he doesn't know that. We start all over again."

A Note on the Author

Peter S. Prescott is a Senior Writer and book critic at *Newsweek* magazine. He also teaches a seminar, "Reviewing the Arts," at Columbia's Graduate School of Journalism. He recently received a Guggenheim Fellowship, for work on *The Child Savers,* and the rarely presented George Polk Award for Criticism. A director of the Authors Guild and President of the Authors Guild Foundation, Mr. Prescott has lectured under the auspices of the U.S. State Department in Syria, Egypt and Ireland. He is the author of three previous books, all highly acclaimed: *A World of Our Own: Notes on Life and Learning in a Boys' Preparatory School; Soundings: Encounters with Contemporary Books;* and *A Darkening Green: Notes from the Silent Generation.*

A Note on the Type

The text of this book was set in a computer version of Times Roman, designed by Stanley Morison for *The Times* (London) and first introduced by that newspaper in 1932.

Among typographers and designers of the twentieth century, Stanley Morison has been a strong forming influence as typographical adviser to the English Monotype Corporation, as a director of two distinguished English publishing houses, and as a writer of sensibility, erudition, and keen practical sense.

Composed, printed, and bound by
The Haddon Craftsmen, Inc.,
Scranton, Pennsylvania

Book design by Judith Henry